Rangers and the

My Life with Scotland's Most-Feared
Football-Hooligan Gang

Rangers and the Famous ICF:

My Life with Scotland's Most-Feared Football-Hooligan Gang

Sandy Chugg

Fort Publishing Ltd

First published in 2011 by Fort Publishing Ltd, Old Belmont House,
12 Robsland Avenue, Ayr, KA7 2RW

Printed by Bell and Bain Ltd, Glasgow

Typeset by Kerrypress Ltd

Graphic design by Mark Blackadder

Front cover and Ibrox-disaster commemorative photographs by AC-FotoWorx,
Cambuslang

ISBN: 978-1-905769-28-5

*For my wife, Kerry, and my three kids, Elliot, Nathan and Olivia
(and to Callan, the one who got away)*

CONTENTS

PREFACE

I want to be clear about what this book is. It is an autobiography. It is not a definitive history of the Inter City Firm. I would love to have mentioned every fight and every incident in chronological order, but that just wouldn't have been possible. It is also my interpretation of what happened. I have tried to be fair to everyone and I have respect for every ICF (and SNF) boy I have gone with. But at the end of the day it's my name on the cover. It's my book.

I have a lot of people to thank: all my family and friends but especially Mum, Tom, my brother and sisters, nieces and nephews, my mother- and father-in-law – mainly for putting up with me, and the baggage that goes with me, for all these years.

Special thanks to Paul L, Alan K, Andy McC, Porky, Pedro K and Big F for their valuable contributions and for sharing their memories. Thanks also to James McCarroll of Fort Publishing, Andy from AC Fotoworx and my lawyer, Kevin McCarron, of Turnbull, McCarron Solicitors.

I would like to mention my late uncles, James, Douglas, Sonny, and my late nephew, Grant. Also the Chelsea Youth lads, especially Liam, Big Dan, Ben, Michael, James and the twins. Also Brains and his firm from Birmingham, the Young Guvnors from Man City, Crazy Gaynor from Millwall, Andy and Graeme from the Chelsea/Palace Massive, Big Jan from Feyenoord and finally to all my friends from the Coventry Loyal, especially Tony and Cameron.

A big hello to the parents, and especially the players, of Drumsagard football academy. Come on the Drummie!

Sadly many ICF boys, and girls, are no longer with us. They will never be forgotten.

Rest in Peace

Barry Johnstone, Walesey, Pandy, Joe Bradley, Glen Goodwin, John McNair, Jeanie O'Brien, Ginger Jase (Cardiff), Andy Curran, Peter MacGregor, Big Laff (Airdrie), Deek Smith, Berwick, Andy Sinclair, Billy Kirkland, Colin Bell, Wee Roby and Bert (the auldest casual in town)

Sandy Chugg, Glasgow,
September, 2011

PROLOGUE: BELLY OF THE BEAST

'I can't believe you lot never got murdered,' said the big Glasgow cop. And how right he was. We had just pulled off the most audacious – and foolhardy – attack in our long and glorious history. It is one to tell our grandchildren about. It was that special.

The date was Sunday, 2 May 1999. The day of an Old Firm game at Celtic Park. Every Rangers–Celtic encounter is tense; the anticipation builds for weeks, even months. It is all-consuming. But the importance of this fixture made it even more special. Rangers only needed a draw to regain the league title from Celtic, who had won it the season before, thus preventing Rangers from winning ten consecutive league championships, which would have been a record for Scottish football. A title win would be some consolation for our failure to complete the historic ten-in-a-row, and to win it on the home turf of our bitter rivals would add yet more spice.

As always, the game was a nightmare for Strathclyde's finest, who do their best to keep a lid on one of the most volatile fixtures on the planet. It is not only the ninety minutes or the immediate aftermath the cops have to worry about; nor just the area around the stadium. In packed pubs and clubs the length and breadth of Scotland, the drinking starts early and goes on into the wee small hours as one side savours victory and the other drowns its sorrows. It doesn't take long to light the fire: a roar of triumph, a spilt pint, a throwaway remark. Before the night is over men with stab wounds and broken heads will be carried into casualty departments from Denny to Dumfries.

The ICF didn't need an excuse. We went to the game for one reason and one reason only. To attack Celtic fans. We attacked them whether they were members of their firm, the Celtic Soccer Casuals, or just standard-issue Soap Dodgers. That principle wasn't applied to other clubs, to your Aberdeens, Hibs, Hearts or Dundee Uniteds. We only fought their mobs;

for those fixtures scarfers were civilians, non-combatants. Not so Celtic. In our eyes their scarfers were fair game. We fucking hated them.

It is not an irrational hatred. A significant number of them support the Irish Republican Army and its murderous campaign against all things British. They sing songs that celebrate the IRA, like 'Boys of the Old Brigade'; they proudly wave the flag of a foreign country; they jeer and catcall during the minute's silence commemorating Armistice Day; they deride the Protestant religion and the Protestant people of Scotland.

Yet they are ferocious when the boot is on the other foot, seeing a sectarian slight in the most innocuous situation. Who can forget the daft bastards (some of whom are in prominent positions in the Roman Catholic Church in Scotland) who argued, in 2008, that any football fan who sang the nursery rhyme 'Hokey Cokey' at a match would be guilty of a hate crime? Or what about the (sadly successful) campaign by the Celtic-minded to stop Rangers fans singing the so-called 'Famine Song', which encourages Celtic fans to go back home to Ireland because the potato famine is over. Can these cunts not take a fucking joke? Celtic fans will go anywhere to be offended. They have never been able to shrug off that sense of victimhood. And they never will, despite the fact that the Scottish establishment has been colonised by people sympathetic to their cause.

These things were on our mind before every Old Firm game. The hatred runs deep and violence is never more than a heartbeat away. Even more so with so much at stake. What happened on 2 May 1999 went above and beyond the norm. It took things to a whole new level.

In the early afternoon, with the kick-off scheduled for six o'clock, the ICF, in keeping with tradition, gathered in three Rangers pubs in the east end: the Bristol, the Alexandra and the Louden, all of them less than two miles from Celtic Park. The glory days of the casuals were now no more than a sweet memory; the two- or three-hundred-strong mob had gone forever. But to me that was an advantage, because the fifty boys who turned up were hardened thugs, front-liners, and, just as important, they were all rabid Celtic haters. These boys would give their all and then some. After a few hours of alcohol-and-coke-fuelled banter we set off for the game and within minutes were at the junction of Duke Street and Todd Street, where we noticed that some Rangers scarfers were getting dog's abuse from Celtic fans outside the Netherfield bar, or the 'Nerry' as it is known locally.

That, we thought, is a right fucking liberty. There was no hesitation. We steamed in, forcing their tormentors back inside the pub, where the doors were quickly locked in our faces. In normal circumstances we would have tanned in the windows and stoned the cowardly cunts who were skulking inside. But the Nerry doesn't have any windows so, reluctantly, we had to leave it and move on.

Our mood had changed. Before an Old Firm game we are always in high spirits, full of anticipation at what lies ahead, praying for a fix of football violence, full of the joys of spring. But after what happened at the Nerry we were fucking raging and thirsting for revenge.

It was at that moment we made the fateful decision to head for Parkhead Cross.

The belly of the beast.

Parkhead Cross and the streets that radiate out from it are home to a raft of Celtic pubs. It is a dangerous area for Rangers fans at the best of times; a no-go area half-an-hour before an Old Firm game.

Not that we gave a fuck. As we passed the Pippin Bar, which was a Celtic hotbed on matchdays, we decided it was time to introduce ourselves.

'We're the famous ICF,' we chanted.

That was enough to let slip the hounds of hell. The shutters on the Pippin came up and about forty of them poured out.

'Come on then you fucking Orange bastards,' they roared. For the first couple of minutes we were showered with bottles, glasses, snooker balls and cues. But when their stock of missiles ran out we were able to go toe-to-toe, quickly forcing them back inside the pub. It was our second easy victory of the afternoon.

The next item on the agenda would be a very different proposition.

Twenty yards further on, milling around Parkhead Cross, there were about a thousand Celtic fans. Some were on their way to the game while others knew what had happened at the Nerry and were lying in wait for us. But when they heard our signature tune of 'ICF, ICF' every one of them put thoughts of the game to one side and got ready to deal with the alien presence in their midst. If you have ever had any doubt about the hatred they feel for us you should have seen the looks on their faces at that moment.

A hundred of them squared up to us and battle was joined. They were punching and kicking and mouthing sectarian insults. The other nine hundred were no less vocal but they held back from the fray and contented themselves with launching volleys of bottles and stones, hoping that their braver compatriots would put us down or force us to run. The numbers we faced grew rapidly as Celtic fans streamed out of the pubs to either join in the fight or to launch missiles at us from a safe distance. Within minutes we were confronted by upwards of two thousand Beggars, surrounding us on every side. We were fighting for our lives.

When a new recruit joins the IRA he is given the Coldwater Strategy by his commanding officer. 'You will either be killed in action or spend the rest of your life on the run.' Neither option is particularly palatable. We had our own Coldwater Strategy that day. Stand and fight and risk serious injury, or perhaps even worse. Or turn tail and run, which would give us the chance to get away but with the distinct possibility that we would be tripped or pushed to the ground, leaving us helpless in the face of a mob baying for blood.

We stood and fought. And we didn't give a fucking inch, despite the constant waves of attacks. All around me boys were going down; some got a right kicking, one was slashed across the back. But we didn't retreat; we didn't let them push us back. It seemed to go on for a lifetime, much longer than any fight I have ever been involved in. That reflects the danger we faced; if we had been pushed back the rest of them would have joined in and we would have been annihilated. It was vicious, no-holds-barred stuff, with both sides fuelled not only by drink but also by naked sectarian hatred. One of our mob, Rico McGill, later told me that he will never forget the terrified look on a traffic officer's face when he saw what was unfolding; understandably, the cop made himself scarce.

We were close to exhaustion when the main body of police arrived and separated us. They escorted us down Springfield Road, where the Celtic fans continued to pelt us with an array of missiles. The cops would never admit it but I believe they were impressed by our audacity, by our willingness to do whatever it took to get at Celtic.

When the game kicked off the atmosphere inside the ground was poisonous. Later my Celtic pals told me that what we had done swept through their support, ratcheting up the tension to a degree I have never experienced before or since. It caused, I have no doubt, the trouble inside the stadium, which erupted after Celtic's Stephane Mahe was sent off in the forty-first minute for a second bookable offence. Mahe was outraged and angrily confronted referee Hugh Dallas, before being persuaded to make his way down the tunnel.

Cue mayhem.

A few minutes later Dallas was struck on the forehead by a coin thrown by a Celtic fan and, in pictures that flashed round the globe, was left bleeding and disorientated on the Parkhead turf. As the game boiled over two more Celtic players, as well as Rod Wallace of Rangers, were dismissed, while a number of Soap Dodgers entered the playing area in an attempt to get at Dallas. A Celtic fan, in fuck-knows what circumstances, fell forty feet from the upper tier of the stands and almost killed himself. At the final whistle, as Rangers players celebrated a 3–0 win and regaining the league championship, the so-called greatest fans in the world, 'sportsmen' to the last, pelted them with coins and spat on them.

The fun didn't stop with the final whistle. In Duke Street, minutes after the game, Rangers scarfers taunted the Celtic hordes about winning back the league, which resulted in a full-scale riot. Later that night, Hugh Dallas, relaxing at home with his family, had his windows smashed by a Celtic-supporting neighbour, someone he had known socially for twenty years. As passions ran high in the wake of the most explosive Glasgow derby for decades violence erupted across the west of Scotland, with police reporting more than a hundred arrests, including many serious assaults and several stabbings.

In the wake of the match our rivals went into, what to me and most Rangers fans, was full paranoia mode. Celtic employed the services of a psychologist to examine Dallas's performance during the game and duly presented his findings to the SPL's commission of inquiry.[1] Maybe that is one reason they got off so lightly; the £45,000 fine for 'on-field disturbances' was a slap on the wrist for a club with their resources. Referee assaulted; the opposition abused, attacked and spat on; three players sent off. What do these cunts have to do to get a real punishment?

That game changed football forever. Never again would the Old Firm be allowed to play a title decider. Never again would the two sides meet in the early evening on a Saturday or a Sunday. For its part the Scottish government, disturbed by what had taken place, also got involved, demanding an urgent report on the debacle from the SFA and SPL. That ninety minutes also made Hugh Dallas the most famous, and controversial, Scottish referee in history, prompting many Rangers fans to have 'DALLAS 12' sewn onto the back of their replica strips.

Not that any of us in the 'famous fifty' were concerned about the historical implications. That night in the pub we toasted the greatest feat of arms in the history of the ICF. We had marched into the middle of enemy

---

[1]   Celtic also asked that Dallas should not be considered for the next Old Firm fixture at Celtic Park, in December 1999, a request that was denied.

territory, outnumbered but never disheartened, and stuck it to them. The players had done their jobs on the field of play and we had done ours off it.

Football doesn't get any better than that.

1

MEAN STREETS

As a boy I was a Celtic fan.

There, I've admitted it. People who know me as Billy Britain will be surprised but, unfortunately, it's true. My only defence is that I was a victim of circumstance. You see I grew up in the Gallowgate, in Glasgow's east end. The Gallowgate – an area strongly associated in the popular imagination with Glasgow's Irish Catholic community – is a stone's throw from Celtic Park but about three miles from Ibrox. So if I was going to the football, which I did from the age of seven, the Piggery was the logical choice.

Like many boys I was attracted by the sights and sounds of the professional game and, let's face it, Celtic Park was a very atmospheric ground in those days. One day my brother Christopher, who is four years older than me, took me to watch an Old Firm game there. He lifted me over the turnstiles and into the Jungle, the area occupied by the hardest of hardcore Celtic fans, while he went into the traditional Rangers end without me in tow. At that first game Celtic won 1–0 and the passion exhibited by the supporters was overwhelming. I was hooked. I think I also supported Celtic to wind my brother up. At the age of eleven he was already a committed Rangers fan and in our bedroom his wall would be covered in Union Jacks and Red Hands while mine was festooned with Irish tricolours.

My childhood infatuation with the Hoops was short-lived. I was becoming more and more aware of what was happening in Northern Ireland and it slowly began to dawn on me that most Celtic fans identified with the Irish Republican Army. They would belt out songs like the 'Soldier's Song' and vile ditties like 'Ooh Ah, Up the Rah'. I knew British troops were being murdered by the IRA and as my ambition at the time was to join the army I began slowly to turn against the Republicanism that infected Celtic Park. By the age of eleven I was a fully fledged Rangers fan and have been ever since.

I was born in Rottenrow, Glasgow's famous maternity hospital, in 1972. It was a good year to make my entrance. Just three months earlier, Rangers won the European Cup Winners Cup by beating Moscow Dynamo 3–2 in Barcelona's Nou Camp stadium. For good measure the Rangers fans also gave the Spanish police a fucking good hiding at the end of the game, of which more later.

We weren't the typical nuclear family and that's putting it mildly. As well as Christopher I have a sister, Carolyn, who is twelve years older than me. The three of us have different fathers and although my father's name is William McDonald I was given the surname of my sister's dad, Chugg, a moniker that has caused me a little local difficulty over the years.

My family are all Protestants, but not churchgoing, and, like most people in the Gallowgate, we loved going along to watch the Orange parades that are such a feature of Glasgow life in the summer months, the traditional marching season. Despite the fact that many of our Roman Catholic, Celtic-supporting neighbours enjoyed the colourful spectacle and the music there was nearly always trouble. However, my abiding memory of the parades is seeing people pissed out of their minds at seven o'clock in the morning.

I use the word 'family' advisedly. The truth is that my father left the family home when I was five and after that I never saw him. He was already married with children when he met Mum and eventually he got an ultimatum from her and my sister along the lines of 'come home now or it's all over'. Clearly, the pull of his other family was too strong. I only have a couple of vague memories of him: once when he picked me up from nursery school; the other when he gave me a Tonka truck for Christmas.

It is only in the last few years that I have realised just how traumatic that breakdown was for me. I was always a quiet child, especially in comparison to Christopher, who was very outgoing, but my parents splitting up pushed me further into my shell. I found the only way to compensate for the lack of a secure family life was to become part of a group. Having pals I could rely on became incredibly important; it gave me a sense of belonging, a sense of purpose. Having read a number of books by people involved in football violence it is clear that many of them also came from broken homes of one kind or another. They, like me, were seeking some kind of consolation for whatever had happened to them at home. That will sound like psychobabble to many people; I don't think it is.

Everyone knows about Glasgow's gang culture from books like *No Mean City²*. Although it came out more than seventy years ago there are probably as many gangs in the city today as there were then. The place is full of them despite the best efforts of the authorities to break them up. Hardly a week goes by without Glasgow being named in this crime survey and that as the murder capital of Britain or the place in which young men are most likely to carry a blade. Like it or not gang members are prepared to fight, and often to die, to protect their little patch. Given my family background, my personality and where I lived it was inevitable that I would join a gang and when I was seven I became a member of the Young Gallowgate Mad Squad. It was far from kid's stuff: if you got caught by a rival mob you ended up with a sore face or worse. Sometimes the pain was self-inflicted: I remember chasing a rival gang with a bottle in my hand and tripping over on the pavement; my hand was cut by the broken glass but instead of telling Mum I applied a bandage and tried to keep out of her way for a few days.

We weren't short of rivals. The east end is awash with gangs, including legendary outfits like the Bridgeton Derry and the Calton Tongs, both of which we had run-ins with. But our closest and most bitter rivals were the Spur and the Torch, whose members hailed from Barrowfield. For those of you who are unfamiliar with Glasgow's geography, Barrowfield is within spitting distance of Celtic Park and has a reputation for being the toughest scheme in a city full of tough schemes. Strangers who ventured there would, if they were lucky, get a kicking; if they were unlucky they would not only get a kicking but would also be robbed of their money, their clothes and their shoes. As well as fighting outsiders the Spur and the Torch would fight each other. The dividing line between the two gangs was Stamford Street, nicknamed Nightmare Alley. Such was Nightmare Alley's reputation that it featured in a 1970s documentary on urban deprivation aired on the BBC.

The YGMS was outnumbered by both Barrowfield gangs and they would often give us a chasing. The turning point came this day – I was around ten years old – when the Torch turned up in Slatefield Street in the middle of our estate. They knocked fuck out of a Gallowgate boy who was on his own at the time, which enraged the whole scheme. Within minutes the YGMS mobilised, helped by a number of grown men and a

---

² First published in 1935, Alexander McArthur's best-seller explores the life of 'razor king' Johnnie Stark, a fearsome street-fighting man from the Gorbals.

well-known boxing family from the area. There were twenty of us against thirty Torch but helped by a fearsome array of weapons, including base-ball bats, we chased the cunts down Slatefield Street and right out of the Gallowgate.

That little incident gave the YGMS no end of confidence and from that day on we took them on as equals, even when the Torch and Spur merged into one big gang. Parkhead Forge – once home to one of the biggest steelmakers in the world but by then a vacant industrial site – was our battleground. We came at each other armed to the teeth; it wasn't just fists and feet but also machetes, coshes, knives and bats. There would be a fight almost every day and the rate of attrition was frightening, with boys regularly getting carted off to hospital suffering from stab wounds and head injuries.

The respectable middle classes often wonder why guys like us are so drawn to gang culture and thousands of bearded academic types have researched and probed and analysed the 'problem' until they are blue in the face. I could have saved the taxpayer a fortune. Young men are natu-rally territorial and when you add in the boredom that comes with living an urban desert with fuck-all in the way of facilities it's easy to work out why it kicks off. Of course cheap drink, like cider and super lager, plays a part, as does glue, the drug of choice for skint inner-city youth. But they are symptoms, not the cause. We had one red-ash football pitch in the Gallowgate, not exactly ideal when you live ten floors up in a multi-storey block and never get to see a lawn. I guess that around half the boys in our area were in gangs and you couldn't blame us.

My mother did her best to keep me on the straight and narrow. From the balcony in our multi-storey flat in Whitevale Street she would often see me having a square go and give me a telling off. I could not have wished for a better mother or a more loving upbringing. The problem was she had to put in long hours in her job as a barmaid at the Drum in Shettleston Road and so for long periods I was left to my own devices. I was the typical latchkey kid, hanging about the house on my own for hours, jealous of my pals who were at home with their mums and dads. In his formative years Christopher had the benefit of being under the watch-ful eye of Carolyn. She really kept him in line and my abiding memory is of her chasing him round the house after he had pulled yet another stroke. By the time I was at the age when I needed a firm hand she had upped sticks and emigrated to Canada, where she is now happily married to a business executive. Had she stayed I am sure I would have turned out to be a different person.

I was also getting the piss taken out of me because of my surname. 'Chugg' is a slang word in Scotland for masturbation and older boys would never let me forget it. I well remember my tormentor-in-chief, who was about four years older than me and lived in the same high rise. That boy teased me mercilessly about my name, often throwing in a hiding for good measure. He died at the age of eighteen, in the early Eighties, which was very good news for me because I might well have murdered the cunt.

School could have been my passport out of the east end but not when it was run by Glasgow Corporation. My first alma mater was Thomson Street primary school, a dilapidated, red-sandstone heap and, I believe, the oldest school in the city. Despite its many deficiencies I was delighted to be there not just for the company of the other kids but also because I was a pretty able student and was regularly in the top three in the class. I was particularly good at English and I recall that an early ambition was to become a football reporter, to which end I would compose little stories about my exploits on the pitch.

The main problem at Thomson Street wasn't the age of the school or my fellow pupils. It was our teachers. There might have been one or two good ones but to me most of them didn't give a fuck. It was a chore for them even to turn up and an even bigger chore for them to teach us. They were going through the motions. I had my own, very personal problems to contend with. When I was in primary six, Mum met the love of her life, Tom, and although I now consider him to be my father I resented him at the time. As a result my behaviour at school became disruptive; I got lippy with the teachers, threw my schoolbooks around the class and played truant on a regular basis. The inevitable suspensions followed.

Worse was to follow. One day in class I was swinging a desk on my feet when the teacher slammed her hands down on the lid. My feet were squashed but instead of saying 'That's no' fair miss,' as most of my classmates would have done, I picked the desk up and threw it at her. I missed by inches but it was enough for me to receive the ultimate punishment: expulsion. In my six weeks away from school I was referred to a child psychologist, which seemed to calm me down and after that my classroom behaviour improved.

The same couldn't be said for my life outside of school. By the time I arrived in primary seven I was already a prolific shoplifter. One of my favourite haunts was the toy department of Fraser's store in Buchanan

Street, from which I stole huge numbers of those little Corgi cars. I was bound to get caught and sure enough on an expedition to What Every Woman Wants I was picked up by store detectives and handed over to the police. I was referred to the children's panel and placed on a supervision order. Mum was worried sick but she knew it was a phase I was going through, a youthful rebellion against the arrival of Tom. As I said we are like father and son now but it took me years to accept him.

Fights were a daily occurrence at Thomson Street, as they were on the streets of the east end, and it was at this time that my readiness to take on all-comers became evident. I am not the biggest but that was never a disadvantage. In fact I think my lack of stature was an advantage by forcing me to stand up for myself. My personality also helped. I try never to back down, no matter who I am up against. I also discovered that verbal aggression from someone my size has a huge impact on potential opponents because they just don't expect it from someone who is smaller than they are. I must have been in a scrap every other day, mainly with guys my own age. I would say I won about half of them, which is a decent batting average considering my size. I didn't care about the punishments until one day in a final attempt to stop me fighting the teachers pulled the Thomson Street team out of an inter-schools tournament. The decision punished everyone and it was designed to bring home to me that I was letting my teammates down as well as myself. As a member of the team, and a football fanatic, it hurt.

It certainly helped me when I made the step up to Whitehill secondary school in 1984.[3] I was looking forward to going there, not least because on a tour of the school while I was still in primary I noticed two lovely-looking girls. 'That will do me,' I thought. The reality of life at Whitehill however was very different.

The first problem was my blazer or should I say my sister's cast-off blazer, which I inherited. I didn't want to wear the fucking thing but Mum insisted. It was twelve years old and really looked its age. I knew the minute I walked through the school gates for the first time that I would get the pish ripped out of me. And so it proved. On my first day I ended up battering a loudmouth who wouldn't stop going on about it. After that I hid the blazer in bushes on my way to school and picked it up again when I was walking home.

---

[3]   Whitehill luminaries include Lulu and Ford Kiernan of *Stlll Game* fame.

The second thing I had to deal with was the extreme levels of violence, which came from both inside and outside the school. The boys in second year saw the new intake as easy meat and picked on us from day one. You had to stick up for yourself or your life would become unbearable, although sometimes the odds were just too great no matter how brave you were. I vividly remember being chased for two miles round the Powery area of the east end by a mob of second years wielding coshes and wooden hammers. Luckily for me I gave them the slip and by the time school came around again they had moved on to another target.

Whitehill only really came together when we were faced with a threat from outsiders. In our case it came from the pupils at St Mungo's, a Roman Catholic school that was also in the Dennistoun area of Glasgow and less than a mile from Whitehill. That is the Catholic Church for you, creating divisions wherever it can, separating children from the same estate, the same street, the same block. It started at the age of five and I will always remember my Catholic pals from Gallowgate trooping off to St Ann's while I went off in the other direction to Thomson Street. There is no need for it; quite simply it is a form of apartheid. On their way to and from school the St Mungo boys would shout 'dirty, smelly, Orange bastards' at us while we would reply with 'dirty Fenian bastards'. Fights were an everyday occurrence, made more vicious by sectarian hatred.

That was life in an east-end school. And just like at primary school most of the teachers, it seemed to me, couldn't have cared less about helping us to fulfil our potential. The gym teacher did his best to keep me and my pals in line and gave us what Sir Alex Ferguson later made famous as the 'hair-dryer' treatment. My geography teacher realised that I had ability and encouraged me but the rest in my opinion were a waste of space. It was more about childminding than education. Given proper encouragement I could have passed a lot more exams than I did but it wasn't to be.

2

THE SOCCER BABE

I was inspired by my brother's stories about the violence he was experiencing as a Rangers fan. Christopher had attended the infamous Scottish Cup final of 1980 when both sets of Old Firm fans invaded the Hampden pitch at the end of the game and engaged in running battles. At the age of eight I watched the television pictures of the fights and felt contrasting emotions; worried for my brother but exhilarated by the violence. He followed Rangers all over Scotland and would come back with tales of how the light-blue legions would dominate the towns and cities they visited, rubbing the locals' noses in it in the process.[4]

But that was old-fashioned stuff: scarfers getting pissed up and running amok; there was no planning, no organisation. There was a new phenomenon in the world of football hooliganism: the casual. The word 'casual' was now becoming well known to the media and football fans in Scotland, thanks to the mass outbreak of trouble at a Motherwell–Aberdeen game in the early Eighties, when scores of smartly dressed young hooligans fought each other on the Fir Park terracing.

By this time my Celtic-supporting days had been over for a couple of years and I was now a regular at Ibrox. It was 1983 and although in those pre-Souness days Rangers were rubbish on the pitch I found the terracing fashions inspirational. More than anything else it was shame that made me a football hooligan. When I was growing up, families like ours were given clothing grants and when Mum got ours she would buy me Y cardigans, polyester shirts and waffle trousers. The naffest clothes known to man. It didn't matter that every other working-class Glaswegian was wearing

---

[4] This was a major factor in the development of casuals firms in places like Aberdeen, Edinburgh and Motherwell. The locals got sick of Old Firm fans coming onto their manor and taking the piss.

them; they still made me self-conscious, as they did all self-respecting twelve-year-olds.

What a contrast with the fashions sported at Ibrox. Boys just a little older than me had wedge haircuts, and wore Adidas Trim Trab trainers, Lois jeans and Lyle and Scott shirts. Some guys, those with a few quid to spend, had Ellesse tracksuits as well as the latest gear by Segio Tacchini and Fila. Others adopted fashions from American sports, with Rangers fans wearing the blue colours favoured by the New York Rangers or New York Jets, providing a clear contrast to Celtic fans with their green Miami Dolphins outfits.

The Rangers casuals, the Inter City Firm, led by guys like Barry Johnstone[5], had come into existence by 1984. I was desperate to join but the problem was my age. The older boys didn't want a thirteen-year-old hanging around cramping their style and they told me in no uncertain terms where to go. Desperate to get a foothold in the new, exciting world of football violence some of my like-minded pals and I set up the Rangers Soccer Babes. It wasn't long before we were called into action.

Hearts were our first opponents. One Saturday in 1985 their main mob, the Capital Service Firm, was in Glasgow city centre, on their way to Central station to catch a train to Paisley. Never ones to let a promising shoplifting opportunity pass them by Hearts cruised down Buchanan Street looking for opportunities to plunder the fashionable shops that line both sides of Glasgow's most exclusive shopping destination. About twenty Rangers Soccer Babes, including me, were outside Fraser's department store when we heard the unmistakeable hiss of 'CSF, CSF'. No hesitation, we steamed in. As bottles flew in both directions the two mobs came together, scattering terrified Saturday-afternoon shoppers all over the place. The CSF initially got the better of it and pushed us back but we quickly regrouped and chased them down Buchanan Street and under the Hielanman's Umbrella in nearby Argyle Street.

I was exhilarated. It was my first experience of FV and the adrenalin rush was incredible. I had never experienced anything like it and I am sure everyone who has ever been involved in the scene will back me up. Drugs, sex, alcohol; nothing comes close. I prayed that my next fix would not be long in coming.

---

[5]   Johnstone with an 'e' is the correct spelling; it is not, as some people think, Johnston.

Our main opponents were the Celtic Soccer Babes, no surprise there. Although I only ever rated the main Celtic mob, the Celtic Soccer Casuals, for a season or two their baby offshoot was a different kettle of fish. For a start it was bigger than our baby crew, and vicious with it. I discovered just how vicious before an Old Firm game at Celtic Park in 1985. Seven of us were standing outside Greaves sports shop in Gordon Street, talking to two boys who had come up from Leeds to savour the Old Firm experience. We spotted two Celtic Soccer Babes and verbals were exchanged. I thought to myself, 'These cunts can't be out on their own,' and no sooner had the thought gone through my mind than forty of them came charging round the corner. We scattered; we had no chance. Forty against seven doesn't compute, which just goes to show that we all have to run some time despite what some so-called hooligans claim in their books.

With the rest of the boys I sprinted down Mitchell Lane towards Argyle Street but Celtic caught up with me. I did my best to resist but was quickly knocked to the ground. That pack of wolves didn't need to be asked twice. They were all over me, pushing each other aside to kick, punch and stamp all over my body. I put my hands over my head but the blows kept raining down. One well-directed kick caught me on the nose, splitting it wide open and splattering my assailant's trainer in blood. I fell in and out of consciousness, one thought flashing through my mind.

'I am going to die, right here in the middle of Glasgow, in my city, in my home.'

And then salvation came from the unlikeliest of sources. A passing Good Samaritan saw what was happening and shouted:

'Enough is enough.'

He was wearing a Celtic scarf and that was probably what saved my life. It gave him a degree of moral authority with the CSB lads and they reluctantly backed off. The Celtic scarfer helped me to my feet and I was able to stagger off and rejoin my pals.

Having taken a beating like that some people might have walked away from the hooligan scene, never to return. Not me. It didn't put me off for a second; all it did was to intensify my hatred for all things Celtic, a hatred that became even more pronounced the next time I ran into the Celtic Soccer Babes in the city centre. A few months later I was walking along the Trongate, heading for one of my many hearings at the Children's Panel. I had stopped to look in a shop window when I felt a hand on my shoulder:

'Excuse me mate.'

I turned round to find six CSB surrounding me. I tried to throw a punch but they set about me, leaving me with a bloodied nose and boot marks on my clothes. 'This will make a good impression on the panel,' I thought as I made for the nearest toilet to clean myself up.

I had by now fully embraced the casual and gang cultures, and everything that goes with that way of life. I was desperate to look the part but not having the means to buy the gear I wanted there was only one alternative: shoplifting. An early expedition came one Christmas Eve in the mid Eighties. I had had my eye on an Aquascutum shirt in Fraser's for some time and when the shop was jam-packed with people buying presents I took my chance and stuffed it up my jacket. Although it was a woman's shirt and the buttons went the wrong way I thought I was the coolest guy ever with that shirt on. After that stealing from shops became a way of life. That's how I got most of my clothes and, so that Mum wouldn't worry, I told her I had bought them from a shoplifter. I even sold her clothes I had nicked and gave her the same cock-and-bull story. Being part of a big firm helped in the shoplifting game. About forty of us would charge in, so ensuring that the security staff couldn't lock us in, and then lift as much as possible before scarpering. We were particularly fond of our expeditions to the upmarket boutiques of Edinburgh, where there was also much less chance that we would be recognised.

Fighting was not confined either to match days or to other groups of casuals. The Rangers Soccer Babes was made up mostly of guys from the east end of Glasgow and we spawned two offshoots in that area: the East End Firm and the Duke Street Firm, both of which were largely, but not exclusively, made up of Rangers casuals. A favourite haunt was McKinlay's nightclub in Shettleston, where we would attend the under-eighteen disco. The first time we went there was to give our pals from Shettleston a hand against a gang from Tollcross with a truly wonderful name: the Tollcross Wee Men. During the disco, one of our guys got it on with a Wee Man and the whole place went up in a full-scale, thirty-a-side rammy. I picked up a chair and brained the nearest Tollcross boy with it but in return got a blow to the head with another chair.

Although the Tollcross mob were thrown out by the bouncers the trouble spilled onto Shettleston Road and then into Pettigrew Street where, funnily enough, my aunt lived. It was a dangerous moment: two formidable gangs facing each other, thirty on each side, most of them tooled up. I have always said that your true character reveals itself when the chips are down, and the chips were well and truly down that night.

I didn't hesitate. I picked up a 'four by two' (a wooden shaft used in joinery) and ran straight at the Wee Men, screaming like a banshee. Although it was one-man assault the Tollcross boys panicked, turned on their heels and ran. At the risk of blowing my own trumpet it did no end of good for my reputation. Even at the tender age of fourteen I was being recognised as a top boy.

Not that our little firms were invincible. Far from it. In the city centre our club of choice was Henry Afrika's, where we battled inside and outside the premises with gangs from the Gorbals, Castlemilk, Possil and of course with Celtic casuals. I remember one night I was there with the East End Firm and got my head split open by a Celtic boy, who hit me with a Coke bottle. Celtic got the better of it that night and chased us all the way along Clyde Street.

Celtic were our most frequent opponents at that time and the venue for our tussles with the CSB was often the grounds of Duke Street hospital. I had a reputation for 'sneakies', which meant going round behind the rival mob and running straight into them. This night I set off on a sneaky and made straight for their top boy. Unfortunately, he spotted me, picked up a metal bracket and hit me full in the face with it. I went down like a sack of spuds and would have been kicked to fuck and back if the rest of the boys hadn't steamed in and rescued me. When I got home Mum had one look at my bloodied face and took me straight to hospital, where I got ten stitches inside my mouth and fourteen on the outside.

My reputation as someone who could handle himself must have reached the right ears because just a year after I had been told to stay away from the main mob I was invited to join. I had also done some work for them as a spotter and I think they came to realise I was a handy guy to have around. Fourteen years old and a member of the best mob in Britain.

I had won my spurs.

3

MEET THE MOB

Fast forward to 2 January 2011.

A hundred ICF are ensconced in the Swallow hotel, a stone's throw from Ibrox. We had just watched the traditional New Year's Day Old Firm derby and had arranged to meet after the game. It wasn't just for sentimental reasons, although it was as always great to see the boys. We were there to lay a wreath marking the fortieth anniversary of the Ibrox disaster in 1971, when sixty-six Rangers fans tragically lost their lives on Stairway 13 after that year's traditional Old Firm fixture. Our floral tributes, placed carefully next to the John Greig statue outside Ibrox, were featured heavily on the television news that night. It was the right thing to do. We may be hooligans but first and foremost we are Rangers fans. We love the club as much as anyone.

We also wanted to remember our fallen comrade, Andy Curran, who had been murdered a few months earlier. What a waste of a life that was. There was a collection in Andy's memory, which raised £1,200 for his family. I hope it helped.

As I looked around the bar that afternoon the memories came flooding back. The shared dangers, the dashes, the broken bones and burst lips, above all the laughs we had. I wouldn't have missed it for the world. There were so many great boys there, boys you could rely on when the going got tough. But as my eyes panned round the room I also realised that many of my old friends had passed away, far too many, in fact. That saddened me. I miss every one of them.

Although Strathclyde police might disagree, I am no longer involved in football violence. The torch has been passed to a new generation, the Rangers Youth. Many of the Youth were in the Swallow and I was chatting happily to them. I think they are well capable of carrying on the good work we did. Mind you they will have to go some to match the boys of the ICF. Just have a read of the eight profiles below and you will see what I mean.

I could have written about so many more people because we have had dozens of outstanding boys over the years, including Bomber, Rab Anderson, the Pedros (K and McL), Deak, Swedgers, Jeff, Scott N and Craw. I have listed them and many more besides in the Hall of Fame at the end of this book.

Barry Johnstone

Anyone who was ever a member of the ICF will put Barry Johnstone in the top three Rangers boys of all time. He was outstanding in every way: a real leader, a great organiser and possessed of bottle you wouldn't believe. Barry hailed from the Anderston area of Glasgow but he later moved to Duke Street, the epicentre of everything ICF during our heyday of the mid-to-late Eighties. He was already considered an older lad when I started going and I think he was about four years older than me.

It was easy to see why he was so respected and why people followed him. He was a big, good-looking man, very popular with the ladies and he had the personality to match. Loud and brash, you always heard Barry before you saw him. But that wouldn't have mattered one jot if he couldn't handle himself. And boy could he handle himself. He was as game as anyone I have ever seen in the UK or Europe and believe me I have seen my fair share.

Barry lived and breathed the ICF and FV. He was one of the first to have 'ICF' tattooed inside his lower lip and he would proudly display the tattoo to visiting mobs. Like most of the lads he had an almost patho-logical hatred of all things Celtic. He played in a couple of flute bands, The Sons of Ulster and the YCV, and he was a staunch supporter of the Loyalist cause in Northern Ireland. You may have seen him in a *Panorama* programme about football hooliganism, which was broadcast sometime in the 1990s.

My abiding memory of Barry stems from the first leg of the League Cup semi-final against Hibs in September 1985. We were walking back to Waverley station after the game when we were ambushed by a group of CCS who had disguised themselves in Rangers colours. It was a very dangerous situation but Barry held us together, enabling us to repel wave after wave of attacks. Then when it looked like we could lose it he played his trump card, spraying CS gas into the Hibs front line. Those cunts were choking and spluttering and cursing but their consternation was nothing compared to a police horse, which reared up on its hind legs after inhaling some of the gas. It looked fucking funny but I bet the poor old nag wasn't laughing.

Sadly, Barry is one of many boys no longer with us. He died a few years ago, around 2006 or 2007, but had given up hooliganism a long time before that. He had been attracted to the rave scene in the early 1990s and after that he never came back to the ICF.

RIP, Barry. You are a legend.

Harky

What can I say about this man that hasn't already been said by other mobs the length and breadth of Scotland?

He is probably the most famous Rangers hooligan of them all, more famous even than Barry. He is tall and has a blond mane that ensured he always stood out in a crowd. In the early days Harky modelled himself on Paul Weller in his Style Council years, sporting the same hairstyle and clothes.

He was from Shettleston, which I regard as my spiritual home, and when I started to get involved in the scene, Harky, who is about four years older than me, took me under his wing. I was, if you like, his protégé, not just in a football-violence sense but also on a personal level. He was an older brother and he was always there for me during my teenage years, even when I was inside thanks to a conviction for drug dealing.

Harky was totally fearless and I can still picture him steaming in, regardless of the numbers he was up against or the reputation of the opposing mob. He was the gamest boy I have ever seen.

He'll kill me for mentioning it but he was also, like me, a childhood Celtic fan, which is ironic because two more rabid Celtic haters you will not find this side of London Road. Harky wasn't at the Swallow that afternoon. He got out of the scene fairly early on. But I wished he could have been there to savour the great days we shared.

Walesy

Walesy, who was from Garthamlock, enjoyed cult status in the ICF, especially in the early years. He caused havoc everywhere he went. Walesy was a game wee cunt, so game that his small stature and wiry frame never put him at a disadvantage in a ruck. He was also known for his amazing ability to rob and steal when we were on our travels. But those weren't the main reasons for him becoming a cult figure.

That was down to the number of people he slashed. In fact he was probably the main reason our boys became known – wrongly in my view – as blade merchants. He was a fucking fiend with a Stanley knife and in a tight spot would cut anyone who got in his way.

Walesy moved down south where he died, tragically young, more than a decade ago.

RIP wee man.

Davie Carrick

Like the boys I have mentioned above Davie was as game as fuck, a real front-liner. Always first into a fight, and the last to run, he would be a stick-on to be inducted into any hooligan hall of fame. Like me he wasn't the tallest and like me he worked his way through the ranks to become one of the main faces.

It was thanks to Davie's drive and enthusiasm that we kept the mob going through the dark days of the early Nineties when FV became very unfashionable, with people preferring raves and getting loved-up. He always ensured we pulled a mob, even if the numbers had dwindled to as little as twenty. For that reason alone he is the most-important figure in modern-day (that is post-rave-scene) hooliganism.

Davie was also instrumental in the formation of the Scottish National Firm, which, although opposed by some older Rangers boys, ensured that at least we had an outlet for FV. That helped us get the ICF up and running again after the 1998 World Cup and since then we have enjoyed something of a renaissance.

My most vivid memory of Davie is of him going into his bag and handing out claw hammers when we got off the train at Slateford, prior to facing Hibs in what turned out to be our most humiliating defeat of all time. He was of course the first to steam into Hibs, helping us to back them off for the first few minutes of that battle.

It is just a pity that the book he wrote on his ICF experiences (*Rangers ICF*, published in 2008) didn't do him justice. I blame the publisher and the ghost writer for that, not Davie.

Big Boris

Boris is another close personal friend. He was a latecomer to the scene, only really getting involved after the demise of the SNF in the late 1990s. Boris is another larger-than-life character, whose six-foot-plus frame and shaved head make him instantly recognisable.

He has enjoyed a rapid rise through the modern ICF and is now one of our top boys, thanks in large part to an extrovert personality, great networking skills and superb organisational ability. Those personal qualities have also enabled him to set up and run a very successful business. Boris likes nothing better than getting the boys together for a piss up or a day out.

But don't run away with the idea that he is just a strategy bod. Boris can more than hold his own in a fight and has served two terms in prison for football-violence-related offences.

Warren B

The biggest compliment I can pay Warren is to tell you that he was the only Rangers boy to come from Edinburgh at the onset of the casual scene. It is a testament to his strength of character that he made the trip to Glasgow week in, week out despite many threats from Hibs and Hearts. These threats were not of the idle variety and Warren got attacked by one of the CCS boys while he was in hospital. That was a disgrace but I am afraid the knuckle draggers who run with the Hobos don't know any better.

He was of course as well known for his love of right-wing politics as he was for following Rangers. He became head of security for the British National Party in Scotland and helped to guard its leader, Nick Griffin, when he ventured north of the border.

It may surprise some people to learn that Warren is one of the friendliest, most amiable lads you could ever meet. He is just a genuinely nice guy. That doesn't mean he can't handle himself because he is no mean scrapper, someone you would always want alongside you in the trenches.

Alan Christie

Clydebank's finest, another ICF stalwart, and someone who has been on the scene since the early 1980s. In his pomp he was a slim, tall, wiry boy and always in the front line, earning him the respect of the likes of Barry,

Harky and Carrick. AC was another who kept going through the dark days of the early Nineties.

Fun to be around and great company, he and his pal Sick Mick were a great comedy duo and kept us well entertained, especially during our forays abroad.

I will never forget him and Harky going at it with thirty hoolies from down south on Jamaica Bridge prior to a Scotland–England game in the late Eighties. I was sitting in a police heavy-eight, having just been arrested, and the way those two got stuck in despite being massively out-numbered was awe-inspiring.

Big Fin

Springburn's answer to Shane Warne. Tall, burly, blond hair, suntanned. Fin first got involved with the ICF in its John Street Jam heyday in 1993/94. With his two pals, Davy and John, they were affectionately dubbed the 'Christmas casuals', a phrase used to describe budding casuals who appeared in January having got new clothes for Christmas but then disappeared off the face of the earth after a few months. Happily, Fin stuck around and became a front-liner. He had the uncanny knack – as I witnessed on many occasions – of being able to knock out an opponent with a single punch.

He should be eternally grateful for my testimony in Manchester Crown Court, which helped him get off scot free from a charge of affray. That's a drink you owe me big man!

4

THE NOT-SO-DANDY DONS

I hate Aberdeen fans almost as much as I hate Celtic. To me they are the lowest of the low. They can't accept that they are no longer number one, that the Sir Alex Ferguson glory days are over and that Rangers became top dogs in Scottish football after Graeme Souness arrived at Ibrox in 1986. Their insane hatred of everything Rangers dates from that time. They just love singing their vile songs about the Ibrox Disaster of 1971, when sixty-six Rangers fans were crushed to death on the stadium steps after an Old Firm game. That is what I mean about the lowest of the low.

For good measure they take great delight in the tackle that nearly ended the career of one of the best players Rangers have produced in the last thirty years: Ian Durrant. The tackle was made by Neil Simpson during an Aberdeen–Rangers game at Pittodrie in 1988 and to me and most Rangers fans it was reckless to say the least. Wee Durranty, a bluenose to his fingertips, was out of competitive football for almost three years, and, when he did manage to make a comeback, was never the same player again. Not that the Sheep gave a fuck. They even made up a little ditty about the incident.

Nice one, Simmy,
Nice one son
Nice one Simmy
Let's have another one.

As for their mob, the Aberdeen Soccer Casuals, I have mixed feelings. Yes, they were instrumental in establishing the casual culture in Scotland. Yes, they could turn out huge numbers of lads. Yes, they fronted up at Wembley and Hampden when England were around. In fact probably my first experience of a real mob came at a Rangers–Aberdeen game at Ibrox in September 1985. Two hundred ASC came down and, although we were very much a fledgling firm and not that well organised, the Aberdeen lads got a hard time from our scarfers, who took exception to the large alien presence in their midst. The scarfers did their best to get at them but Aberdeen were penned in by police horses and the best our guys could do was to pelt them with missiles. Aged thirteen I was impressed not only by the numbers of boys Aberdeen put on the street but also by the bottle they showed.

All of that would have earned them my respect but too often they blotted their copybook either by attacking non-combatants or with other cowardly acts. Where Rangers were concerned they didn't care who got hurt, whether it was ordinary scarfers or even young kids. My other problem is that under the umbrella of a police escort they would mouth off but when it came to meeting us away from the prying eyes of the Old Bill they would, as often as not, fail to front up.

A good example of how they were out of order came one afternoon early in season 1998/99, when I travelled on a normal supporters bus up to Pittodrie. There were five ICF on the bus, but that was it. The rest of the rest of the seats were occupied by scarfers and no one was looking for FV. After we had got parked up in Aberdeen about fifteen of us walked into the city centre, where we split into two groups. I went with the other ICF boys to get something to eat. On the way we passed a pub that was heaving with ASC. About fifty of them steamed out and before you could say 'sheep-shagging bastards' punches were being thrown. We couldn't hold out for long against the sheer weight of numbers and we had to back off. I got on my toes and ran into a chip shop, which was full of Rangers fans, some as young as six. I stood my ground in the doorway and took on four of the cunts. As their boys could only get to me one at a time I managed to hold my own and fought them off, using my fists and a mobile phone as weapons.

'Hello, Sandy. How's it going?' the voice at the other end of the phone said.

I couldn't believe it. My fucking phone had rung while I was fighting for my life in the middle of enemy territory. Maybe I should have let it go to voicemail but, 'you never know,' I thought, 'it might be an important call'.

'Can I call you back? I'm busy right now,' I replied as the blows continued to rain down.

It was a moment of light relief but what happened next was no joke. More ASC arrived on the scene and without further ado they tried to kick in the shop's big plate-glass window. The kids inside the chippy were terrified and started to cry. Not that the ASC cared. Their only priority was to inflict harm on Rangers fans and if a few kids got in the way so what. It wasn't an isolated incident. I have had reports of thirty ASC attacking lone Rangers scarfers and giving them a hell of a doing. It's out of order and well they know it.

It wasn't long before we were able to compete with them. On the day of the Skol Cup final in 1987/88 there was a massive battle on Aitkenhead Road, where the big ASDA is today. There were a hundred and fifty of them, while about seventy of us had splintered off from the main mob. I have to admit it was scary. They were on the front foot, helped by their superior numbers and if it wasn't for a large police presence we would have got a right kicking. One thing will always stick in my mind from that day: Harky steaming right into the cunts on a real suicide mission; the guy is pure class, one of the greatest hooligans of them all.

Being outnumbered by the ASC, even in Glasgow, is a recurring theme. There is a great video on You Tube of us getting it on with them in George Square one holiday weekend in 2001. Rangers didn't have a game that day but about twenty of us were drinking in the Merchant City. We knew they were playing in the west and that they would be in the city later, mobbed up. We got on the phone to them and through the various conversations and a bit of scouting we discovered they had about eighty boys. Despite our best efforts to entice them they wouldn't front up at our pub, which was to become par for the course.

It was time to pay them a visit.

That wasn't the most sensible decision we had ever made. The pub we were in was full of football-intelligence officers and the whole area is closely monitored by closed-circuit television. It was also a holiday weekend, which meant we could be lying in a police cell from the Saturday until the Tuesday, a fucking horrible thought. But we had never knowingly passed up an opportunity for FV and we weren't going to start now. Followed by the FI cops we marched round to the Counting House, a big Wotherspoon's pub in George Square. There was a police van on our route and we expected to be stopped in our tracks. However, much to our surprise we were allowed to keep going and as we walked across the Square, Aberdeen came flooding out of the pub.

Given the relative numbers it was a suicide mission but as the chants of 'ICF, ICF' grew louder and more insistent we gathered speed and were soon engaged in some brief fisticuffs. There were fights all over George Square, including a particularly bloody encounter next to a tourist bus full of foreign visitors. They must have thought it was some kind of street theatre put on for their benefit. Maybe we should have passed round the hat after the 'performance'. The fight itself didn't last long because within a minute we heard the dreaded wail of police sirens. Before we disengaged there was still time for the piece de resistance, a peach of a punch from one of our boys, Wee Moose from Townhead, who, despite his lack of inches, knocked an opponent right on his arse. It was scant consolation because despite the disparity in numbers we knew Aberdeen would claim it as a victory.

We had another reason to worry. The large police presence, backed up by images from the television cameras, meant that one day soon we would face the dreaded knock on the front door in the early hours of the morning. And so it proved: I got my visit, was nicked and then charged. I got a result, though. The procurator fiscal took a decision that six ICF should be prosecuted and he didn't give a fuck who they were. So Davie Carrick put our names in a hat and the six unlucky losers got drawn out. I wasn't one of them.

*

Aberdeen were also at the heart of one of the two or three most memorable days I have ever experienced as a casual. It resulted in me being charged for violent offences in not one but two cities, all of them carried out on the same day. Rangers played Arbroath in the Scottish Cup on 25 January 2003 and before the game we stopped off in Dundee and had it big time with Hibs, who also happened to be in the city.[6] After that fight we headed back to Glasgow and forty of us ended up in the Auctioneers pub, which is just off George Square.

It was a sociable night. We had a few pints, then a few lines to keep us going, then a few more pints, then a few more lines, and so it went. Two Clyde casuals came in and joined us and they too sneaked off to the toilets to do a bit of snorting. We heard the ASC were in town, on their way back to furry-boots city after a game with Queen of the South. After a few hours the boys started to drift off home in dribs and drabs and I was about to call it a day myself when two of them, Ecky and wee Geo Mac, came back into the Auctioneers.

'We were attacked by a mob of ASC,' they told us.

---

[6]   The fight with Hibs is also on YouTube and at the time of writing has been viewed by more than 300,000 people.

It was the proverbial red rag to a bull and in the state we were in there was only going to be one outcome. We grabbed our coats and bounded out of the door.

As soon as we hit the street we saw them. They could tell by the looks on our faces that we were not best pleased by what had happened to our boys and when we charged they turned tail and ran like fuck. We pursued them right round George Square to the Counting House. They now had two choices: stand and fight or get themselves arrested, because the cops were less than a hundred yards away, outside Queen Street station. Some, clearly unnerved by our anger, went straight to the police lines; some to their credit stuck around and got wired in. I was in a right scrap, as were most of the boys, when, suddenly, the lights went out.

I remember being hit hard on the head, staggering and slumping to the ground. It didn't seem that hard a blow and I thought my grogginess was down to the beer and cocaine kicking in. I was also bleeding profusely from a head wound. By this time the cops were on the scene in big numbers and it was time to leave. Big Boris helped me to my feet.

'I'm fucking okay, Boris,' I assured him, but when he let me go I slumped to the pavement again, my brain scrambled. Even in such a befuddled state I knew we had to get away or we would be lifted and as the police approached we ran back in the direction of the Auctioneers. Aberdeen saw it a chance to run us and they chased us all the way back to the pub. Of course they hadn't run us; we were trying to avoid arrest, not run from them, but that is typical of the way they think.

Back in the Auctioneers I knew we might be in trouble. It was a dark night but there was still a chance we would be seen on the CCTV images and arrested at a later date. Sure enough, the next week I got the dreaded chap on the door. I was pissed off for another reason; I had bought a new house in Robroyston and had invited my niece and nephew to stay with me for the night. The last thing you want when you have two young kids sleeping over is for a big, daft polisman to march in with his size tens. Because they were using the bedrooms I slept on the couch and woke at half six with an impending feeling of doom. My sixth sense proved right when, half an hour later, I heard the Old Bill rattling my letter box. I sprang up and went to the back door, to be greeted by two cops waving and smiling.

'Do you know what this is about?' one of them asked.

'No, I haven't a clue,' I lied.

I was bundled into the back of an unmarked police car and driven to Helen Street police station in Govan, which is near to Ibrox. I was taken to the charge desk to hear the counts against me. By now I realised I faced the possibility of being held in a grotty police cell for several days and my mood had darkened considerably. Glasgow's top football intelligence cop, Kenny Scott, was in the room and I thought he was trying to stare right through me in an attempt to unnerve me. The words 'What the fuck are you looking at?' were on the tip of my tongue, but I resisted the temptation.

Later that day I was hauled out of my cell for the trip to Glasgow Sheriff Court. Scott was there to wave me off.

'How do think you'll get on today?' he asked.

'I'll get bail, no problem Kenny,' I blustered, trying to look more confident than I felt.

'Aye, but that wasn't the only place we got you on camera last week,' he replied, in what to me was a really smug tone of voice.

He was right and didn't I know it. Being caught on film for the rucks in Dundee and Glasgow meant I was looking at a seven-day lie down after which I would have to apply for bail again. If that failed I could be remanded for up to 110 days pending a trial. Not a happy prospect. But I got a result; bail for Glasgow and then eventually for Dundee as well. Now all I had to worry about was my trials.

The trial for the Aberdeen incident took place a year later in Glasgow Sheriff Court. The atmosphere in court was tense and dozens of extra police had been drafted in to prevent it kicking off with Aberdeen, which to me was a total overreaction. My lawyer told me there was a deal on the table for a few boys from the ICF and the ASC to plead guilty and for the rest of us to walk free. I was sure the procurator fiscal would insist on me being one of the ones to cop the guilty plea but to my surprise – and delight – he didn't have me on his list. I had been caught on a George Square closed-circuit camera but it was some distance away and I had been wearing dark clothes, which made it hard positively to identify me. Six of our boys weren't so lucky: three had been arrested at the scene; the faces of the other three were clearly seen on the video and when that was taken in conjunction with the police evidence they had no alternative but to hold their hands up. It was no laughing matter. They got up to twenty months for assault and breach of the peace, as did the three ASC who had pleaded guilty.

I later found out that the cops were raging that I had my charges dropped. In fact I heard there was an unholy row between football intelligence and the procurator fiscal about me being let off the hook. The problem for Strathclyde's finest however was that due to the shortcomings of the video evidence there was no way I could be convicted. That I am sure stuck in their craw and made them even more determined to get me on a charge that would stick.

The score was Sandy Chugg 1, police intelligence 0, but I still had another mountain to climb for the fight with Hibs in Dundee. I was worried. I really was. The twenty-month sentences handed down for George Square were to my way of thinking excessive and no doubt due, to some degree, to the pressure the police were exerting. The incident with Hibs was on a bigger scale and looks much more dramatic when you see it on screen. In addition I had no illusions about the attitude of the Old Bill; they would be keener than ever for me to get sent down for a long time, having lost out in Glasgow. The sensible thing would probably have been to plead guilty in the hope of a lighter sentence but when I watched the closed-circuit tapes with my lawyer we noticed right away that although I had been caught much more clearly you could only see the back of my head.

I had a big decision to make, one made even more difficult because by that stage in my life I had a mortgage to pay and two young kids to support. 'Fuck it,' I thought to myself, 'I'll go for not guilty and hope for two in a row.' But when I got to the initial hearing I realised what a stupid mistake I had made: one of the CCS pleaded guilty and got off lightly, with a heavy fine and community service. With a full trial coming up I was facing a lengthy jail term – for mobbing and rioting – when I could have held my hands up and got the same lenient sentence as the Hibs boys. Just before the trial started, after a meeting with my lawyer, we decided to switch from not guilty to guilty. With my form I was still looking down the barrel of some serious bird but I hoped that the last-minute change of plea might persuade the sheriff to cut me some slack when it came to the length of the term.

Lucky for me I had an excellent lawyer, Kevin McCarron, who is actually a Celtic fan. He argued strongly that the sentence had to be comparable with the Hibs guys and so I was fined £1,500 for a reduced charge of breach of the peace and given time to pay.

I have never been so relieved in my life.

*

Because of the way we felt about the Sheep we were regular visitors to Aberdeen. Our problem in the frozen north was getting even a sniff of FV. There were two reasons for this. The first was football intelligence, which by the late 1990s, early 2000s was taking a much more pro-active stance.[7] The FI Old Bill watched us like the proverbial hawk when we got within fifty miles of the place and they kept on watching. You had to be up early in the morning to get one over on the cunts. Our other difficulty was in getting Aberdeen to front up away from the CCTV cameras and the Old Bill. A visit we made in 2001 was fairly typical of the challenges we had to overcome up there.

Our bus left from Glasgow city centre, packed with fifty full-on hooligans, every man jack determined to do the ASC some real damage. When we got to Dundee, instead of taking the main road to Aberdeen, the A90, we decided to go the scenic route via Arbroath and Montrose, figuring that was the best way to avoid plod. We reached the small seaside town of Stonehaven, fifteen miles from Aberdeen, and made straight for the pub. Our task now was to get to the area around Pittodrie without being spotted by Grampian Constabulary. As we sank a few beers and hoovered a few lines one of the boys came in and said there was a souvenir shop along the main street that sold not only the usual tartan tat but also Aberdeen scarves and hats. It was then that someone came up with the bright idea of buying the Sheep gear and pretending to be home fans.

The aim was to get to the main Aberdeen coach park and surprise the ASC. If they weren't there it wouldn't be a wasted journey; we would attack some ordinary fans as payback for the number of times their mob had attacked our scarfers. It all went according to plan. Dressed as Aberdeen scarfers we sailed through several police cordons and drew nearer to the city centre.

Then our luck ran out. When we reached the harbour area, not far from the stadium, the bus was stopped by police motorcyclists. One of them, a real fat bastard, strode onto the coach. He could see that some of us were dressed in casual gear but because a lot of the boys had Aberdeen scarves on he seemed happy enough, walked down the steps and closed

---

[7]   The media firestorm surrounding the 1998 exploits of the Scottish National Firm in Spain and France was undoubtedly a factor in the clampdown.

the bus door. We were on cloud nine. Our plan had worked and the ASC were about to get a bloody good hiding.

The good mood lasted for all of thirty seconds. A dark-coloured, unmarked car screeched to a halt in front of the coach and two senior FI cops promptly got out and boarded the bus. They walked up and down the corridor, peering intently at our faces. Thanks to the contented looks on their faces I could read them like a book.

'Did they really think we would fall for a trick like that? There's Sandy Chugg, that's Davie Carrick and that must be Boris,' they were no doubt thinking.

We were well and truly screwed.

'Are you boys having a fucking laugh?' one of them chortled.

The air blew out of our tyres. We were close to despair. The most heartbreaking thing was that we had come so close, now we were going to be sent straight back down the road. Surprisingly perhaps, we were not escorted out of the city and back down the A90. One of the FI cops radioed in for instructions and was told that any of us with match tickets were to be escorted, on foot, to the stadium and allowed in to watch the game. Those without tickets were kept on the bus and driven, with a police escort, to the car park at the Aberdeen exhibition centre.

For the next hour-and-a-half we were confined to our seats on the coach, which we felt was an infringement of our civil liberties. At that point we were becoming more and more agitated, not to mention very hungry, and to relieve the mood, which was turning ugly, the Old Bill took an order for McDonald's. As everyone shouted out 'burger and fries' or 'cheeseburger' one well-known ICF boy, who is deaf and dumb, wrote 'Twix' on a piece of paper, at which point the whole bus, including the cops, burst out laughing. He was quickly clipped round the ear and told it was a Big Mac or fucking nothing. Let me tell you he has never lived it down to this day.

At the end of the game the bus was driven to the coach park occupied by Rangers supporters and we phoned our mates who had gone to the game to let them know where they could get picked up. As we walked back to the bus a group of thirty ASC appeared from nowhere and tried to set about them. Seeing they were outnumbered Rangers scarfers joined in and Aberdeen were sent packing before the cops could get there and make arrests.

We were accorded the honour of a police escort out of the city and on the way down the road we stopped off in Dundee for a carry out. Our only consolation was a wee drink and a few snorts. Once again it was a case of what might have been where Aberdeen were concerned.

Despite the disappointment of that day in 2001 we were still determined to get the Aberdeen mob on its own patch. We had heard so many stories of our scarfers getting a doing up there and that was a situation that couldn't be allowed to stand. We were now number one in Scotland and we had a duty to stick it to the other leading firms every chance we got. A year later, in January 2002, we put together one of the most formidable mobs I have ever been a part of. There were at least a hundred and fifty of us there that day; from hardened veterans to Rangers youth. In Schooners pub in Aberdeen I looked around in awe at the legends that had turned out. Guys like Barry Johnstone, Davie Carrick, Harky, Andy Curran, Craw and Bomber Morrison, to name but a few. We would have been a match for any mob in Britain with faces like those on our side. The police presence inside and outside the pub and in a pub close by, which was also full of ICF, was massive. Aberdeen knew we were there in numbers and one of their leading boys – Muirhead, I think – stuck his head round the door of Schooners and did a quick head count.

We got an escort to the ground and were channelled into the area reserved for Rangers, which is adjacent to the stand occupied by the hardcore Aberdeen fans and their mob. I remember that the atmosphere – it was a Saturday evening game, if memory serves – was poisonous. We had been drinking and taking lines for hours and were well up for the fray. Most of us would have taken a jail sentence just to have a crack at Aberdeen.

As the mood turned uglier one of the Aberdeen players, Robbie Winters, came over to the touchline in front of our stand and lifted the ball to take a throw in. As he limbered up one of the ICF threw a coin, hitting him right on the head. Pittodrie was in bedlam and as the referee and police came over to Winters we saw our chance and tried to get onto the park. Our aim was to goad the Aberdeen mob and get them onto the pitch for a ruck. But as we surged forward the police drew their batons and pummelled us, forcing us back into the stand. The ASC, give them their due, weren't about to take this lying down and tried to get onto the pitch but they too were beaten back by the filth. As tempers flared Lorenzo Amoruso, the Rangers captain, came over and pleaded with us to calm down. It didn't seem to do much good because the referee decided to take the players off the field while the police tried to restore order by lining the track with officers in full riot gear.

It was at that point the Aberdeen mob showed their true colours.

We were aware of a commotion but it was only after the game that we got the full story. In another part of the stadium, which we couldn't see, some ASC had got onto the track and were attacking Rangers fans. They didn't give a fuck who they hurt, whether it was scarfers, young boys, women, or, in a particularly cowardly move, a seventy-year-old man called Tam Perry. Mr Perry later told a newspaper what happened:

> These young guys started running up the pitch towards the Rangers fans. As they passed me one of them swung a punch and hit me in the face. I couldn't believe it. I was absolutely raging. . . . Then, a few minutes later, bang; something, part of a seat, I think, hit me on the back of my head. I don't think I'll be going back to Aberdeen.

Real fucking heroes. And you wonder why we hate them.

After the game we spread out and went hunting for Aberdeen. But it was always going to be difficult because of the huge number of cops on duty and the presence of closed-circuit-television cameras. There were a few skirmishes but nothing to write home about.

The press had a field day after that one. In the *Daily Record* Jim Traynor, noting the long-standing animosity between Rangers and Aberdeen fans, wrote a long piece arguing that both clubs, the Scottish Premier League and the police had 'turned a blind eye to this hatred' while other observers took the view that it was the worst violence seen in Scottish football for many years. Of course there were the usual attempts to blame the English and the far right, with the papers reporting that every bogeyman from Combat 18 to the Chelsea Headhunters were behind the violence. 'Nazi Link to Thugs,' screamed one headline; 'Football Riot Yobs Are English,' splashed another. Pathetic. There was no evidence that anyone apart from the ICF and the ASC were to blame. When will the Scottish media learn that we don't need the English to do our fighting for us?

That was yet another example of us doing everything in our power to meet Aberdeen head on and of them being chancers who attack women, children and the elderly. For some reason they never wanted to meet us mob-on-mob away from the prying eyes of a police escort or the cameras. We did our best to engineer them away from the surveillance apparatus but they very rarely played along. They were great in the Eighties but have been living on their reputation for too long. I am retired from the FV scene but I will always regret that we never gave Aberdeen the pasting they deserved.

5

CELTIC

When it came to Celtic nothing was out of bounds. And I mean nothing. We ambushed their scarfers, trashed their pubs, took the piss out of their mob, invaded their heartland and threw them off motorway bridges. We even held slashing contests, with the gold medal awarded to the boy who gave the highest of number of their fans a stripe.

I made sure I was always at the heart of the action for our encounters with the Soap Dodgers and, as I became more prominent in the ICF, I became well known not only to their mob but also to whole swathes of their ordinary fans. As well as my penchant for attacking them I am sure my reputation as a staunch supporter of Loyalist causes got right up their noses. In the eyes of the ordinary, everyday Celtic supporter I was public-enemy-number-one.

That was fine with me. I hated them, they hated me. With Celtic there was never any quarter asked for, nor given. It was all-out war. Despite the size of their support I never worried about retaliation. Their mob was only decent for a couple of seasons and as for their scarfers they would only fight when you pushed them into a corner and only then if they had vastly superior numbers. So I felt able to have a go at them every chance I got and not give a second thought to the consequences.

Until, that is, they played their joker.

Fed up with the constant attacks Celtic fans contacted the IRA and asked them to shoot me.

It was 1997. Although I was then in the Scottish National Firm (of which more later) we could always pull a mob for Old Firm games. For years we had targeted the Celtic pubs in the Gallowgate but the closed-circuit-television cameras that now panned every inch of the street had made that impossible.[8] We moved on to the Candleriggs area, just east of the city centre. Candleriggs also had a raft of Irish-themed bars that were popular with Celtic fans and after we had played them they would be full to the gunnels with their scarfers. Their mob was in terminal decline by then but we saw their ordinary fans, many of them hard-line Republicans, as a legitimate target. It was also a good training ground for the Rangers Youth firm, which was pulling healthy numbers at that time. It gave them a taste of real FV.

It became a regular occurrence, panning in those pub windows and pelting the customers inside with bricks and stones. You might even call it a turkey shoot, simply because the pubs were so crowded that they couldn't get out of the way. And if a few brave souls did come out to fight we would wire right in to them.

This went on for a long time. We thought it would never end. But as sure as night follows day there had to be a backlash. One day Davie Carrick and I discovered that our names and addresses had been printed in a Republican magazine. I was outraged. It was a fucking liberty and it had potentially serious consequences for both of us and for our families. I phoned a friend, TB, who, ironically, was a prominent Republican himself. He had shared a cell with a good mate of mine and even though my pal was in the UDA, and the Republican was doing time for firearms offences, the three of us had become firm friends, which shows that you can reach out across the sectarian divide if there is mutual respect.

'What the fuck is all this about?' I asked him.

'Leave it with me. I'll see what I can do. But you've obviously pissed someone off,' TB told me.

A couple of days later the phone rang. It was TB. When he started speaking I noticed it was in a very serious tone.

'The good news is you won't be appearing in the magazine again. The bad news is you've pissed off some prominent Republicans because you keep attacking Celtic fans when they're having a drink.'

There was a pause and then he delivered the news I didn't want to hear.

'Your names have been mentioned with a view to finding out how much it would be for you and Carrick to be sorted.'

---

[8]   See chapter 6: 'Assault on the Gallowgate', written by one of our top boys, Mr Blue. It is an excellent account of our attacks on the pubs in that area.

'To be sorted.' I knew only too well what that meant. It was a euphemism for 'to be shot'.

TB advised me to be careful about my movements, because he had information that thousands of pounds had been raised to pay someone, most likely an IRA soldier or associate, to shoot us. I was worried, who wouldn't have been. This was a step up from football hooliganism. TB was a player in the Republican movement and I knew he was on the inside track.

Despite my anxieties, it didn't stop me from attacking Celtic fans, or their pubs. I was worried but I wasn't about to give into their threats, no matter how credible they were. I am still in one piece and I probably have my Republican mate to thank for that. TB phoned a few weeks later and explained that I was now off the IRA's radar. Whether he had persuaded them not to go through with the hit or they had changed their minds for operational reasons I will never know. As soon as he hung up the phone I breathed an enormous sigh of relief.

The attacks on the Candleriggs pubs did come to an end but not because of the threats. By the late 1990s the ICF numbers had dwindled, with many boys, including me, getting more heavily involved with the Scottish National Firm.

*

As I explained earlier my history with Celtic's mob goes back a long way, to the time they nearly kicked me to death in Mitchell Lane. However, I was well aware of the potential for sectarian clashes long before that episode. That was because my brother, Christopher, would come home from a night's clubbing in the city and tell me all about the fights he had had with Celtic supporters.

In the early 1980s there was such a divide between the two sides that we even went to different nightclubs. Rangers used Viva in Union Street (which is now renamed the Cathouse) while Celtic frequented Daddy Warbucks on West George Street. When the clubs spilled out at three in the morning there would be thousands of drunken young people on George Square desperately looking for a bus or taxi. Celtic would congregate on one side of the Square, Rangers on the other. Mass battles would break out, with both sides backed up by gangs sympathetic to their cause: Possil and Springburn would side with Celtic; Barrowfield and other east-end gangs with us. While the police had their hands full, shops would be looted. We targeted the ones that sold the good gear, like Hoi Polloi and

Olympus, although you had to be careful when you kicked the windows in as they were huge sheets of plate glass that seemed to explode when they shattered. Chris's tales intrigued me and I couldn't wait to go out clubbing and get into the fighting.

By the time I reached my late teens, early twenties I was a regular on the scene and it was then I discovered just how dangerous Glasgow was. It wasn't just the neighbourhood gangs or the football mobs; there was also the Troubles in Northern Ireland to consider. There is no doubt in my mind that what was happening across the water during the mid-to-late Eighties made things infinitely more tense, and therefore more danger-ous, in Glasgow.

A good example of how gang, football and sectarian violence seemed to blend into one came at a Scheme concert in, I think, 1987.[9] Despite his Irish Catholic-sounding name Joe Bradley was an ICF boy who also happened to be in the Possilpark gang and had gone to see Scheme at the Pavilion theatre. A fight broke out with a gang from Barmulloch and Joe was stabbed to death by one of the Barmulloch team, who also happened to be a prominent member of the Celtic Soccer Crew. No one knows why it happened. Was it gang-related, a football thing, or religious? Or, Glasgow being Glasgow, a lethal cocktail made up of all three ingredients? The next day the ICF played the Rangers Soccer Babes at football. Quite understandably, we mourned Joe's loss but it also brought home to us just how dangerous the city had become. We knew that we were targets for a whole network of gangs and, of course, for the CSC and that we could be attacked anytime, anywhere. There was another emotion: a hatred for Celtic that had become even more intense, if that was possible.

As I said the Celtic mob was pretty good in those days and I remember many battles with them. I would only have been twelve at the time but one of the most-talked about incidents came before an Old Firm match at Ibrox in 1985. We had arranged to meet the CSC at Kinning Park industrial estate, which is not far from the ground. We had a mob of about two hundred and I will always remember the sense of anticipation as we walked down Paisley Road West. As we approached the narrow footbridge over the M8 motorway it became clear that Celtic were as keen to get it on

---

[9]   Scheme was a band from one of Glasgow's toughest housing estates, Easterhouse, and hugely popular in the city at the time.

as we were. As they headed for the bridge both sides picked up pace and within seconds we were going hell for leather. A cry went up.

'ICF, ICF. Let's get into these Fenian bastards.'

The police – worried that someone would be thrown off the bridge – did their best to head us off but seventy of us managed to evade them and met Celtic head on. It was chaos on the bridge, where there was room only for three boys on each side. But despite the crush we quickly swamped them and pushed them back to the other side of the motorway.

Most of them managed to scurry back to safety. One wasn't so lucky.

Amongst all the confusion I heard a thud and looked down to see a Celtic boy called Joey Laird lying on a patch of grass. I suppose he was lucky. If he had landed on the concrete he would have been dead, but as it was he suffered brain damage. It was no accident; it wasn't because of the crush. Two Rangers boys had lifted him up and deliberately thrown him off.

As you might imagine the cops were outraged by the Laird incident and it was all hands to the pump to find out who did it – or, the Glasgow polis being the Glasgow polis, to stitch some poor cunt up for it. And that's exactly what they did. After rounding up dozens of ICF and taking us for interview at the procurator fiscal's office it became clear that they were intent on putting Barry Johnstone in the frame. Not because he did it – it was nothing to do with him – but because he was our top man and probably the most feared hooligan in Scotland. We stood firm. Every single one of us stonewalled them and no one was ever prosecuted.

How did we feel about Joey Laird? To be perfectly honest most of the boys were buzzing. They felt it was a right result. Me? I knew Joey and had mixed feelings about what happened to him.

While that was an interesting day out I had been too young to make a real contribution. Two years later, however, after another Old Firm encounter, again at Ibrox – older, bigger and stronger – I really came of age, not least in the eyes of the more experienced ICF boys. It was January 1987, which would make me fourteen. After the game, we met the CSC behind Ibrox primary school and a vicious battle broke out. There were no cops around to break things up so you had to choose whether to get into the fight or to cower on the sidelines. It was one of those situations that define you as a hooligan.

We had some Chelsea boys with us; members, it was said, of Britain's toughest mob. Don't make me fucking laugh. They stood and watched, paralysed with fear, as it went off. Those 'hard men' from London took one look at the reality of Old Firm violence and stayed in their front-row seats. That was their choice. That was how they would be defined.[10] Meanwhile the teenage Sandy Chugg got wired in. That was my choice. That was how I would be defined. It helped cement my reputation and afterwards our older boys were full of admiration for the 'game wee cunt' who had gone toe-to-toe with Celtic.

*

As the 1990s dawned there was no let-up in the war between us and Celtic. One night we would be looking for revenge for an attack on our boys, on other nights they would come looking for us. It was a deadly game of tit-for-tat, one that could easily end in tragedy. That is the way Glasgow was in those years. It may sound melodramatic to say that it was like a war zone but for many guys of my age, on both sides of the fence, that's exactly how it felt. Trouble came out of nowhere. It could happen anytime, any-where. You had to be on your guard at all times. There was no alternative.

It was 1990. We still frequented different nightclubs; Celtic used Tin Pan Alley in Mitchell Lane, while we favoured the Hacienda, which is close to Glasgow Sheriff Court. This Friday night, no doubt enraged by another doing at the football, they came looking for us. We weren't there that night but some of our associates were. It kicked off and the CSC got the worst of it, forcing them to butt out, chased by our pals. One of the Celtic boys, Gary McGuire, was cornered on the steps of the Sheriff Court. He had no chance. He was stabbed and left to die.

The murder of Gary McGuire had nothing to do with the ICF. I even printed a newsletter explaining that we weren't anywhere near the Hacienda that night. Later a boy nicknamed Wee Semi was convicted of the murder and given a life sentence and he was certainly never a member of the Rangers mob. None of that cut any ice with the CSC. They blamed the ICF for what happened to Gary and after that they were hell bent on taking revenge on us. There were skirmishes almost every night, with boys on both sides getting badly beaten up. Glasgow's streets were as dangerous as they had ever been.

As time went on however we began to get the upper hand on Celtic and by the end of the Nineties we were completely dominant, with our

---

[10]   These lads would claim to be Chelsea bods but were most probably back-liners at best. In the years to come we got to know the real Chelsea Headhunters and their youth mob. They were, and are, a top firm.

success mirroring what was happening on the field of play.[11] In fact the CSC deteriorated to such an extent that it rarely if ever turned out, even for games at Celtic Park. We didn't have a mob to fight so there was only one alternative open to us: attack their scarfers. That was the period when we really turned the screw on the ordinary Celtic fan. We hounded them mercilessly, especially when we went to the Piggery. I will never forget those days of glory, when we left Celtic Park with a mob of four hundred, belting out 'The Sash' as we celebrated yet another victory. Soon our thoughts turned to FV and we went through our full repertoire of war chants and songs:

We are the Section Red[12]
Celtic are dead

Or my favourite, which we sang to the tune of 'Don't Dilly Dally on the Way (My Old Man)':

My old man said be a Celtic fan,
Fuck off father you're a wank
Well take the Hibs and their casuals with it
We'll take the Jungle and the shite that's in it.

With hatchets and hammers,
Stanley knives and spanners
We'll show the Fenian bastards how to fight.

So come all ye lads to the Ibrox stands
And join the Inter City,
We're so pretty
The Inter City
The Inter City Firm

---

[11]   Rangers' dominance on the park was quite incredible. From 1988/89 until 1999/2000 we won eleven league titles out of twelve, provoking Celtic's 'Sack the Board' campaign, the ousting of the families who had run the club for decades and the takeover by the 'talking bunnet', Fergus McCann.

[12]   Section Red was an area of seats in the Govan and Broomloan stands at Ibrox. We even thought of changing our name from ICF to Section Red because we didn't want to have the same name as West Ham, but the name didn't catch on.

We walked proudly along London Road, went through Bridgeton Cross, past the back of the Barras and down to the Gallowgate, where all the Celtic pubs are. I have lost count of the number of times we smashed the windows in with volleys of bricks, traffic cones and metal poles. One time an undercover cop tried to stop us and was laid out by a single punch from one of our leading boys. With the windows tanned we did our level best to force our way into the boozers to get at the Great Unwashed who were lurking inside. It was always chaotic, with patrons and police coming together in an attempt to repel us.

Before some games at Parkhead we would even mingle with the Celtic scarfers, using every tool at our disposal to provoke them. One afternoon, after a drink in the Bristol, fifteen of us marched up Millerston Street, where there would be thousands of them on their way to the game. We didn't give a fuck about being outnumbered and gave them several choruses of 'Rule Britannia' to announce our presence.

'Fuck off you Orange bastards,' they retorted, which set off several little skirmishes. A Celtic fan threw a bottle at us, which one of our boys caught on his knee and proceeded to play keepy-uppy with. That made them even angrier and as we got closer to the ground it became more and more dangerous for us. By now, in that swelling ocean of green and white, they could see how few of us there were, which I always thought was the equivalent of feeding them 'game pills'. The police knew a bloodbath was a distinct possibility and one of their vans, a 'heavy eight', hove into view. The cops got out and after a great deal of pushing and shoving, managed to form a cordon around our little group. Then they herded us inside the van and took us to Parkhead Forge, which is on the route to Celtic Park traditionally used by Rangers fans.

The hatred we felt for all things green and white led us down some dark alleys of the soul. One such alley was a slashing contest between two of our main and iconic lads after an Old Firm game. The rules of the game were simple: whoever slashed the most Celtic fans would be declared the winner and inducted into the ICF hall of fame. To make sure we didn't get detected by the coppers we took an alternative route through Duke Street and along High Street, one that would give us exposure to the maximum number of Celtic fans. The two contestants weren't satisfied with an ordinary, common or garden knife. They attached Stanley blades to ice-lolly sticks to give then a tramline. It meant that when you were slashed it would be much harder for the doctor to stitch. Who won? It was honours even. They got ten each and we declared it a draw.

*

Although by the twenty-first century the golden days of the casuals had gone forever there was still huge potential for trouble any time we played Celtic. After one Old Firm game the ICF were drinking in the city centre when twenty of us decided to go to the Merchant City to look for them. Due to the number of police on the streets we got split up and I found myself in a group of five, made up of four Youth and me. I don't know why but I had a sixth sense that we were going to come unstuck. We ended up in a pub in Trongate and we knew that the CSC had also been drinking in the area. So it was no great surprise that when we walked out there were twenty of them in front of us. Two of the Youth panicked and ran away. I had two bottles in my hand and I said to the two who were left, 'No matter what happens I'm not running away.'

I knew one of the Celtic boys. I had helped him out in the past and now he was about to return the favour. He did his best to get me to leave quietly.

'Sandy, just put down your bottles and walk away. We will let you off this time,' he counselled.

I took his advice and calmly walked away, without panicking. I went into the pub that the two Rangers Youth had run into. I wasn't going to leave them. Nobody owed them any favours and they would have been given a right doing if Celtic got a hold of them. In the end they bailed out the back door of the pub. Their mistake was to panic and run away. You should never do that.

That wasn't my last encounter with Celtic. In 2005 after an Old Firm game the ICF were drinking in the Orange Lodge in Rutherglen, after which, funnily enough, we moved to a former Celtic boozer, which was then called The Edge. We had been on the phone to Celtic but as usual they were hiding in the pubs of the Gallowgate. First the Rangers Youth got in touch with them but no joy. Then I belled their top boy but he didn't want to know either.

At eight o'clock I heard a commotion at the front door when a couple of the Youth lads left the building. When I went out to find out what the fuck was going on I saw that twenty Celtic were in a confrontation with our Youth. By this time all the main ICF boys were outside and they steamed into Celtic. I was fighting this fat lad when, all of a sudden, I was picking myself up off the pavement. I had no idea who, or what, had hit me. I tasted blood in my mouth and began to spit out bits of my teeth. I saw five Celtic boys lying on the ground and it was then I realised that I had been knocked out, because the fight had moved on up the street.

'Sandy, Sandy,' someone was shouting.

I looked up and saw an old pal, Scooby, a Rangers fan from Haghill. He had been driving past and had seen me on the deck. Realising how bad I looked he drove me to the Royal infirmary. When I found out it would be several hours before I would be attended to I made a few phone calls to find out what exactly had happened. While I was told that several Celtic boys had been knocked out I didn't find out what had happened to me until later. It turned out that one of the Rangers Youth had inadvertently hit me with a traffic cone while he was attacking the CSC. He denies it to this day even though I have reassured him there are no hard feelings.

I decided not to wait for treatment but to go home and lie down on my own bed. However, when I woke up I not only had a pain in my mouth but also on my neck and, to make matters worse, I had a blinding headache. I had recently (and temporarily) split up with my wife so a pal drove me to Monklands hospital. They were too busy to see me so on we went on to the accident-and-emergency unit at Stobhill.

I was seen pretty quickly at Stobhill and they took a precautionary X-ray, after which I was put in a neck brace and strapped to a trolley. I began to panic and asked the staff what was wrong. I was told there was a serious abnormality: an injury to one of my vertebrae, and that it might have moved. The worst-case scenario was that I might need a spinal operation, although they also said it could be an undiagnosed medical condition.

For the next three hours I went through hell. All sorts of thoughts swirled around in my head. What would the effect be on my kids, my employment prospects and my already fragile marriage? And all because of a fight after the football. As usual a drunk was abusing the nurses and I said to him, 'If I could get up I'd fucking strangle you.'

I had another X-ray, after which I was made to do some exercises with my neck. They discovered I had a congenital vertebra defect, which had gone undetected. It wasn't as bad as they thought and when the tests were completed I was discharged. I have never been so relieved in my life. As I made my way home I weighed up what had happened. It was another lesson about the hazards of being a hooligan and I couldn't stop thinking about the effects that a serious injury could have on my sons. I also realised that one of the reasons for my temporary split with Kerry was because of the football violence. Of course none of that put me off. I loved Rangers and I loved running with the ICF. Nothing was going to change that.

6

ASSAULT ON THE GALLOWGATE: MR BLUE'S STORY

It is ironic that I was raised in the Gallowgate, which is without doubt the spiritual home of the Celtic support. Their shining city on a hill. It was always thronged with Celtic fans and Republican sympathisers before and after Old Firm games and was therefore a hard place for the ICF to go. Until that is one day, sometime in the mid-to-late Eighties, when we went there and fucking annihilated anyone who got in our way.

What follows is Mr Blue's experience of that fateful day.

Looking back, going to Celtic Park was a weird situation in the 1980s. There are three main roads into Celtic Park from the city centre and Rangers, despite being the away team, dominated two of them. London Road was always a no-go for Celtic mainly because they would have to negotiate Bridgeton Cross, which was always a bridge too far due to Bridgeton being the predominant Rangers, Protestant and Loyalist area in Glasgow. Another entry point to the Piggery was through Duke Street, which has always been known as a Rangers area, however it wasn't unusual to find Celtic fans wandering through en route to that dump, until of course the ICF came on the scene around 1983/84. For the rest of the Eighties, Duke Street became our domain, even on days when we weren't play-ing at Parkhead. From 1983 until 1989 it was defended vigorously from many Celtic invasions. Quite often Celtic's firm would ignore their opposition that day/ night and try to get through Duke Street unscathed. It also wasn't unusual for us to ignore our game in order to defend our 'headquarters'. Being from Glasgow we looked down on everybody else in Scotland anyway and, to many of us, only Celtic mattered – so missing some games to get one over them wasn't a problem.

Whilst holding superiority on the streets leading to Celtic Park was great for us we didn't quite have what the military call 'supremacy'. Generally speaking when Celtic came to Ibrox they had to scurry up back streets as we had total dominance on the roads from the city centre to Ibrox. Whether we were at home or away we ruled supreme on the streets of Glasgow . . . with one exception.

That fly in the ointment was known as the Gallowgate!

The Gallowgate is to Celtic what Bridgeton has always been, and Duke Street became, to Rangers. It was their base, their spiritual home. They were safe there. They couldn't be touched there. Their firm were surrounded there by many active IRA men who in turn were surrounded by hundreds – which became thousands on match days – of IRA sympathisers who drank in the Gallowgate's many Republican pubs. Take the murderers, terrorists, hard men, Celtic's firm and throw in the odd nutter – it's fair to say the Gallowgate was a pretty ferocious place for anyone of a bluenose persuasion.

To the east-end lads in the Rangers firm the Gallowgate was a bit of a bogeyman. Although there had been whispers about 'taking it', and even some half-hearted plans about how we would achieve that feat, it remained the untouchable green fortress on the hill.

The first Old Firm game of the season always brings a unique sense of antici-pation. When early August comes around you are straining at the leash to get going. I made an early start that day, meeting Jinks and a few other lads on Duke Street. Although lads from Duke Street and elsewhere in the east end often made their own way directly to Celtic Park, having their own battles, we decided to head into town to have a drink in Minstrels, our pub of choice at the time. We got to Minstrels at half twelve and there was a decent seventy or eighty lads already in there. By two o'clock our numbers had grown to one hundred and fifty or so. 'We better make a move,' somebody said, to be met by the usual moans and groans: 'Fuck off you, I've just got a pint in,' and 'I canny be arsed walking, you won't find Celtic until after the game, I'm jumping in a taxi.'

About forty of us left, walked up onto Argyle Street and began the couple of miles walk to the Piggery. We came across small pockets of Celtic's firm, who had been dispatched to keep a close eye on us. Then, somewhere on Argyle Street, it was said.

'Mon go up that fuckin Gallowgate and do these cunts there.' 'Aye mon,' another voice said 'they are fucking shit.'

Those fateful words had been uttered. It had been said. Now it had been said many times before but this time it was seconded. Before long it was 'thirded' and we were off.

I looked around at the boys with us and realised it was far from our top firm. We had maybe seven or eight top-table lads and a collection of dependable, but by no means main lads, in which category, incidentally, I included myself at that time. As we approached Glasgow Cross it was time . . . time to decide. I was thinking 'It's one thing chasing off fifteen of them bastards here, and twenty there, but this is the Gallowgate for fuck's sake, they will have their main firm, backed up by a good few hundred others, who'd be delighted to murder us.'

Being 100 per cent honest I was half hoping we would choose the right-hand side of the Glasgow Cross fork and head for the safety of Bridgeton via London Road. That wasn't because I was a shitbag – quite the contrary, I was beginning to make a decent name for myself in our firm – but because I wasn't into suicide missions (this would change!) and this was a suicide mission and a half. As we approached the fork I knew we were heading left because after it had been said and backed up there was no fucking way we could do anything else.

'Oh fuck,' I thought. Again, being 100 per cent honest, it briefly crossed my mind to accidentally lose our lads in the crowd. 'Fuck that, get a grip ya cunt,' I was telling myself. As we got into the middle of Glasgow Cross our forty or so had became thirty: possibly one or two of the lads had the same concerns as me; possibly others had accidentally lost us; and possibly some had been carried away chasing the little pockets of Celtic we'd done. Whatever the reason our already small number of boys had been reduced by a quarter.

As we got closer to the Barras, where Celtic pubs are everywhere, all I could see was a sea of them in front, behind us, around us, everywhere. I felt it like I'd never felt it before. The fear, the dread, the expectation that we'd struggle like fuck. We were on the enemy's doorstep; we were about to face the bogeyman with seriously depleted numbers. I fucking loved it.

As we got closer, Harky, Chugg and one or two others walked into the middle of the road and swaggered towards their main pub without a care in the world. That helped: being a relatively young lad I needed a display of confidence like that to reassure me. We got to within thirty yards of the front door, our pace quickening, when I saw John O'Kane, Celtic's main lad, running down the middle of the road towards us. He had a few others behind him but it was impossible to work out how many due to the number of shoppers and scarfers who were thronging the street.

As O'Kane got closer I noticed he was carrying a pint with some lager still in it. He poured out the beer and bent down to smash the glass on the road, but as the glass broke, bang, Harky had put him on his arse. That alarmed the rest of the Tarriers, who seemed shocked to see us on the Gallowgate. By now they were hesitant. We weren't. The shout went up 'ICCCF ICCCF' as we charged forward. By now Celtic were off, not just backing off, but fully turned and running past their pubs, through the Barras market. They were in full fucking panic mode. A few of the local loons came out of Baird's and Norma Jean's (as it then was) well tooled up. But we had the momentum, we were unstoppable and lads who've been part of a firm will know the feeling. The momentum was with us.

'ICCCF, ICCCF.'

Hearing that chant as we obliterated the Gallowgate sent shivers down my spine. Then we heard that familiar sound. Sirens! As the police came flying down the Gallowgate we ran through the market and came out the other side at London Road, by which time, amidst the mayhem, our thirty had become fifteen.

'Lets go back and do them again,' somebody said.

'Aye, mon, that was fucking brilliant.'

'Walk down here and come out one hundred yards fae Baird's and we'll walk up again.'

I was buzzing like fuck and was delighted to carry on. In fact looking back I possibly even suggested it. Fuck knows, whatever the case, we were going back into the lion's den. We cut through one of the side streets that run from London Road onto the Gallowgate. There was a tentative peek around the corner to check for the police. Nothing. Great, we were on again, and as we walked back towards their pubs it slowly dawned on me that before the last battle the actual road was a heaving mass of people, people we could blend in with. However, now it was us, just us, fifteen-handed!

As we got within ten yards of Baird's they spotted us and this time they were tooled up to fuck. After a brief exchange they had us backing off, and, within seconds, I heard a commotion from behind. It was the other part of Celtic's firm who we had chased off in dribs and drabs along Argyle Street. Fucking hell, we were in serious trouble now. Then, as we made for the safety of London Road, I heard the beautiful sound of sirens. Luckily, the market was still crammed full of shoppers – it takes more than a spot of football violence to stop a Glaswegian in search of a bargain – so we were able to blend in and get to safety, almost in one piece. By now there were only six in my group.

'Naw, don't even fucking think about going back again,' I said with feeling.

I had a black eye and Jinks had a broken nose, a few of our expensive garments were totalled and I believe that was the sum total of our casualties. It was now quarter to three. As we made our way up London Road we bumped into other ICF, some in groups of five or six, some twenty-strong. As we told our stories there was a mood of envy amongst the lads who weren't there and of what might have been among the lads who were.

'If even half of the lads in Minstrels were there we'd have ran them cunts all the way into their shithole of a stadium,' I said, to general agreement.

The atmosphere in the Rangers end was fucking phenomenal. By now all our firm knew what had happened. We could see their main lads in the Jungle and they looked gutted. I can't blame them. I think the final score was 1–1 but I couldn't be sure; I couldn't have cared less. What I remember very clearly is that *after the game we mobbed up outside and our firm was at least five hundred-strong. Word had got around about what happened before the game and, although nothing was said, we all knew we were going back for seconds. As we headed along London Road we came to Baines Street, and, without anybody saying a word, we turned right and walked the couple of hundred yards to the corner of Baines Street and the Gallowgate.*

'ICCCF, ICCCF,' we chanted.

There were thousands of Celtic fans around but that didn't matter. Confronted by five hundred Rangers they lost it; you could taste the fear radiating from them. They were shiting themselves. Their firm, the Celtic Soccer Casuals, and various other groups of terrorists, local nutters and hard men tried to front us but they were utterly destroyed. They were chased everywhere. They tried to make a stand several times but the tone had been set when just thirty of us had done them before the game. It had been like the Alamo in reverse.

We had the momentum, we had the belief and we were beheading a bogey-man on behalf every Rangers fan in the city. No more would the Gallowgate be tiptoed around and over the course of the next four or five years we terrorised those cunts in that shithole whenever we chose. Possibly the biggest clue to our utter domination was the fact Baird's, Norma Jean's and the other Celtic dumps closed their doors whenever we played at Celtic Park. Before that day we were already dominant against Celtic's firm, after that day we moved into another stratosphere.

We knew, better still, they knew.

7

I WILL FOLLOW ON

I am not a bigot. That statement will surprise some people, given the team I support, the mob I joined, my antipathy towards Celtic and even the title of this book. But it's true.

While I disagree strongly with the teachings of their church I have nothing against individual Roman Catholics. I even married a Catholic in a Catholic chapel. People are entitled to their own beliefs and that includes adhering to whichever religion they choose. Freedom of speech, freedom of conscience, freedom of worship; these things are what Britain is all about and what made this country great.

I was glad when Rangers started to sign Roman Catholics. I was glad when Rangers made a Roman Catholic the club captain. I was glad when we appointed a Roman Catholic manager, even if he did turn out to be a dud. Those were the right things to do. And I don't just mean in a moral sense, although that was important too. Opening the floodgates meant that we could draw on a much wider talent pool; it has made Rangers stronger on the field and that for me is what it's all about. In fact I would go further: I believe that had the old signing policy been scrapped earlier Rangers would have won the European Cup before Celtic did.

The change in the signing policy had another beneficial spin-off: it meant that Celtic supporters and their many camp followers in the media and in politics no longer had that particular stick to beat us with. It was something they raised at every opportunity and in every forum and it took its toll on our reputation. That said I don't think Celtic fans have been entirely honest about this issue. It seems to me – and to many of a light-blue persuasion – that the only reason Celtic signed Protestants was because there weren't enough Catholics in Scotland for them to choose from. Celtic had to broaden its horizons, not for principled reasons, but to put a competitive team on the park. Just think of the way they treated Jock Stein, the most important man in their history. They should have given Stein a seat on the board when he stepped down as manager but chose instead to give him a job in the pools department. That to me was an insult and I believe that had he been a Catholic he would have been a shoo-in for the boardroom.

While I defend the right of people, including Roman Catholics, to worship as they see fit, that does not mean the Roman Catholic Church, or Roman Catholics, should be above criticism. Some questionable things have been done in their name. Scottish Catholics like to make out they have been discriminated against in Scotland, and, while there is some truth in that, it doesn't tell the whole story. Let us consider 1920, when the conflict over Irish independence was boiling over, a conflict that the Irish in the west of Scotland took more than a passing interest in. In that year Charlie Diamond, editor of the *Glasgow Observer* – the main newspaper for Scotland's Roman Catholics – was sent to prison for advocating terrorist attacks on British troops in Ireland. Nor did a jail sentence stop Diamond from supporting extremism. In the late 1920s and early 1930s the *Observer*, under his editorship, praised the fascist regimes of both Hitler and Mussolini in the most glowing terms. The *Glasgow Observer* in those days was also consistently and fiercely anti-Semitic, describing Jews among many other things as 'odious and unscrupulous exploiters'. It is significant that there were no protests at the *Observer*'s vile editorial policy from Scotland's 'downtrodden' Catholics or from the Roman Catholic hierarchy of the day.

There was also a strong link at that time between fascism and Irish Republicanism. In May 1945, shortly after Hitler committed suicide, the government of the Irish Republic sent a wreath to the German embassy in Dublin. While almost every country in the world celebrated the death of the cruellest man in history Ireland mourned his passing. It is also well documented that the Irish Republic was a haven for Nazi war criminals after the Second World War.

But for some Scots from an Irish Catholic background it wasn't enough simply to incite violence against the Crown. They went even further, bringing Republican terrorism to the streets of Glasgow. In 1921 an IRA commander, Frank Carty, was being transported in a Black Maria from the High Court to Duke Street prison. The van was attacked by a ten-man IRA unit, who shot dead a police inspector, Robert Johnston, before turning their guns on his two fellow officers. It was only thanks to the courage of these two officers that the raid was foiled. Carty was safely delivered to his prison cell.

Inevitably, there was anger at the atrocity perpetrated by the IRA. In the aftermath of Duke Street there were sectarian riots in Glasgow, most notably in the Gallowgate, which left many people injured and caused extensive damage to houses and commercial property. The police did their best to find those who had planned and carried out the raid on the van and discovered that the IRA men had been helped by some members of Glasgow's large Catholic population. In St Mary's RC church in the east end the police found a huge cache of guns and bomb-making equipment. A priest and seven parishioners were arrested, but due to lack of evidence no one was ever prosecuted for the 'Glasgow outrage', as it became known.

In the field of education the Roman Catholic Church is responsible for the most divisive policy of the last hundred years. I am talking of course about the educational apartheid forced on this country by the presence of separate Catholic schools. 'Rome on the rates', as it was once known, is to my way of thinking deeply damaging. In the already divided west of Scotland it divides people even more, breeding distrust and exacerbating sectarianism. The vast majority of Scots agree with me, if opinion polls are to be believed. Given that they asked for and were granted their own state-funded schools I am not sure how Catholics can square this with their contention that they are seriously discriminated against.

Then there is the scandal of the paedophile priests, a scandal that the RC Church desperately tried to cover up. It was systematic abuse that lasted for decades, perhaps even centuries. One wag summed it up when he said, 'At one time young Irish boys wanted to enter the priesthood, now it's the other way around . . .' The whole thing was a disgrace; it turned my stomach. You have to question the morality of the bishops and the cardinals, supposed men of God, who not only turned a blind eye to what was going on but also actively conspired to get the perverts off the hook.

Despite the claims by Catholics about unfair treatment today the boot is firmly on the other foot. It seems to me that the Scottish establishment now actively favours people of that religious persuasion. By contrast we Protestants have been made to feel ashamed of our religion, our background and even our football team. We have been cowed by the relentless propaganda that pours out of Holyrood and the media, all of it designed to make us feel like second-class citizens. Celtic fans wallow in their Irishness, even those whose only connection with Ireland is to have once drunk a pint of Guinness.

This new state of affairs is accurately reflected at Ibrox. Rangers fans hate Celtic as much as they ever did but are now afraid to say it. While Celtic fans feel free to sing songs praising the IRA and other murderers, or to boo a minute's silence commemorating British soldiers who died for this country, we sit on our hands, unable to celebrate our heritage. The atmosphere at Ibrox has been ruined by bans on this song and that chant, even when they are clearly humorous, designed only to wind-up Celtic supporters. Take for example the 'Famine Song', a witty little ditty which suggests that as the potato famine is over Celtic fans might like to go back home to Ireland ('The famine's over/Why don't you go home?', sung to the tune of 'Sloop John B'). Some daft bugger with green-tinted spectacles complained to the Irish embassy in London, who in turn passed the complaint along to the Scottish government. Meanwhile Celtic too jumped on the bandwagon, with Dr John Reid, club chairman, describing the 'Famine Song' as 'vile, racist and sectarian'. Then, in November 2008, came the most ludicrous overreaction of them all, when a young Rangers fan was convicted of breach of the peace for singing it at a Kilmarnock–Rangers game.

The establishment in Scotland hates what Rangers stand for. Politicians, the media and churches portray anyone connected with the club as right wing, bigoted and old fashioned. To them we are an embarrassment. It came as no surprise to me that the anti-sectarian organisation, Nil by Mouth, was set up following the murder of a young Celtic fan. Since its inception in 2000 it has been handed substantial amounts of taxpayers' money to help meet its running costs. The murder in question was horrific, and as a father my heart goes out to the boy's parents, but I strongly believe that if it had been a young Rangers fan who had been murdered the Scottish establishment wouldn't have bothered. Nor have I, and most other Rangers fans, been impressed by NBM's campaigns. To me they lean towards helping Celtic and Celtic fans. Nil by Mouth even gave evidence against the Rangers fans accused of singing discriminatory chants by UEFA.

The Scottish government proudly proclaims that it is fighting racism, sectarianism and discrimination. One of its campaigns had a slogan 'One Scotland. Many Cultures'. That's right, but not if you're Protestant, Unionist, working class and a Rangers supporter. I am of course a member of that endangered species – and I do mean endangered, because everything I believe in and hold dear is under attack in modern-day Scotland.

First and foremost I consider myself Scottish and British. But I am also a proud Glaswegian. This is a great city with a proud past, at one time a world city that produced more ships and railway engines in a year than the whole of Germany. Shettleston, my spiritual home, is a microcosm of Glasgow, full of hard-working, down-to-earth, friendly people; they are the salt of the earth. I have strong links with Shettleston: my mum worked there; I had a house in the area; my aunt lived there; many ICF, including Harky, come from the place. I also happen to like the many Roman Catholics who hail from Shettleston; they are a welcome addition to the community.

To me an essential part of being British is an appreciation of our armed forces. They epitomise everything that is great about this country. They are the real heroes. As a boy I read about the 36th Ulster Division, and was inspired by the heroism of its soldiers. The 36th grew out of the Ulster Volunteer Force, which was formed by Sir Edward Carson to prevent Northern Ireland from being subsumed into a united Ireland. The Ulster Division fought bravely throughout the First World War and on a single day at the battle of the Somme in 1916 suffered more than five thousand casualties. Reading about those brave Ulstermen gave me ambitions to serve. I wanted to be a Royal Marine and at the age of seventeen I was all ready to join-up but Mum wouldn't sign the papers granting me permission and the opportunity to serve my country slipped away. I never miss the chance to defend our servicemen and women and the great job they do. I am regularly on radio phone-ins, where I go toe-to-toe with people I believe are trying to put down Britain and its values. One such person, I would argue, is the socialist politician, George Galloway, and I have had more than a few ding-dongs with him on the airwaves.

In political terms I am on the right of the spectrum. I admit to attending the odd British National Party meeting when I was younger and, yes, I did sign the nomination papers for a BNP candidate but that is my right in a free society. For the record I should make it clear that I agree with some of the BNP's policies. Immigration has become much too easy and has to be more tightly controlled – but on the other hand I do not agree with the forced repatriation of immigrants. That said people moving here from abroad have to integrate and to respect this great country of ours and all it stands for. My message to immigrants when it comes to Britain is. 'Love it or leave it.' Simple as.

My political hero or heroine if you like, is Margaret Thatcher. She stood firm against so many challenges, whether it was militant trade unions, the Soviet Union or General Galtieri. She also allowed tenants to buy their own council houses, giving people who would never normally have got the chance a foothold in the property market, freeing them from the yoke of municipal socialism. I certainly wouldn't be as well off today if it wasn't for Maggie freeing up the economy, although on the negative side I do admit that the country became a little more selfish when she was prime minister. Most importantly of all she refused to capitulate in the face of violent Irish Republicanism. Without her the proud Protestant people of Northern Ireland – who have fought so bravely for Britain through the ages – might now be part of the Republic of Ireland.

I am still opposed to, and suspicious, of the Republican movement. Its leaders say they are now wedded to the democratic process but I remain to be convinced. There is a new danger on the horizon, as younger Republicans become disillusioned with the peace process and join organisations like the Continuity IRA, which has recently been involved in terrorism. Everyone of a Loyalist persuasion will need to be vigilant.

My Loyalism is the main factor in my antipathy towards all things Celtic. I just can't accept that Celtic fans, who have benefited greatly from living in this country, sing songs that praise people who have murdered British soldiers, not to mention many innocent women and children. Celtic apologists will argue that only a small minority sing the 'Boys of the Old Brigade' and suchlike but I am not so sure. And if it is just a 'small minority' then why do the majority let them get away with it? If they really wanted to they could stop the hatemongering tomorrow by putting pressure on those who are doing the singing. But they don't and that tells its own story.

My sense of Britishness, of being a Loyalist and a Protestant, has cemented my love of Rangers. We have signed Catholics, we have had Catholics in positions of authority; one day we may even be owned by a Roman Catholic. But to the supporters we will always be a Protestant club despite what I see as the apparent desire of the powers-that-be at Ibrox to suppress our traditions and rewrite our history. I have attended hundreds of games, at home and away, in Scotland and across Europe. I played for the club as a schoolboy and dreamt of becoming a defensive midfielder in the mould of Lee McCulloch or Rino Gattuso. I have bought the replica kits and the memorabilia. I am bringing up my two sons in the true Rangers way. I have risked life and limb to defend Rangers scarfers when they have been attacked by opposition mobs or the Spanish police. But what thanks have I had?

Three life bans from Ibrox. That's what.

As the letters in the plate section of this book show Rangers have seen fit to ban me from the place I love, most recently in 2007 (although the ban was rescinded in 2009).

The bans hurt but they never affected my feelings for the club, which I consider to be the greatest in the world.

I *will* follow on

8

HIBS: THE ROAD TO SLATEFORD

I had never felt so low. I was sitting in Deans's pub in Shettleston, a great wee howff frequented by ICF, gangsters and assorted local hard men. I couldn't get the disasters of the afternoon out of my mind. It had been the most humiliating episode in ICF history. My mood was hardly lightened when in bowled Harky, full of the joys of spring as per usual.

'What's the matter Sandy? I heard you got your baws kicked in Edinburgh,' he said sarcastically.

'Fuck off ya dick. At least I was there,' was my considered response.

But, despite my retort, deep down I knew he was right. We had been annihilated that afternoon in October 1994. Many ICF, a good proportion of them young and inexperienced, got a doing. Several were hospitalised.

I had also taken a beating. Hibs had landed volleys of kicks, punches and missiles on my body. I was cut and bruised and my legs were aching, a result of my vain attempts to ward off the CCS.

The emotional pain was much worse and the constant, albeit light-hearted, ribbing I got that night in Deans's didn't help. It wasn't just from Harky. The regulars, most of them formidable scrappers in their own right, didn't spare my feelings. They gave me pelters. I was in turmoil and the copious quantities of drink and drugs I was ingesting were no help at all. I went over Slateford again and again in my mind. One thought predominated.

What could I have done differently?

*

Hibs were always formidable opponents. Over the piece they were the best mob we ever faced, at least in Scotland. It wasn't just their fighting abilities. They had style, an abundance of self-confidence and a cockiness that came with being the top mob. They didn't walk, they swaggered.

What made them so good? I think one of the main things was their unity. They were a tight-knit group, at least in the early days. Most of them came from the same, relatively small, areas of Edinburgh. That was a unifying factor and helped to bond them. They were so close that, when they were formed, consideration was given to calling their firm The Family, before they settled for the name everybody knows them by today, Capital City Service. They wholeheartedly embraced the casual lifestyle, from clothes and music to fighting and organised crime.

The CCS produced some top, top boys. Names like Taylor, Girvan, Lynch, Welsh and 'Fat' McLeod will be familiar to anyone who has ever folded a Millwall brick. And then there is Andy Blance, author of the book *Hibs Boy: the Life and Violent Times of Scotland's Most Notorious Football Hooligan*.[13] While some of the Hibs main faces (including Fat McLeod) would splinter off and join the Scottish National Firm in the late 1990s, Blance stayed loyal to the CCS. That loyalty steadied the ship and ensured that Hibs remained a leading player on the hooligan scene.

The CCS would do whatever it took to get to the top of the heap and stay there. After one of their lads, Raymie Morrell, was nearly kicked to death by Aberdeen they took revenge in the most spectacular way possible. They threw a petrol bomb at the ASC in the middle of Princes Street and, as Blance notes in *Hibs Boy*, they had also planned to petrol bomb the Aberdeen train as it left Waverley station, a manoeuvre that was detected just in time by the Old Bill. That is just one example of the extreme violence they were prepared to use in pursuit of their goals. You knew that anytime you faced them you had to be right at the top of your game.

One of my earliest memories of the CCS was the afternoon of the Skol Cup final at Hampden in season 1985/86. Rangers weren't involved; it was a match-up between Hibs and Aberdeen. Hibs travelled through to Glasgow on the train, getting off at Queen Street and walking the short distance to Glasgow's other mainline station, Central, to catch a train for the national stadium. To an 'Under-Fives' hooligan it was an awe-inspiring sight. It was one of the tidiest mobs I had ever seen. I reckon they must have numbered close to five hundred that day, every one of them dressed from top-to-toe in to-die-for gear. With a couple of my pals in tow we tracked them through the city centre, entranced by their style and their swagger.

---

[13] See also *These Colours Don't Run: Inside the Hibs Capital City Service* by another leading Hibs hooligan, Derek Dykes.

They didn't think as highly of us. We were wearing Paisley-pattern jumpers, which clearly didn't impress our visitors from the east.

'Where did you get those jumpers you Weegie cunts?' they asked.

There were major battles that day, right across Glasgow, but we played no part. It was a day for Hibs and Aberdeen to enjoy. We were interested spectators, watching as two of Scotland's top firms fought each other to a standstill on the streets of our city. It was magnificent to behold.

Seeing the CCS in its pomp had whetted my appetite. I was itching to take them down a peg or two. Despite what some people think it was never sectarian where Hibs were concerned. The Easter Road men may have formed the original Irish Catholic club in Scotland and in recent years – probably due to the James Connolly marches in Edinburgh – their fans have become more Republican in outlook. But that never applied to the CCS. They were game lads, dedicated to their club and to FV. We wanted to take them down because they were the top mob. It was out of respect for their achievements.

My only real beef with Hibs is their contention that Rangers always used tools and they, the wee souls, didn't. That sticks in my craw. Andy Blance and his pal were jailed for attacking Dunfermline at the Kronk nightclub, and almost every CCS boy who was there that night was holding. Maybe a battle in the Gorbals in 1991 has also slipped their mind. I was in jail but I was told that in the course of a brutal encounter one of our boys got his ear sliced off. You can't do that without a knife.

One of my first confrontations with the CCS didn't coincide with a Rangers–Hibs game. In 1985/86 we were playing Hearts at Tynecastle in the Scottish Cup and I went through to the capital with a few boys in my own age group. We couldn't get match tickets so we took a diversion to Princes Street, where we hoped to relieve some of the bigger stores of their choicest clothes. What we didn't know was that the favourite haunt of the CCS was the former Wimpey bar at the east end of the street. We were happily strolling along, identifying the best shops to steal from, when, all of a sudden, we were pulled up by ten Hibs Baby Crew. They gave us the third degree. Where were we from? What were we doing there? Which team did we support?

We were outnumbered two to one and discretion being the better part of valour we tried to bluff our way out of a tense situation. I thought they were satisfied with our answers but one of them had clearly run out of patience.

'It doesn't matter who you are. You're Weegie bastards. You shouldn't be in this city.'

With that he cracked one of our lads in the face and from there it kicked off big time. We did our best to hold them but the disparity in numbers was just too great and we had to retreat. Bizarrely, me and one of my pals ended up in a shoe shop, where we threw an assortment of boots, shoes and sandals at our assailants. The shop staff, visibly upset, picked up the phone and dialled 999. Within a few minutes the cops were on the scene and they hauled the two of us into an old Tardis. For the second time in ten minutes we were asked the same questions. Where we were from? What were we doing there? Which team did we support? We explained that we couldn't get tickets so we had decided to come into the city centre. The cops seemed happy with our answers and sent us on our way but not before giving us a rather strange piece of advice.

'Let that be a lesson to you. The Hibs Baby Crew are no mugs and they won't accept outsiders, especially Weegies, coming onto their turf.'

An officer of the law was happy that Hibs had attacked us! To most people what he said would have seemed strange. But the reason for his attitude I think is that many police forces across Scotland had grown tired of thousands of Old Firm fans turning up in their towns and cities and running riot. They were glad the boot was on the other foot, that it was Rangers and Celtic fans who were getting a hard time.

That was the Hibs baby crew but I soon found out just how formidable, and devious, their main mob could be. It was a Skol Cup semi-final in 1985/86 and we took healthy numbers with us on the train for the first leg at Easter Road. The game itself was a nightmare. It fucking pissed down all night and as we were getting drenched on an open terracing Rangers contrived to lose two-nil. There were many skirmishes inside the stadium but it was after the ref had blown for time up that things got really tasty. We were walking back to Waverley, surrounded by our fellow Rangers fans.

At least we thought they were Rangers fans.

We heard the chants of 'CCS, CCS' and before we could work out what was going on about fifty 'Rangers' fans were steaming in to us. Hibs were wearing Rangers colours and had taken us, and the Old Bill, completely by surprise. Once we had got our composure back it went off with a vengeance and there was some vicious close-in combat. The CCS got the best of it but we stuck to it and they didn't run us. It was memorable for another reason. As I outlined in a previous chapter Barry Johnstone used CS gas on Hibs but it blew back, almost knocking out a police horse. We watched in disbelief as the poor beast reared up violently, clearly disorientated after inhaling the gas.

Hibs came to our place for the second leg and I was again struck by their organisation and discipline. They were as cocky as ever, taking the tube to Copland Road station, where they knew they would be surrounded by tens of thousands of Rangers scarfers and casuals. The flash cunts also carried early examples of the mobile phone, those big half-brick jobs that are so reminiscent of the Eighties. There were verbals before and after the game but we couldn't get near each other due to the large police presence.

It took us until 1987 to get a right result against the CCS. It was a league game at Ibrox and they were striding down Paisley Road West after the game, arrogant as ever. That was the cue for Rangers and a big mob of our lads attacked. I was actually on my way home on the bus when I saw it kicking off. I rang the bell and when the driver slowed down I leapt off the bus and ran to join the fray. By this time Hibs had been split into two groups and they were both under siege from hundreds of ICF. There were fights all over the street with boys going down and getting a right kicking. Some of the ICF lifted scaffolding poles from a nearby building site and were whacking the CCS with them. I will never forget the dull thuds as metal connected with muscle, knocking the Hibs boys clean off their feet in the process. We chased them all over Govan, the formerly invincible CCS. It was a real coup. The two mobs, even they would have to admit, were now on a par.

Our rivalry got even more intense. There was one afternoon in either 1989 or 1990 when the CCS took on, and ran, a small group of ICF in Govan. I wasn't there and nor were most of our front-liners but we heard about it and were desperate to avenge what had happened. About twenty ICF drove to Edinburgh in five cars, every last man armed to the teeth. Some had knives; others carried baseball bats or coshes, while I was in possession of a Samurai sword. We cruised up Lothian Road, the heart of Edinburgh's social scene, scouring nightclub after nightclub. We drew a blank. At club after club there was no sign of them, either that or the bouncers told us the ICF were barred. We even phoned some of their main faces but they wouldn't come out. Just as well. Those weapons weren't for show. It would have been a bloodbath.

That era was the real deal, the peak of FV, and our clash with the CCS in August 1990 at Easter Road is a good example of that. I had arranged for two buses to take us along the M8 and I remember being delighted at the turnout. All the main ICF were there, supported by a healthy complement of baby crew. All in all we had about eighty that day, every last man completely reliable. The buses dropped us at Haymarket and we walked through the back streets, knowing they would have spotters the length of Princes Street. We turned right, and came onto Princes Street at its eastern extremity. Hibs were taken completely by surprise, a real plus for us, but they still made a fight of it. Imagine the scene: more than a hundred and fifty of the country's most formidable thugs going at it hammer and tong. It was bedlam. Fights spilled from the pavement onto the street, stopping the Saturday-afternoon traffic in its tracks. I was in a stand-off with their baby crew, fending off blows from every angle and then coming back in with a few digs of my own. No one gave an inch.

It would have carried on a lot longer but we heard the wail of sirens and then a fleet of police cars and vans screeched to a halt. One motorcycle cop wasn't so lucky. As he braked the silly cunt fell off the bike. When he got back to his feet I noticed the dark scowl on his face and immediately realised that someone was going to pay for his mishap. I was right. He drew his baton and lashed out indiscriminately at the boys nearest to him. Harky was particularly unlucky; Evel Knievel caught him on the leg with a bone-jarring blow that must have hurt like fuck.

When the police broke us up we mobbed up again and made for Easter Road. On the way it kicked off again and it was the same after the game as we made our way along Princes Street, shadowed every step of the way by the CCS. All of a sudden the air was thick with missiles, as the two mobs came together for the third time in as many hours. Purely by coincidence there were dozens of Japanese tourists leaving their hotel for a coach trip and they must have thought it was something to do with the Edinburgh Festival.

'Ah, what interesting street theatre they put on in Scotland,' they must have been saying, because their cameras were clicking non-stop as they took a few choice snaps to show the folks back in Osaka.

I have no idea what our Japanese friends thought when the cops arrived and shepherded us into vans but that was the end of our fun for one day.

*

'Come to Slateford. Get the slow train. The bizzies won't expect it to go off there,' Hibs told us on the phone.

It sounded like a really good idea. Slateford was in south Edinburgh, in the suburbs, well away from the city centre and the football hotspots. We could have a battle with the CCS away from the prying eyes of Lothian and Borders police. That was it. Sorted.

But I wasn't so sure. For one thing I knew Hibs would have been staking out the station at Slateford, the entrances and exits, the vantage points and the nooks and crannies. We had never set foot in the place; we would be heading into territory that was completely unknown. The fact there would be no police around was a double-edged sword. Yes we could have it with Hibs without the cops breaking it up, but, if the CCS got the upper hand, it might end up a bloodbath.

I was even less sure when we got to Central station and saw our mob. It wasn't the best. By 1994 football hooliganism in general, and the ICF in particular, was going through a rough patch. Many boys had been lost to the rave scene, others had been deterred by the increasing sophistication of police surveillance techniques and the ever increasing resources the authorities were putting into combating hooliganism. It meant we only had about thirty-five boys out, many of them teenagers, inexperienced in the ways of FV. I had brought two young guys along with me from Shettleston and like the rest of the youngsters I could see they were excited at the prospect of facing Hibs. They didn't realise what they were getting themselves into.

My mood wasn't lightened by a hangover of Charlie Sheen proportions. The previous night I had hit the booze hard, supplementing it with copious amounts of ecstasy. I wasn't sure if I was sweating because of the drugs or my nervousness about what lay before us in south Edinburgh. I tried not to show how I felt because that would have spooked the younger guys, who were nervous enough about facing a top firm.

We also had spotters out that day. Warren B, one of our top boys, lives in Edinburgh and he was in Slateford, trying to discover what Hibs were up to. He was on the phone to Davie Carrick throughout the journey, giving him regular reports. The news wasn't good. Warren said there were forty CCS in the immediate environs of the station and another forty in two big furniture vans. His advice to Davie was clear: stay on the train, don't get off at Slateford. It was a message that Davie relayed only to other leading members to prevent the younger boys losing their nerve.

As we were about to pull into Slateford station we were well fired up, fuelled by an hour-long orgy of lager, ecstasy and coke. One of the guys was carrying a bag of claw-hammers. 'These are our insurance policy, Sandy,' he confidently assured me. He was right. We would need them.

The CCS would be well tooled-up, despite their bullshit propaganda about not carrying weapons.

We saw two CCS on an adjoining platform. They motioned to us to come to an industrial estate that was just yards from the station. Fuck off, we thought, that is Indian territory; the perfect place for an ambush. We walked out of the station and onto Slateford Road. There were twenty Hibs at the bottom of an incline that leads to a railway bridge. Our twenty front-liners immediately charged and as the two mobs came together another twenty CCS appeared, giving them a numerical advantage. We gave as good as we got and those claw-hammers certainly came in handy. I was wildly swinging a hammer at them, but they kept backing off and I couldn't land a meaningful blow.

After what seemed like five minutes – in reality it was a fraction of that – the furniture vans drew up and forty more CCS, led by Fat McLeod, poured out. That was the game changer. We were swamped. The CCS attacked us from the front and the sides and as the tide turned in their favour our boys were getting knocked over like ninepins. It was carnage, that's the only word I can use to describe it. Even amidst a brutal fight for survival I will never forget the sight of two of our top lads going down and having the shit kicked out of them by large groups of CCS.

To increase the psychological pressure Hibs shouted 'slash them, slash them'. On hearing this many of our younger lads, already in a state of shock, ran. It was the worst decision they could have made, because Hibs clipped them and when they were lying helpless on the road they too took a fearsome kicking. The main danger was the cosh. It looked like every Hibs boy was carrying one and many of us were coshed repeatedly around the head. One of my young Shettleston pals didn't fare too well either: he was struck on the head by a sickening blow from a heavy glass ashtray and fell glassy eyed onto the tarmac.

The attacks from Hibs grew more and more frenzied. Each new act of violence spurred them on to even greater ferocity. It was the only time I have ever felt my life was in danger. I had to stay on my feet. If they had decked me I would have been going home in an ambulance, or even a hearse. All around me there were ICF boys lying on the pavement and on the road, many bleeding profusely, all of them in pain. Five of them would be hospitalised.

That was probably the only time in my life I was glad to see those flashing blue lights. I managed to make myself scarce and an hour later was on a train back to Glasgow, tail stuck firmly between my legs.

After Slateford our priority was revenge. A day like that could not go unpunished and from then on we obsessed about getting our own back. When Hibs were next due at Ibrox we had a huge mob out. There were one hundred and fifty of us in the Glaswegian, tooled up to fuck and itching to get at them. They told us they would front up but then said a couple of their boys had been involved in a violent incident the night before and that they had changed their mind. To me it was a feeble excuse. They knew we were raging and they didn't fancy it.

The same thing happened the next time Rangers were at Easter Road. A coach-load of our top guys went through, armed to the teeth. I had two small coshes and a huge meat cleaver, which I hid in the toilet of John Robertson's pub on Gorgie Road where we had plotted up for a pre-match drink. We belled Fat McLeod but he was vague about meeting us and we went back to our pints and our lines while they made a decision. All the while we could see the CCS going past in their cars, weighing us up. As the hours went by we got higher and higher and also more and more frustrated. Where the fuck were they? It was now half-seven and we had been in the pub for about eight hours, much to the disgust of the wives and girlfriends back home in Glasgow. There was nothing else for it. We would have to go and look for them and so thirty of us went into the city to track them down. Once again, they were nowhere to be seen. I realise the CCS were in the midst of a power struggle at the time – one faction led by McLeod, the other by Blance – but that was no excuse. Not fronting up on home turf is no way for a top mob to behave.

In fact it took us five years, until August 1999, to exact revenge on Hibs for Slateford. We ran a bus from the Pitz five-a-side centre in Townhead. There were fifty top hooligans out, a real hardcore, all of whom drank in Dr Brown's in Queen Street. Guys like Jeff, Boris, Ricky C, General Jamie, Andy Mac, Big Gary, Davie, the usual suspects. I was wearing a white England rugby shirt, so bright it dazzled anyone within ten feet of me, which in hindsight made me a little too conspicuous. However, I was outdone in the dodgy-fashion stakes by Smoothy, who had an equally bright white Stone Island jacket on, which earned him the nickname Dr Death. Lager was swallowed, cocaine snorted, ecstasy popped and then we were off.

We drove straight to Edinburgh where we plotted up at the Haymarket bar. The plan was to use Edinburgh corporation buses to avoid police detection so half of us jumped on one bus while the rest got the next one that passed. We mobbed up again at Leith Walk and made straight for the

CCS's spiritual home: the Royal Nip. Fair play to them, Andy Blance and one other Hibs boy came out to face us. And despite getting a doing they gave a fair account of themselves before the Old Bill arrived and broke it up.

Half of our group went to the game but the rest, me included, went back to the Haymarket. Football wasn't our priority, being ready for Hibs was. During the game (which Rangers won 1–0 thanks to a goal from Jonatan Johansson) Ricky was approached by one of the CCS and phone numbers were exchanged. It looked promising.

The Haymarket contingent left the bar about fifteen minutes before the final whistle and made its way through the back streets to avoid the cops. As we passed the Scottish Parliament, which was still being built, we phoned the CCS and were told they were well up for it. We hooked up with the lads who had gone to the match and marched on, desperate to get to grips with the enemy.

Then we saw them, fifty CCS, standing outside the St James centre. I felt a warm glow. It wasn't the usual adrenalin-fuelled nervous tension. We were just so confident; we knew we were a match for anyone. I remember thinking, 'This is our time. We are the top mob now. We are taking no shit.'

When it went off we had them on the back foot right from the off. Taylor, one of their top men, was knocked out within seconds. I was desperate to get as many of them as possible, to pay them back for Slateford. This time it was me who was shouting 'stab them'. They had no answer to us and we managed to inflict some hospital-grade injuries before the police arrived and spoiled the party. On the bus back to Glasgow we were elated and the celebrations in Doc Brown's went on long into the night.

Five years of hurt had been erased.

9

SLATEFORD: MR BLUE'S STORY

I thought it would be interesting to include other memories of Slateford. So here is Mr Blue's story. Blue of course was with the ICF that fateful afternoon in 1994 and ended up being hospitalised. Interestingly, he puts the ICF mob at twenty-two, much smaller than I thought. I suppose that makes our efforts all the more commendable.

A week before the game at Easter Road (which was in October 1994) word got round this would be football violence with a twist. No football! The police were an important factor in our calculations. By the late 1980s they were getting the upper hand and the last time we had gone to Hibs on the train about two hundred of us got sent straight back due to having no tickets. This would be around 1989. That said we did manage to have a memorable day up there when two coach-loads of us wrong-footed the boys in blue and did the business, but, that apart, they had things nailed down.

So we had to think of a way of avoiding the Old Bill. After much thought it was decided we would leave from Central station and go the scenic route, meeting Hibs somewhere along the Edinburgh rail network. I got into the bar in Central at one o'clock expecting to find a decent-size firm. There were two! We were looking to leave around 2.15 so that left about an hour for the numbers to grow. I needn't have worried because by that time our firm had grown . . . to an astonishing twenty-two. As we sat in the bar there wasn't even a decision to be made. We were going, 22 or 222, it really didn't matter. We'd arranged it, so we were going. But I'd be lying if I said I was confident. Out of our twenty-two around half were what is known these days as 'youth' and half were solid, experienced lads. We got on the train as planned, no police in sight. I was laughing at the thought of those smug cunts hanging around Queen Street – the normal station for Edinburgh – content in the knowledge today was going to be another peaceful day on the football front.

On the train we didn't have a care in the world. Then we got a call from one of our lads who lived in Edinburgh.

'How many?'

'Twenty-two,' we replied.

'Stay on the train,' he firmly advised.

After a quick discussion a consensus emerged. There was no fucking way we were staying on the train. As the announcer said 'next stop Slateford' I felt the butterflies. I fucking love this time, just before the battle. You know it's coming, you don't know what's coming but it's definitely something. The train stopped and in the station there was a firm of Hibs waiting.

'Come on Rangers, there they are,' someone shouted.

'ICCCCF'.

There might only have been twenty-two of us but that chant makes it sound a lot more. The CCS in the station got on their toes. 'Strange,' I thought. I had no idea how many were in the station but I assumed that wasn't their full firm. Unfortunately, I was right.

Faced with a much bigger mob I had one thought in mind: 'If we keep tight, we'll be okay.' We got out of the station and the first thing that occurred to me was how wide a road we were on. 'Shit,' I thought. I had no idea how many Hibs had with them, although word had got through there would be eighty-plus. Those odds didn't overly concern me when I was on the train. That may sound like bullshit to those who've never been involved in football violence but most firms have their frontline of twenty or thirty doing the business and the rest may as well not even be there. This isn't because everybody else is a shitbag; it's simply due to the width of a road. Hence my initial concern about Slateford Road being wide.

We left the station and to our left we noticed a firm coming round a corner. They were, from memory, about a hundred yards down the road. A couple of our lads were tooled up, not with weapons of mass destruction, but with a couple of little hammers and a chain. As our walk towards them turned into a jog they just kept walking around this corner, more and more of them. An unspoken 'Fuck it we've come this far' spread through our ranks as our jog turned into a full-blown charge.

'ICCCF ICCCF' and with that the lads with tools got them out. When we got to within ten yards their frontline began to back away; they weren't running but they were definitely on the back foot. By now I realised their firm was well over a hundred, possibly 130. 'Come on Rangers, these cunts are off,' I shouted. I could see their main lads trying to hold them together. Shouts of 'Fucking stand Hibs' were clearly heard, along with 'Stay Hibs, fucking stay'. There was a strange tone in their voice, not fear, more disbelief. That is a good indicator of how close it was at that stage.

By now almost every one of us was going at it with them and the next few seconds would decide which way this was going. After trading a few blows I felt a punch on the side of my head. Behind me, the lads in their firm who had melted away were coming back into the fight and I could see the right-hand side of our line getting backed away. On that side of the road they had the same problem as us: Hibs either side and behind them, although they may have had it even worse. There was no choice, we had to retreat. We ran about ten yards and now it was our turn to rally the troops.

'Fucking stand Rangers,' some of us shouted. We did stand but our left flank got completely overrun leaving Carrick, Broony and others exposed on the right. They had to fall back and as we attempted another stand a few yards up the road it was obvious the battle was lost. I had lost contact with the rest of our lads and I was running back towards the station with Hibs in front of me. I felt a click on my heels and went down. I saw Millsy about five yards ahead of me. He was my only hope.

'Miiiilsy,' I shouted, as I went down, taking a few kicks along the way. I expected the worst. However, within seconds I was being dragged back to my feet. Millsy – who could give Linford Christie a run for his money – could have got away unscathed, but he came back for me. However, being upright was short lived as both Millsy and I went down under a hail of blows.

'Wake up, wake up.'

Some silly cunt was slapping my face.

'Fuck off,' I replied.

'Do you know where you are?'

'Aye am outside Hampden ya fuckin' nutcase.'

'Lie down, you're lucky to be here.'

'How? It's only two miles away fae my hoose and we always get tae Hampden.'

Next thing I knew I woke up. I could tell from the feel of the uncomfortable mattress I was lying on that this was either a jail cell or a hospital ward. When I went to look at my watch I realised two things. Firstly, I didn't have a watch, had that peasant mob nicked it? And secondly, my wrist was at a right angle. I managed to get myself up from the bed and noticed it was half five. Half five for fuck's sake, we got off the train at half three! I got off the bed, pulled back my curtain and had a peek in the next cubicle. This ginger nut was looking up at me. It was Millsy.

'Look at the fucking state of you,' I said, pissing myself laughing.

'Have you seen yersel?' he laughed back.

Within a minute a nurse came in. 'Stitches or staples Mr Blue?' she asked. 'Whit?'

'Stitches or staples? You've got a two-inch laceration on your head that needs stitches or staples.'

'I don't really mind to be honest but thanks for the choice. Do whatever you choose, suit yourself. I respect and admire the job you do. What time do you finish?'

Miserable cow never even raised a smile, it was only later I realised I looked like the elephant man's ugly brother! Six stitches on my head, four butterfly stitches in my jaw, a plaster cast on my arm, eight butterfly stitches on my leg and an armful of painkillers later I signed myself out. When I got out the sister-in-law of one of the younger lads gave me a lift home, which was much appreciated as I could hardly walk.

In the days that followed I found out that of our little firm of twenty-two, eleven ended up in hospital. I had had no choice. I took a right beating and was going to hospital anyway. I got surrounded and, as speed was never my strong point, hospitalisation was inevitable. Millsy, however, the proverbial whippet, could have fucked off unharmed. He didn't. He came back for me. I respected him before that day, as did everyone in the ICF, but I will never forget what he did at Slateford. Sadly, I've lost touch with him now but, if you are reading this, cheers pal.

In my opinion very few firms would have taken on those odds. We always did. Looking back it was always going to end the way it did but we gave it our best shot. We lost that battle; there is no doubt about that. Some people took the view that Hibs overstepped the mark, and a lot of them who thought that way were lads who hadn't been active over the previous few years. Lads like me who'd been going to raves or bringing up the kids, lads with work commitments. Word about Slateford got around to those who hadn't been involved and everyone was of one mind: what happened that terrible afternoon would be avenged.

'Scotland's number one' would be knocked right off its fucking perch the next time we played them. Between Slateford and the return match our firm grew, week by week. Old faces returned and before long we were on the road again. Dundee Utd were dispatched in Dundee. We went to Aberdeen, nothing major happened but they knew we were back.

Then the day came. Hibs at Ibrox!

People think I must hate Hibs. I don't. They did to me what I'd do (and have done) to them. Our pub by then was The Glaswegian and I got there expecting a good firm. This time I wasn't disappointed. We had eighty solid lads. No idiots, no mates of lads, no voyeurs; this was our main firm. A bag of tools was hidden away for use later, fair enough, but it was what I heard next that sent a chill down my spine.

'Two shotguns there, one of those bastards is getting it.'

'Oh for fuck's sake,' I thought.

The CCS overstepped the mark in Edinburgh – even when we were down they still kept putting the boot in. They also used weapons. However, getting nicked on a murder charge for a spot of football violence would be ridiculous. By now things were becoming 'pre-arranged', with the two mobs calling each other's pubs. The phone went. It was Hibs.

'We're not coming through; there's not enough of us,' they said.

'How many you got?'

'Only forty.'

'Only forty,' we repeated, disbelief in our voices.

If they had come to Glasgow that day they would have been routed. I'm not one for ifs, buts and maybes but it isn't even worth debating. They would have got smashed. Part of me would have loved to have seen them get destroyed but part of me is glad they never showed up. I genuinely feel at least one of them would have died, especially as I know who had the artillery. It would have been used, without a shadow of a doubt.

Another reason I'm glad they never came through is that it proved that, despite gaining a result a Slateford, Hibs were still wary of pushing their luck. In our world bottling out is worse than being turned over. One firm was turned over, one bottled out. Hibs, wisely for them, avoided Glasgow for a few years after Slateford. Next time they were on the scene they were kissing our arse.

In the meantime . . . Rangers were back.

10

A HISTORY OF VIOLENCE

'Sandy, why the fuck do you do this?' asked one of Glasgow's top football-intelligence officers. 'You're giving Rangers a bad name with your antics.'

'On the contrary,' I countered. 'Rangers fans have been involved in violence since time immemorial. We're carrying on a great tradition.'

And it's true. 'No Surrender' is much more than a slogan. We have a proud tradition for football violence and all the ICF are doing is keeping that tradition alive. Take 1909. After the replayed Old Firm Scottish Cup final also ended in a draw, thousands of Rangers and Celtic fans rioted. But they did not attack each other. Their target was authority in general, and the police in particular. The fans thought that extra time should have been played and suspected there had been collusion between two clubs looking for a second replay and another lucrative payday. Hampden was trashed: the stands were torched; the goalposts ripped down and burned. Dozens of police were attacked, as were the firemen and ambulancemen who had arrived to put out the flames and tend to the injured. It was only by sheer good fortune that no one was killed. The official response was decisive: the 1909 Scottish Cup was withheld and there is no winner's name on the famous old trophy for 1909. Forget casuals. This was probably the worst outbreak of football violence in British history.

That martial tradition was carried on into the Twenties and Thirties and one gang in particular stands out: the Brigton (from the Glasgow district of Bridgetown) Billy Boys, named in honour of King William of Orange. The Billy Boys, led by 'King' Billy Fullerton, numbered eight hundred at its peak and had an excellent flute band, the Bridgeton and Purple and Crown, which Fullerton played in. With the flute band in tow the Billy Boys were regular visitors to Belfast for the marching season and were prominent in many of the sectarian riots of the time. In Glasgow their main rivals were the Norman Conks, a local Catholic street gang, and the two mobs fought many battles in and around the east end armed with knives, bottles and open razors. The police were slow to react to the new threat and it was only when chief constable Sir Percy Sillitoe threw all the resources at his disposal at the gangs that their power was broken. That police response would be repeated half a century later – but this time the police target was the ICF.

Although many people have compared the Billy Boys to the ICF I believe that modern football violence began with the advent of European football in the late1950s, early 1960s. Rangers regularly got to semi-finals and finals in those days and would often meet English clubs along the way. There was trouble when we played Wolves in 1960/61 and Spurs in 1962/63 and also when we met Leeds in 1967/68 – and that was despite Rangers putting up giant screens at Ibrox to beam back the away leg from Elland Road. Incidentally, that initiative attracted 43,177 to Ibrox, which I believe is a record crowd for a match televised inside a stadium. And unlike Manchester in 2008 the technology actually worked!

However, it was the semi-final of the Fairs Cup (the equivalent of the Europa League) with Newcastle United in May 1969 that really put us on the map. The first leg was at home and a crowd of 75,580 rolled up to Ibrox, which was yet another attendance record, being the biggest ever crowd for a Fairs Cup match. Although Rangers could only manage a goalless draw the demand to see the return, as you might expect, was phenomenal. When the allocation of 12,000 tickets went on sale the queues stretched for miles around Ibrox and tens of thousands were left disappointed. Although the police on both sides of the border advised fans not to travel it was obvious that Rangers fans were going to follow on to Newcastle in huge numbers.

Before considering what happened before, during and after the game we need a little historical context. Rangers had just been trounced 4–0 in the Scottish Cup final by a Celtic team that was in the middle of its nine-in-a-row run under Jock Stein and the Fairs Cup was the last chance we had to regain some pride after an awful domestic season. In addition, a week before the cup final, England had beaten Scotland 4–1 at Wembley, a result that according to the *Daily Record* the English press 'were still sniggering about'. So losing to an English team in Europe was the last thing Rangers and their fans needed at that point.

The return leg was a huge disappointment. The light blues went two goals down and were on their way out of the competition. The Rangers fans inside St James Park (many of whom were ticketless but had got into the ground when one of the main entrances was stormed) took it badly. In fact, as Samuel L Jackson might say, 'they went medieval on their ass'.

With ten minutes to go thousands of bluenoses invaded the pitch and engaged in running battles with the police. As the fighting raged Rangers chairman John Lawrence came onto the pitch to make a plea for calm but such was the ferocity of the fighting that he had to be escorted off for his own safety. Despite the fact that many of the cops were in full riot gear, and had squads of dog handlers to back them up, it took a full eighteen minutes before the pitch was cleared. Nor was it just the Old Bill who felt the wrath of the Rangers fans: one paper reported that 'some of the Rangers fans kicked the Newcastle players' as they scurried for the dressing room. Not that Rangers fans are bad losers of course, but there is only so much you can take. The citizens of Newcastle were next in line. After the game the fans went on a rampage, as the *Evening Times* of 22 May 1969 notes, 'smashing house and shop windows' all over the city. A spokesman for the Newcastle police said it was, 'the worst violence I have ever seen in the city,' a statement backed up by local hospitals, which had to deal with dozens of walking wounded.

After Newcastle our violent outbursts became, if anything, even worse. Our notoriety was sealed in the aftermath of the European Cup Winners Cup final of 1972, in which we beat Moscow Dynamo by three goals to two to seal our first European trophy. On this occasion it was those thugs in uniforms who sparked the trouble. I am speaking of course of our old friends, the Spanish police. Our fans were understandably excited about winning the cup and in the last ten minutes there were three mini pitch invasions, each of them repulsed by the police. Nothing malicious, just exuberance; they wanted to celebrate with the players.

At the final whistle there was no stopping the happy Rangers fans. They flooded onto the playing surface to hail their heroes. There was no hint of trouble but this time the cops lost the plot. Instead of letting the happy throng celebrate they charged, 'swinging three-foot batons like windmills among the Scots,' as the *Daily Record* noted the next morning. The police lashed out indiscriminately, hitting not only the grown men amongst the Rangers support but also innocent women and children. Angered by the brutality they were witnessing the Rangers fans launched a counter-charge, pelting the riot police with bottles, cans, stones and bricks. When the police backed off most of the fans retreated to the stands but by this time the 'thugs in uniform' were out for blood and continued to bludgeon any fan within range of their long batons. The fans launched another charge, breaking up the wooden seats to use as weapons. It would be a full half hour before the situation was brought under control, which I can tell you is an age in football-violence terms.

After the game the Rangers support, understandably upset after the way they had been treated, went on the rampage, not only in Barcelona but also on the Costa Brava, smashing up cafes and bars, breaking shop windows and overturning cars. The authorities of course blamed the Rangers fans, who they described as 'dervishes' and this was echoed by the morning newspapers in Scotland, many of which rushed to judgement without having all the facts in front of them. The *Daily Record* was typical, its front page carrying the headline 'The Shame in Spain' and star reporter Alex Cameron describing what happened as 'the worst mass invasion ever at a big game in Europe'.

But there was of course another side to the story and the evening papers, with their later deadlines, were able to speak to dozens of Rangers fans, most of whom had not been involved in the violence. They confirmed that the invasion had been peaceful, a celebration, and that there was no problem until the Spanish cops turned nasty. That version of events was endorsed by the *Evening Times*, as this extract from its edition of 25 May 1972 confirms.

> The fans were happy and boisterous as they waited for the cup presentation. But after allowing them a brief few minutes of glory, the police staged a baton charge. Some drew their guns while the remainder laid into the fans with batons.

Of course UEFA didn't give a flying fuck. Rangers were banned from Europe for a year, while the Barcelona Old Bill, despite their brutality, got away scot free.

Shafted by UEFA. Set upon by Spanish police. Slated by the *Daily Record*. That rings a bell . . . .

The trouble continued throughout the 1970s, especially when we travelled south of the border for friendlies. There was now a new twist to the saga: the media used the violence as an excuse to take Rangers to task for our supposed sectarian signing policy. It was the start of a sinister trend, one that has continued to this day.

In March 1974, on a Saturday afternoon, we played Manchester United in a friendly at Old Trafford. The Red Devils also had a well-earned reputation for football violence and as soon as the game was announced the dogs in the street knew there would be trouble. They started it. Before kickoff our midfielder, Graham Fyfe, was hit on the head with a bottle, thrown from the Stretford End, as he carried a goodwill banner round the track. Then United hooligans came onto the pitch, ran up to our end and dared us to come on and have a go. We didn't need to be asked twice. The Red Army got a bloody good hiding and if you don't believe me read Tony O'Neill's book *Red Army General*. O'Neill and his boys are no mugs but he admits they were no match for Rangers on that afternoon. It was the start of a feud that has continued to this day, and one that would be played out again and again before and after Champions League games.

As general manager Willie Waddell said at the time there was 'a plot by Manchester United fans to bait Rangers fans' – and it succeeded. They did provoke us but they forgot what happens when you grab a tiger by the tail. Many of the Scottish papers blamed the trouble on so-called religious bigotry, which of course was nonsense. British football was going through one of its regular violent phases, with mass riots kicking off on a weekly basis, north and south of the border. Somehow I don't think the trouble at West Ham, Notts Forest or Everton was down to those teams refusing to sign Catholics.

But the ridiculous notion that religion was behind football hooligan-ism really took off after our friendly away to Aston Villa in October 1976. There was trouble almost as soon as the game started, but it got worse at half time, when Rangers fans launched bottles and cans at the police who were patrolling the perimeter. The cops waded into the Rangers end and a battle ensued, with a semblance of order eventually being restored. Then in the second half, when Rangers went two goals down, fighting again broke out. It got so violent that the referee had no option but to abandon the match.

Deprived of a game to watch Rangers fans turned their attention to the city of Birmingham. It was mental, as the *Glasgow Herald* reported: 'In the city shop windows were smashed, men and women assaulted as they tried to do their shopping and pubs became battlegrounds as the crazed fans went after more drink.' The disorder prompted a famous outburst from Willie Waddell, who said, despairingly, that: 'These louts are cruci-fying us. They're making it impossible for us to play in England.'

Looking for an explanation the papers immediately jumped on the signing policy. In an editorial on 13 October 1976 the *Daily Record* hit out at Rangers: 'Now it is time – long past time – for Rangers to renounce an employment policy [not signing Catholics] which is as despicable as it is intolerable.' The *Glasgow Herald*'s chief sports reporter, Ian Archer (a prissy cunt with an English accent who pretended he was Scottish) went completely over the top, arguing that 'Rangers . . . are a permanent embarrassment and an occasional disgrace. This country would be a better place if Rangers did not exist.' And Celtic fans have the cheek to say that the media favour Rangers!

Of course the fact that we had not knowingly signed a Catholic had fuck-all to do with it. In England there was trouble on a weekly basis. In one of the worst examples – and just a few months before we played Villa – Manchester United and Derby County fans fought a running battle on the pitch at the Baseball Ground. The Birmingham police got it right – alcohol was the real problem. Rangers fans had arrived in the city early on the Saturday morning and had been drinking for hours by the time kickoff came around. That is the problem with the Scottish media. They will never pass up an opportunity to have a go at Rangers, and that was as true in the 1970s as it is today.

That era of pre-casual football violence came to an end with the most infamous battle of them all. It happened after the Old Firm Scottish Cup final of 1980, when hundreds of opposing fans came onto the pitch from both ends of Hampden and set about each other. The fighting was intense and vicious and, as an eight-year-old watching from my flat in the Gallowgate, it thrilled me. What happened at Hampden that sunny May afternoon is the best-known incidence of football violence in the history of the British game. Those iconic images of mounted police chasing Rangers and Celtic fans over the lush turf of the national stadium are shown every time a documentary about football violence is broadcast. Soon, I hoped, it would be my turn.

So, yes, we in the ICF had a proud tradition to uphold, one that stretches back a more than hundred years. I hope we have played our part and that we did our bit to enhance the reputation that Rangers fans rightly have for defending a way of life, with our blood if necessary. We bend the knee to no cunt and we never will.

No Surrender.

Legends. To my right is Davie Carrick and to my left is the H man. You will not find two more formidable football hooligans anywhere in Britain.

The Beach End, Aberdeen, in the early 1980s. I wasn't there among the dodgy wedge haircuts and the naff knitwear but you will be able to spot Carrick, Anderson and Hillan among the Rangers scarfers.

The soccer babe

On the bus to Hibs, in 1990, aged seventeen.

I once played for Rangers, for the youth team, and my medal haul was pretty impressive, as you can see.

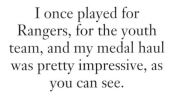

Some of the boys from the early 1980s. Brucie is second from the left while Walesey, a cult figure in the mob, is second from the right. RIP wee man, you were a legend.

The Loyalist

I have always had a strong commitment to the Loyalist cause and I have visited Northern Ireland on several occasions.

Next to a Belfast mural commemorating those who have fought and died for the cause.

Wearing a bulletproof vest in a Belfast safe house, 1999.

Life didn't mean life! I have had three life bans from Ibrox but thanks to a change of heart on the part of Rangers I am now allowed to go and watch games again.

LM/rb

RANGERS
FOOTBALL CLUB plc
Founded 1873

19 March 2007

Mr. Alexander B.M. Chugg

Dear Mr. Chugg,

LIFE TIME BAN

It has been drawn to my attention that despite the life ban currently imposed on you from attending ALL Rangers FC matches you have continued to do so.

This leaves me no alternative but to ban you for life from attending ALL Rangers FC matches.

You are reminded of this life time ban and should also be aware that if asked by Strathclyde Police or any other agency that might pursue a Football Banning Order through a criminal court, I will make information at my disposal available to them.

Yours sincerely,

LAURENCE MACINTYRE
HEAD OF SAFETY AND FACILITIES

THE
RANGERS
FOOTBALL CLUB plc
Founded 1873

AA/rb

13 January 2009

Mr. Alexander Bannerman Milne Chugg

Glasgow

Dear Mr. Chugg,

BAN RESCINDED

I refer to our meeting of 13 January 2009 and can confirm that the ban imposed on you following misbehaviour at Rangers matches has been rescinded.

You are now free to attend all Rangers matches and will be expected to follow the principles set out in the Club's 'Blue Guide'. Lifting the ban provides you with the opportunity of demonstrating that you have indeed moved away from the misbehaviour which brought you into conflict with other supporters, the Club and the Police.

The Season Ticket removed from you at the Rangers –v– Celtic match on 27 December 2008 has been forfeited without compensation.

I will review your situation again in 12 months.

Yours sincerely,

ALISTAIR ANDERSON
SAFETY MANAGER

The ICF in action

Heading for High Street after an Old Firm game, hunting for Celtic.

Taking on Aberdeen in George Square, one bank-holiday weekend.

I am in among the Rangers fans in Belgrade, where we played Red Star. You can just about make me out: I am close to the RAF flag, next to the guy with the white T-shirt.

During the 1998 World Cup the press alleged that the Scottish National Firm were fascists. We thought we would play along with their ridiculous allegations and so we got together for this collective salute.

I have always considered Shettleston to be my spiritual home and to carry an ICF/Union flag with its name was an honour.

In January 2011 the ICF and some of our pals, many of whom are normal Rangers fans, gathered at Ibrox for this photograph. We had come together to commemorate the fortieth anniversary of the Ibrox disaster, in which sixty-six Rangers fans tragically lost their lives. Rangers didn't have a clue who we were or why we were there.

That day in January 2011 was special for all of us, because we are all genuine Rangers fans, despite what the media will tell you. We really wanted to honour the dead of the Ibrox disaster and I hope this wreath and our floral tributes do just that.

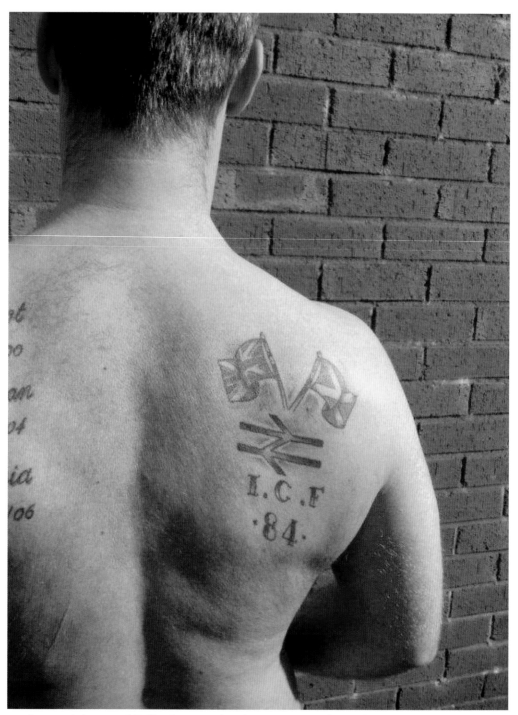

I was nicknamed Billy Britain thanks to my penchant for wearing patriotic colours. I had this tattoo done to symbolise my love for Scotland, Britain and the ICF.

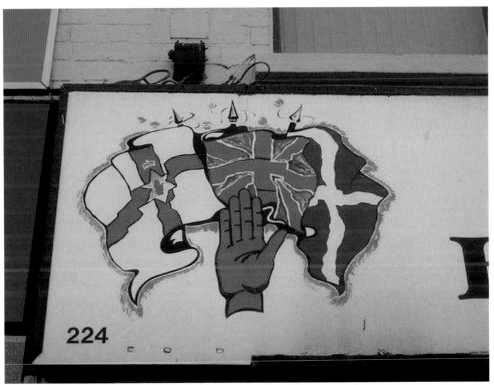

224

To me this shop sign, which depicts the flags of Ulster, the United Kingdom and Scotland, says it all about this great country of ours. I also wanted to include (*below*) a mural from Belfast.

The one who got away. Here I am at the front door of Ibrox (without, I should add, Rangers knowing anything about it). Maybe in another life . . .

Celtic fans are forever claiming that referees favour Rangers. So just to keep in the spirit of things I wore this referee's outfit for the last game of season 2010/11 down at Kilmarnock. I don't know if it helped but we clinched our fifty-fourth league title.

I do have interests away from football. Here I am with my musical hero, Paul Weller, who of course didn't have a clue who I was.

Now that I have given up on hooliganism my main interest is in running kids football teams, along with my fellow coaches at Drumsagard FC.

11

THE UTILITY

Dundee United had a great team in the early-to-mid Eighties, winning the League Cup and then becoming league champions. They even got to a European Cup semi-final for fuck's sake. Rangers were of course shite in those days, at least until Souness arrived in 1986 and changed our world forever.

For a while it was a different story off the field. United could only turn out about twenty boys and their city neighbours, Dundee FC, were just as bad. At a time when Scotland was producing some great mobs, the City of Discovery was a fucking joke in football-violence terms. I remember one time at Tannadice in 1986 when I was just a fourteen-year-old kid. Egged on by my ICF pals I went across to where their casuals were standing and picked a fight. Disappointingly, they didn't want to know. I was shocked that someone so young could take liberties without meeting any resistance.

Dundee had to change. There is only so much humiliation you can take. The city was a laughing stock in casual circles and to their great credit the main faces from United and Dundee did something about it. They formed the Dundee Utility, which became the only mob in Scotland to draw equally on lads from two different clubs. Although I would never rank them as top tier, the Utility was a tidy mob, one capable of turning over bigger and better mobs on its day.

Their progress as a unified mob was however uneven. We went up there again in 1987, on this occasion to play Dundee at Dens Park in an evening kickoff. There were about forty ICF out that night, including my brother Christopher. The game was piss poor and after the ninety minutes had come and gone we walked back to the city via the Hilltown area, landing up in the Wellgate shopping centre. We were confronted by twenty Dundee FC boys, who we promptly charged. They disappeared like the proverbial snow off a dyke. The Old Bill then escorted us through the shopping centre but seven of us broke off from the crocodile and went looking for Dundee. By this time they had regrouped and it went off again in the pedestrian precinct. Although we were heavily outnumbered we fucking smashed them again. At this point the main mob of ICF arrived, along with their police escort. Dundee were sore losers because they proceeded to break the most important rule in the casual code.

'That's them. That's the Rangers mob,' they shouted, pointing us out to the police.

To me that stank. Not only was it cowardly to expect the police to protect them but also they had grassed us up. I was disgusted.

The cops escorted the reunited mob to the station but when we got there the officer in charge of British Transport police took great delight in informing us that we had missed the football special and that there were no more trains to Glasgow that night. It was a serious problem for me. I had school the next day! With great apprehension I phoned Mum from a public phone box and expected her to go nuts but she took it better than I thought, perhaps because Christopher was with me. But she probably suspected, for the first time, that I was now involved in football violence.

We were put onto the Edinburgh train, along with a police escort and, as it was now close to midnight, we expected we would have to stay overnight in the capital, which, to be honest would have been quite a thrill. But when we got to Waverley the BTP told us the train was to be diverted to Glasgow. This was of course completely outwith the normal timetable but the cops didn't fancy the prospect of forty Glasgow hooligans, many of them minors, roaming Edinburgh's streets all night. I don't think the train driver would have been too pleased but he was under orders and had to take us home.

As we got off at Queen Street we agreed it had been a good laugh but once again we had been distinctly underwhelmed by a Dundee mob.

*

Our first clash with the new-look and much-improved Utility came in May 1994 when we played United in the Scottish Cup final at Hampden. We always pulled a great mob on cup-final day; it was an ICF tradition and this was no exception. It was also becoming a tradition that I got lifted on cup-final day. On the day of the 1990 final, I got arrested, not for football violence – Rangers weren't even playing – but on drugs charges. Then, two years later, in May 1992, as Rangers again reached the final, I was apprehended in Shettleston after the game when some high jinks went wrong. Four times in six cup finals I got arrested. It was my bogey day right enough.

After that tale of woe it's back to '94. We met up in our favoured boozer of the time, the John Street Jam, on the corner of John Street and Cochrane Street. It was a great pub and had the added advantage that later on it became a nightclub. We could always make a few quid in there: it was a good place to sell ecstasy, although the pub's management knew nothing about that little sideline. The JSJ was heaving that day with many of our front-liners in attendance, including Carrick, Allen K, Scott N, Ricky C, the Collins brothers, Swedgers, Jeff and the boys from Penilee. We also had fifteen Chelsea with us, genuine members of the Headhunters, and they helped make up a formidable mob, which I put in the region of a hundred and thirty.

There was no particular game plan that day. The loose plan was to take a train to Rutherglen and walk along Prospecthill Road, which is located close to the traditional Celtic end of the national stadium. We knew the Dundee United fans would be massing in that area and all we had to do was to avoid detection by the police. With such a large group we would have stuck out like a sore thumb so we decided to split into two groups and then took an alternative route along King Street. We weren't spotted; so far so good. When we turned into Glasgow Road we could see that the two closest pubs – the Sportsman and the Black Bull – were heaving with tangerine-covered scarfers. Even better, there were forty Utility drinking outside the Sportsman.

I was in the first group of forty ICF and as soon as the Utility saw us they shouted, 'Let's have it.' They thought that was our whole mob; that it was going to be equal numbers.

They got the shock of their fucking lives.

Both mobs steamed in but we were reinforced within seconds by the larger group of ninety, who were about fifty yards behind us. It was like a knife going through butter. We battered them, despite thirty of their beer-fuelled scarfers joining in. They had a major problem. The pubs behind them were so busy they couldn't get back inside and so they had to stand there and take their medicine.

And how bitter that pill must have been. We were picking them off with ease. I saw one of them trying to squeeze back into the Sportsman and caught him with a peach of a right hook, sending him crashing to the ground. I then grabbed a second Utility, pulled his head down and kneed him full in the face. Over at the Black Bull I could see that their scarfers, many of whom had come out to support their mob, were also getting a pasting.

It was inevitable that someone would call the cops and after a few minutes we heard the sirens. I quickly decided that the best way to avoid arrest was not to run but to act like an innocent fan out to enjoy the cup final. I walked nonchalantly over to the Black Bull, trying to look as if the fighting had nothing to do with me. By this time the street was flooded with blue uniforms and as I headed towards the pub a tall and extremely youthful Old Bill grabbed a hold of me.

'Where the fuck are you going?' he spat.

'I am just walking to the game.'

'Which team do you support?'

'Rangers,' I replied.

'You are going nowhere son.'

Given his age the 'son' part surprised me.

'That's rich coming from you. What are you: a YTS?'

Along with a couple of other unlucky souls we were bundled into a van and taken to the nearest police station. I wasn't charged at first but they told me I was going to be held for six hours under some bullshit section of a bullshit Criminal Justice Act. I was gutted to have been lifted at yet another Scottish Cup final but at least I had the consolation that I would be out within a few hours. I would also be celebrating back-to-back trebles for Rangers, the first time that feat had ever been achieved in the history of Scottish football.

After I had been in the cell for an hour a cop came in and took a Polaroid of me, which I found very strange.

'What is going on here?' I demanded.

'A couple of Dundee United fans were slashed and we're going to use the photo as part of an ID parade,' he replied.

One thought flashed through my mind. 'I am being fucking well stitched up here.'

After another hour the same cop came back in and told me that the Utility boy who had been slashed had confirmed it wasn't me who had done it, but that I was a member of the group who had attacked them outside the Sportsman. I was read my rights and charged with breach of the peace and forming part of a disorderly crowd. Although I was relieved not to be charged with the slashing I was informed that enquiries were continuing and that I might be charged with it later.

I was well pissed off. I was not only missing the cup final, and a double treble, but also I was going to be held in a cell all weekend and would then be carted off to the Sheriff Court on the Monday morning. The manageress of the John Street Jam, who was the girlfriend of a childhood pal, came over to plead my case with the desk sergeant, telling him I had a family party in her pub that night. Of course I didn't and she was given short shrift anyway. To make matters worse the turnkey on duty took great delight in telling me that Dundee United's Craig Brewster had scored the only goal of the final – completely against the run of play, I might add – thus denying Rangers that historic back-to-back treble.

I was down for another reason. A fellow hooligan had grassed me up, which left a very bad taste in my mouth. That was the second time a Dundee boy had done that to me. But despite their grassing it was the Utility who were the most embittered about what had happened outside the Sportsman. A few weeks later I got a phone call at the John Street Jam from the boy who had been slashed. He and his twin brother both fancied themselves as hard men, so I wasn't that surprised by what he had to say.

'I want a straightener. How about you and me having a square go to sort things out?' he asked.

This guy was wired to the moon. He must have been to see *Fight Club* at the pictures.

'Nae problem ya bam. We'll book Brockville and start selling tickets the noo,' I scornfully replied.

Funnily enough that blue-collar boxing bout never did take place.

But give them their due the Utility fronted up regularly in Glasgow after that cup final. They formed a bond with Stoke City's Naughty 40 mob, which meant that on occasion they could put a good number of boys out. They even turned up at the John Street Jam one day, and, although they were routed, it at least showed they were game. They also got a bit delusional about that one because a few days later we took another call at the JSJ.

'We fucking did you last week,' they crowed.

'Where did the fight start?' I asked.

'In your pub,' he replied.

'Where did it end up?'

'George Square.'

'You must have fucking done us running backwards then.'

*

As I said, fair play to the Utility. They kept coming despite the many set-backs they suffered and one of their most determined efforts took place in early 1995. We were playing Dundee United in a league game at Ibrox and we discovered that they would not only be bringing a good mob with them but also that they would be hanging around in Glasgow after the game. That was all the encouragement we needed.

We managed to put together a tidy little firm of about forty, half of whom went to the game while the other half, me included, stayed in the Glaswegian, a great wee pub on the edge of the Gorbals. I had been in there from about noon, downing vodka and lager and snorting cocaine. The coke was essential if you wanted to go on what we called 'the skite'; it enabled you to drink all day, get involved in FV and round things off with a visit to a nightclub.

When the boys who had gone to Ibrox got back to the Glaswegian they said that the Utility hadn't been at the game but were drinking some-where in Glasgow. A few phone calls later we discovered they were in Baird's bar in the Gallowgate, probably the most Celtic-orientated pub in Scotland. We were over the moon. The Utility had avoided the police and were now ripe for the picking.

Baird's was a tricky proposition. Many of its clientele were Republicans and if we attacked it head on some of them would fight alongside the Utility. We had a confab and decided that the best thing to do was confront them when they were getting onto their bus, which was parked between the Barras and Bridgeton Cross. We left the Glaswegian in groups of five and headed along Carlton Place to avoid the prying eyes of the Old Bill. We didn't go empty handed either; in fact we were ready for war. It was obvious that the Utility would be well up for it. They had given the game a miss and had been careful to stay off the police radar. We had no doubt they would be well tooled up and we had to be prepared to fight fire with fire. Our arsenal was impressive. Some boys were carrying knives, others coshes. I had an old Samurai sword, a fearsome weapon even if it was on the blunt side.

When we got to where their bus was parked we hid in bushes in front of a housing estate and waited for them to appear. The anticipation grew. We were itching to get into the cunts and to teach them a lesson they would never forget. But as the minutes passed there was no sign of them. Then we saw someone striding towards the bus. It was the fucking driver!

He started up the bus and started driving in the direction of the Gallowgate.

'Shit,' we thought. 'We need a plan B.'

A decision was made to split into two groups and catch them in a classic pincer movement when they came out of Baird's. Half of us walked along Kent Street, the other half down Bain Street. The only problem was that as a few of the Utility were getting on their bus they spotted us. The element of surprise was gone.

There was only one thing for it. Flanked by the rest of the boys I ran at them, wildly swinging the sword. They didn't fancy getting hit by a Samurai and backed off. By this time the rest of them had come out of Baird's, roaring drunk and well up for it. They now had a numerical advantage and as the two groups fought toe-to-toe they began to get the upper hand and pushed us back.

Then a strange thing happened. The other half of our mob arrived and immediately attacked the Utility from the rear. This unnerved the group of ICF I was in because it gave the impression there were eighty of them ranged against us. My group fell back and I was beginning to get more and more isolated. I could also see that some of our lot were getting a really hard time and I did my best to help, whacking two Utility on the head with the sword and knocking them to the ground in the process.

It was a massive thrill. With two mobs going at it in such a confined space the violence was frenzied and bloody, with heads being coshed and faces slashed. There was no hiding place, no respite. It sorted the men from the boys.

It couldn't last. The sirens were getting closer and closer. I knew I had to ditch the sword or I would be facing very serious charges, so I tossed it in a bin and hot-footed it out of the Gallowgate. I managed to escape arrest but several of our boys weren't so lucky. The Utility went back inside Baird's but the cops were wise to them and many of them got locked up for the weekend before being taken to court on the Monday morning.

Back in the Glaswegian we had our usual post-mortem. We had to acknowledge that the Utility had got the better of it. With hindsight we concluded that splitting the mob had not been one of our better ideas as it seemed to sow the seeds of confusion and, eventually, panic. On a personal level I was annoyed that they had got the better of us in my beloved east end, even if it was the Celtic-supporting, Gallowgate part of the east end. Right away my thoughts turned to revenge and the return fixture at Tannadice in a few months time.

*

After the bitter taste left in our mouths by the Gallowgate incident we were determined to get our own back at the first time of asking. We hired a bus and filled it with some of the most formidable thugs this little country of ours has ever produced. There was no way we were going to the game. That was business, this was personal. Having been in touch with the Utility's top boy in the lead up to the game I had been assured they would be well up for it after the game.

The other decision we took was to stay well clear of the city of Dundee itself, away from the prying eyes of the new football-intelligence units that were springing up all over Scotland. I suggested to the rest of the boys that we should plot up in Broughty Ferry, a place I knew well from my time in Castle Huntly prison. Broughty Ferry is just the right distance from Dundee, not too close yet not too far, and being a wealthy seaside suburb hardly the sort of place you normally associate with FV.[14] With any luck it would throw those meddling FI cunts off the trail.

We watched the game in a sports bar, our mood made even brighter by a comfortable 3–0 win for Rangers. At soon as the ref had blown for time-up I was straight on the phone to my Utility contact. He said they would be in Broughty Ferry within the hour. They got there a lot quicker than that because within half an hour our spotters were reporting that they had seen several cars full of Utility driving up and down the main street. We left the bar in small groups, wielding bottles and pieces of wood, ready for the fray and eagerly anticipating the violence to come. We waited and waited but they didn't show. By this time it was pissing down and we were getting a right soaking.

A decision was made to go back to the sports bar where we ordered a final pint and snorted a few lines. Feeling deflated, and calling the Utility all the shitebags in the world, we finished our drinks, trudged out of the pub and got on the bus, which was parked on the main thoroughfare. Then, just as the driver pulled the lever to close the doors, we saw them. Forty Utility. Coming out of the side streets and walking at a fair old clip towards us. Game on.

'There they are,' one of the boys shouted, followed by cries of 'Yes' and 'Ya fucking beauty' from others. I was near the back of the bus and could only watch as the lads who had been at the front got out and immediately engaged their top boys. It should have been very tasty but for some

---

[14] Broughty Ferry was once known as the 'richest square mile in Europe' because of the number of jute millionaires from Dundee who lived there.

reason the Utility didn't fancy it. Within sixty seconds they had backed off and were running for their lives. I had by this time got off the bus but I didn't get a chance to throw a punch because they were legging it as fast as their Trim Trabs would carry them. Some of the boys chased them down to the beach and gave the stragglers they caught a kicking but I was still soaked to the skin and thought, 'Fuck it, I am not running after them.'

We managed to get back on the bus by the time the cops arrived. They knew fine well what had gone on but the driver saved our bacon. He told the Old Bill that we had been for a quiet drink and had been attacked by a group of locals, although he must have realised we were football hooligans. He was backed up by the staff from the sports bar who told the police that although we were boisterous we hadn't caused them any problems. There was nothing the filth could do, apart from giving us an escort out of Broughty Ferry, blue lights flashing.

Revenge for the Gallowgate had been short, swift and decisive.

12

THE JAMBOS

I like Hearts. I like the club's ethos, the fact that they have a pro-British ethos. I like the crest on their strips, which is based on the famous Heart of Midlothian mosaic on Edinburgh's Royal Mile. I like their strong affinity with the British Army, which goes right back to the First World War, when sixteen of the first-team players volunteered for active service. They were the first players from any British club to join up en masse and they became part of the legendary McCrae's battalion of the 16th Royal Scots.

In terms of their mob, I have always found them to be something of an enigma. In the pre-casual days they had the most formidable hooligan gang in Scotland, the feared Gorgie Aggro, which was made up of skins and bovver boys. I remember my brother Christopher coming home from Tynecastle and telling me about fights with the Aggro. It was one of the few places Rangers were met with any resistance in those days.

It is therefore surprising that Hearts didn't become major players when the casual scene got into full swing. They had a mob, the Capital Service Firm, but many of them went over to Hibs, their deadly rivals, and became part of the much bigger and more formidable Capital City Service. Despite their difficulties the CSF still had a reasonable mob and we had quite a few offs with them. That may surprise some people, given that Rangers and Hearts are supposedly Protestant clubs, but football is very territorial. Tynecastle has always been an unlucky ground for me and I got hurt there several times. The first incident was in 1985/86, the season that Hearts were pipped to the title by Celtic on goal difference. I was part of a group of Rangers Soccer Babes and before the game we plotted up in Gorgie Road, close to the Wheatsheaf stand. We ran into Hearts youth and after some pretty nifty fisticuffs backed them off to their own stand. It was still early, so early that there were hardly any scarfers around.

After hostilities had ended we were trooping back to Gorgie Road to meet up with the main mob when I, being a mouthy so-and-so, held back to goad the Hearts boys for running away. I was so busy giving them pelters that I didn't notice one of the guys we had chased flanking me on my right-hand side. Before I knew it he punched me on the back of my head and knocked me to the ground. Within seconds six of his mates jumped on and started to kick fuck out of me. I remember lying on the ground trying to fend off kicks and punches and shouting for handers from the rest of our mob. The force of their blows got ever stronger and it got even scarier when one of them shouted: 'Hold the Weegie bastard and we'll stab him.'

I took this threat very seriously because given the rate they were going they probably would have ended up killing me using just their feet and hands. Thank fuck that someone in the ICF saw what was happening and alerted the rest of the firm. They ran back to help, and not a moment too soon either because I really thought I was going to get a knife in the guts. It was two valuable lessons for the price of one: don't take the piss, and always expect the unexpected. In the end I walked away with just cuts and bruises but thanks to my big mouth it could have been so much worse.

Later in the Eighties we were again in Gorgie Road, this time in a swing park, with about ten other ICF and RSB. We weren't able to get match tickets so we were larking about on the swings waiting for the game to end so that we could walk back to Haymarket station with the rest of the mob. From out of nowhere we were confronted by twenty CSF and although we were well outnumbered we had nowhere to run. The only option was to stand and fight. I have to say that we gave as good as we got, despite them having twice as many boys. I was in the wars again and ended up with a really sore ear after some cunt hit me with a Millwall brick. No wonder I think of Gorgie Road as my unluckiest street.

In the Eighties the walk from Haymarket to Gorgie could be tasty but from about 1990 onwards the relationship between the two mobs became more cordial, with the two youth wings forging a particularly close friendship. The CSF have some great lads on board: the T brothers; Gags; Davie E; Young Claye and his youth firm – all of whom joined us in the Scottish National Firm. The problem for the CSF as an independent mob was that the Hearts support never embraced the casual culture in a big way and, in consequence, they were dominated by their city rivals. Much the same thing happened in Glasgow, where we have lorded it over Celtic for years.

13

THE ENGLAND NATIONAL TEAM

I am proud to be British and I never want to see any of the four nations that make up the United Kingdom break away. Such is my passion for this great country of ours that as a young hooligan I always tried to wear Union Jack boxer shorts, T-shirts and socks, and if it wasn't Union Jack gear I would don clothes with the Red Hand of Ulster logo prominently displayed. My choice of outfit was always a great source of amusement for the older boys in the ICF. In fact it led to Harky giving me the nickname Billy Britain, and it is one that has stuck with me to this day.

Given our strong sense of Britishness, fans of other Scottish clubs claim that the ICF joined up with the English national team's firm to fight Scotland fans. That is crap. We are Scottish and British, not English and British. While we have nothing but contempt for the Tartan Army bampots who denigrate the idea of British identity that does not mean we put England above Scotland. In fact some of the most vicious football violence I have ever taken part in involved Rangers ICF members fighting the English national firm.

My first experience of the England mob came in 1985. I was twelve and a Rangers Soccer Babe, just starting out on the great hooligan adventure. They came up to Glasgow for the Scotland–England game that year and again in 1987. I was in awe. There were just so many of them, and they were almost all massive beer monsters. The England lads had been making headlines all over Europe and when I saw them, and the way they took the piss on the streets of Glasgow, I understood why.

I went down to Wembley in 1988 for the England–Scotland fixture with an old school pal from Shettleston. We travelled by coach on the Friday morning, one out of a convoy of hundreds that clogged up the M6 and then the M1. My mum and my aunt were also on the coach, which made the journey slightly bizarre. They weren't going to the game; their intention was to go shopping on Oxford Street and no doubt to keep an eye on me. We arrived about two in the afternoon and were taken to our hotel in Piccadilly Circus, after which we did the whole London tourist thing.

The next morning me and my pal headed for Trafalgar Square where we ran into a few boys we knew from Blackley's Baby Crew. They had come down with the main mob, the CCS, and I would guess there were about three hundred Hibs there altogether. We didn't get any grief from the Hibs boys and in fact we walked with them the rest of the way. En route the CCS had it with Leeds and then Chelsea and they gave a good account of themselves. At Trafalgar Square it was fucking chaos. There were thousands of Scots milling around, most of them drunk, and fights were kicking off all over the shop with the many English firms who had come along for the fun.

We got the tube to the game and as we were walking up Wembley Way I realised just how special the place is. Wembley is steeped in tradition. But there was another great tradition about to be played out: all-out warfare between England and Scotland. The atmosphere was tense, especially after what had gone off at Trafalgar Square. This time I was desperate to be part of it.

In the stadium I had hoped to be alongside the CCS and those ICF boys, including Harky, who had travelled down. So you can imagine my disappointment when I found myself in the upper tier behind one of the goals, sixty feet above Scotland's top hooligans, who were congregated in the lower tier. It didn't take long for it to go off. Hibs had a massive presence and ably assisted by elements of the ICF they steamed into England. It was a magnificent sight to behold and the Scots fought like lions. I was desperate to get into the fight and eventually I managed to scramble down into the bottom tier but by the time I got there the Old Bill had things well under control.

After the game, boys from every major Scottish firm – Hibs, Aberdeen, Rangers, Hearts, Celtic – mobbed up and went looking for England. There were skirmishes all over the place, with mounted police charging both sets of hooligans. I was in a group that chased some England into a multi-storey car park and we had a memorable set-to, which ended with one of their boys being thrown off a stairwell on the second floor. He was hurt but not, as I found out later, critically. The fighting continued all the way to the tube station until the cops managed to squeeze us onto trains for the city centre.

Scotland more than held its own at Wembley (off the pitch at least) and it gave us a lot of confidence for the next game with England, which of course would be the following year at Hampden. That turned out to be the most memorable Auld Enemy encounter of them all, one that led to questions in Parliament and calls for the fixture to be scrapped.

To say that the 1989 Scotland–England game was eagerly anticipated by mobs north of the border would be an understatement. Everyone was buzzing; everyone wanted a slice of the action. There would be no repeat of what happened in either 1985 or 1987 when the English had wreaked havoc without any real response from us. This time it would be different. We were two years older, we were better organised and our club mobs were more formidable, even if some of them had their own agendas while they were fighting under a Scottish banner.

On the day of the game I travelled into the city centre by taxi, heading for Minstrels bar, which is opposite where the Riverboat casino is today. On the way in I noticed that along with the massive police presence there were huge mobs of England roaming the streets. Their body language left me in no doubt that every last one of them was looking to spill Scottish blood. We would have to be at our very best if we were to stand any chance of competing with that lot.

When I got to Minstrels I was delighted to see that upwards of two hundred ICF were out. We also knew that Hibs would be fielding at least two hundred and that Aberdeen would have about the same. Nor did the other clubs let us down. The Utility was out in force and so too were our provincial colleagues from Motherwell, St Johnstone, Partick Thistle and Kilmarnock. The common denominator that day was that no cunt wanted England to take the piss. I was tooled up. I had a spring cosh in my pocket and most of the ICF were also carrying a weapon of some description. There was no alternative. We knew that the English boys rarely left home without a tool and that they were not afraid to use them.

We left Minstrels and made our way up Hope Street. Almost immediately, at the junction with Argyle Street, we were confronted by a huge mob of Derby County. I was immediately struck by how old they were; I was sixteen but some of them were old enough to be my father. It didn't faze us. The roar of 'ICCF, ICCF' went up and we charged. Drawing my cosh I was confronted by this fat fuck, thirty-five if he was a day. I bounced the cosh off his skull but it must have been a cheap one because it broke into little pieces, leaving me to rely on my fists and feet.

By this time hundreds more England had appeared and they split us into two smaller groups. I was in a group that got backed off to the railway arches and although they were getting the upper hand we were giving everything we had. The Old Bill were doing their best to break it up but their job was rendered nigh impossible as more and more mobs appeared. To our right we were flanked by one hundred and fifty Newcastle and in the confusion I remember steaming into them as well. My run-in with the Geordies didn't last long because out of nowhere a brick shithouse of a cop grabbed me by the ear, wrestled me to the ground and stuck on a pair of handcuffs.

'Fuck off. My day is over,' I thought as I was thrown into the back of a police van with a group of England. There were dozens of these vans in the city, and they were quickly being filled up with boys from both sides. I thought I would be taken to the nearest station and charged but I was to spend four hours in the back of that particular vehicle. The cops were too busy lifting people to take us anywhere and the only consolation for me was that as the van sped from one trouble spot to another I got a great view of some of the best FV in the history of the beautiful game.

Jamaica Bridge was typical. I watched open mouthed as Harky and Christie, with the assistance of a few Rangers Soccer Babes, backed off twenty of Stoke's Naughty Forty crew. I was so proud of their bravery and their fighting spirit. They were outstanding that day; it was in the best traditions of Rangers and the ICF. When we got to Eglinton Toll, which is not far from Hampden, there was an almighty tussle between two hundred Hibs and the same number of English outside a petrol station. I was very impressed by the way the CCS boys handled themselves and I said as much to one of the Dykes boys when he was arrested and bundled into the van.

Finally, the cops took us to Stewart Street police station and on the way there we were joshing the English about what they could expect in Barlinnie prison. 'You're going to the BarL boys. You'll get your back doors booted in there,' we chortled, using a well-known euphemism for anal sex. Some of them were fucking shiting themselves; you could see the fear etched across their faces. They were well aware of Barlinnie and its fearsome reputation and taken out of their comfort zone some of them weren't as tough as they thought.

Inside Stewart Street it was a real Who's Who of football thugs. The place was awash with leading faces from every corner of the United Kingdom. They kept me in a cell overnight and the next day, at five in the afternoon, I was released. I was well pissed off. Not only had I sat out most of the FV but I had now also missed a league decider between Rangers Boys Club and our bitter rivals, St Mary's Guild, a Roman Catholic team (the good news was that the game finished in a draw, which meant we won the league).

In the Sheriff Court on the Monday morning I got a £75 fine, which was paltry by the usual standards. But I did get a double bollocking: one from my mum and the other from my team manager at the Boy's Club. It was becoming apparent to me that I was a much better football hooligan than I was a footballer!

The media reaction to that game was something to behold, and no wonder. There were more than two hundred and fifty arrests, dozens of people were seriously injured and taken to hospital while pubs, shops and restaurants got trashed. The Sheriff Court was so busy that a special thirteen-hour sitting was necessary to deal with the sheer volume of cases. More than £11,000-worth of fines were imposed for offences ranging from breach of the peace to assault.

The headlines in the Scottish press said it all: 'Hampden Mayhem', 'The Battle of Glasgow', 'Battle Stations', 'Thugs Battle on Our Streets', 'Scrap the Bovver Match'. Politicians, as politicians always do, jumped on the bandwagon. The Labour party's official spokesman called for the fixture to 'be put on ice'. John Maxton MP, whose constituency includes Hampden Park, demanded that the fixture be scrapped while Scottish sports minister Michael Forsyth said that he was 'bitterly disappointed' by the violence and called for a report into what had happened.

Interestingly, but perhaps predictably, some of the Scottish papers put the blame squarely on the England boys. One argued that 'Scots soccer fans had been the target for England's marauding morons,' while another took the view that 'English football hooliganism came to the streets of Glasgow yesterday'. We knew different. We were not victims, we gave as good as we got and then some. Never again would the English come to our city, our country, and take the piss. Those days were long gone.

By the time Euro 96 came along my attitude towards the Scottish national team had changed. I was getting a bit pissed off with the Tartan Army's obvious, and growing, hatred of England and such was my frustration with their attitude that I told one paper I wouldn't open the curtains to watch Scotland. Paul Gascoigne was also a factor: he was at the peak of his powers as a Rangers player and I wanted him to do well in the tournament, even if that meant he turned it on against Scotland.

I was by then a leading light in the ICF and Harky and Davie Carrick were keen that I should go south for a crack at England, Holland and anyone else who got in our way. But I wasn't that bothered, mainly for the reasons I have cited above. Then there was my relationship with other Scottish mobs: I had made derogatory comments about some of them and I wasn't sure about their reaction; down there, amid all the confusion, I would be a sitting duck. So, reluctantly, I decided to sit Euro 96 out and watch it in the pub.

It was the wrong decision.

I put a grand on England to beat Scotland and settled down in Deans' bar to watch the game. I was delighted to take the money off the bookie but when I saw the running battles after the game in Trafalgar Square I was in turmoil. I knew the boys would be in the thick of it and I realised that I should have been there, standing toe-to-toe against the English. It got worse. Harky kept phoning me, giving me running commentaries on what was going off. That made my guilt unbearable. I had let my mates down; I had let the ICF down. It is something I regret to this day.

Euro 96 was my last chance to have a crack at England. Although the ICF turned out for the Euro playoffs between Scotland and England in 2000 by then the cops had the whole thing sewn up with their intelligence units, closed-circuit television and banning orders. Although I had been enraged when the Tartan Army booed 'God Save the Queen' before the game at Hampden I was still keen to have it with England. After the game (which Scotland lost 2–0) we mobbed up in the Printworks pub and then moved from pub to pub, playing cat and mouse with the Old Bill. A rumour spread that Man United were in Shenanigan's in Sauchiehall Street and we did our best to arrange a meet but the cops were onto us and the same thing happened when we tried to hunt down Aberdeen's mob. The night just fizzled out and so did Scotland's playoff hopes despite a 1–0 win at Wembley in the return.

It was another glorious Scottish failure.

14

CATCHING THE SMALL FRY

I have always had the utmost respect for the boys who make up Scotland's smaller mobs. They didn't have the benefit of great numbers, with fifty being possible only on a very good day. Nor did they enjoy great longevity; most of them had only two or three of what I would call good seasons. They were also, perhaps inevitably, always stronger at home, the main exception being big cup games when they got their act together and put a decent firm out. But those special days came along once in a blue moon. For the most part the wee guys had to rely on their native courage and daring, and they had both quantities in abundance.

Motherwell

The Motherwell Saturday Service deserves its place in the pantheon of great Scottish mobs. For me the men of the MSS were the founding fathers of the organised-football-violence scene in this country. Their battle with Aberdeen at Fir Park in 1983 was historic. It was the first time two mobs of casuals squared up to each other and it was also the first time that the media got a handle on what was to become such an important social phenomenon in the years that lay ahead.

There were other reasons to admire the MSS. They were game as fuck and, like their team on the field, would take on much bigger and better-resourced outfits without a moment's hesitation. That takes guts. In the early days they were a match for anyone, which speaks volumes for their dedication and forward planning.

And I couldn't help but admire their politics. Many of the Saturday Service were staunch Loyalists and played in a flute band that hails from the town.

Most of the MSS encounters I was involved in came during the mid-to-late Eighties. In December 1985 there was a particularly nasty, thirty-a-side fight at Argyle Street low-level station. It spilled onto the street, panicking Christmas shoppers. We smashed them with a metal crowd-control barrier and then when they were on the run a few of them got a right kicking. Fair play to Motherwell: a week later they attacked some of our boys at St Enoch Square and gave them a bit of a pasting.

However, the best day from that era was 3 May 1986, when we beat them 2–0 at Ibrox and I was beginning to make a name for myself in the firm. I remember it well because the game was played just after the announcement that Graeme Souness was to become Rangers manager.[15] When the ninety minutes were up twenty-five Motherwell walked around from the away end and confronted us in a housing estate behind the Copland Road stand. Despite putting up a spirited fight the MSS got a bit of a doing. Our main man that day was Barry Johnstone, who, as always, was in the thick of the action. I was in awe of the way that Barry steamed into the SS without a moment's hesitation, displaying exemplary courage and leadership.[16] With someone like that on your side you just couldn't lose.

I have to admit taking a bit of a liberty that day. Motherwell had a big, blond-haired boy in their firm and when he got decked a few of the young ones got wired into him. He got a real kicking and in the course of a frenzied attack one of our boys (not me) slashed him across the face. I remember straightening up after kicking him and noticing that my clothes were covered in red stains. 'Where the fuck did that blood come from?' I asked myself. I looked down at Mr Blond and saw that there was a gaping hole where his cheek used to be. I heard later that when he got to hospital he needed fifty stitches the slash was so bad. As I said, a bit of a liberty.

It was always tasty with Motherwell, especially on their patch, and one dash with them in 1991 – just after Graeme Souness announced he would be leaving Rangers – sums that up. Unfortunately, I was in jail and missed it but Mr Blue was there and this is his version of what happened.

Motherwell at Fir Park, 1991: Mr Blue's Story

As Rangers were marching towards the title in 1991 the world was great. Souness had built a team capable of competing with anybody in Europe, the rave scene was

---

15   It seems incredible, but Rangers actually finished fifth in the league that season.
16   The late, and much lamented, Mr Johnstone can be seen talking about this fight on YouTube.

in full swing – meaning great drugs and birds everywhere – and there was still a spot of football violence if that was your thing.

Everything was fucking great, then . . .

'Graeme Souness has resigned as manager of Glasgow Rangers to take control at Liverpool,' announced Rangers director David Holmes.

'What the fuck! Ya hairy lipped cunt,' I thought when I heard the news. Although people trotted out that old cliché 'no man is bigger than the club' Souness had almost single-handedly brought us back from mediocrity to our rightful place at the top of Scottish football. Now the cheeky cunt was fucking off to the land of the robbing-bastard Scouser.

'Ah well, never mind,' I thought. We'll just pick up a world-class manager from Real Madrid or some other little club. It seems like madness now, but that's how Rangers fans thought back then, because Souness not only gave us back our dominance, he also gave us back our arrogance. We lost it for a while but now it was back and, fuck me, we loved it. We rubbed every cunt and any cunt's nose in the fact we were back at the top of the tree. The rest of Scotland fucking despised us and we revelled in it.

Nobody does arrogance like Glasgow Rangers.

Of course, we never got Real Madrid's manager. We got Walter Smith!

Due to injuries, change of manager, loss of form or loss of bottle our 'charge' towards the title was now a bit of a limp. I wasn't too concerned though as we still had two games to pick up the point we needed and one of those was a game against Motherwell, who had a number of ex Rangers players in their side and of course were managed by Tommy McLean and Tom Forsyth, both Ibrox legends.

For fans under the age of thirty, Motherwell may not seem like an obvious place for one of the best spots of football violence I've ever been involved in. But for a period during the 1980s, even into the early 1990s, trips to Motherwell could be fairly lively.

We made our way to the game with a firm of fifty lads from the east end, got off the train at Airbles and walked to the ground unopposed by any locals. We were there to see some goals and Rangers swagger to another title. 1–0, 2–0, 3–0 and that was that – nope, not another title but a 3–0 hammering.

We left Fir Park a bit pissed off and met a few other lads outside. There were around thirty of us and one of the lads had somehow acquired a Motherwell sun hat. We began the walk to Motherwell central when we saw a few lads down a street. There were only a few of them, and they quickly got on their toes as we approached them, but it was obvious they were Motherwell lads. It was even more obvious that their role in life was to tell others where we were. They went to fulfil their role as we happily followed them into their 'trap'. In fact we had a cunning plan. One of the lads said, to nobody in particular, 'Somebody stick that Motherwell hat on. We'll chase you and crack the first cunt that comes to help you.' Wee Johnny, always game for a challenge, volunteered for the assignment.

Our route took us to the football pitches on which it has kicked off with Motherwell's firm several times over the years. We went onto the first pitch at the corner flag and, two pitches away, we could see Motherwell making their way past a corner flag. They were around two hundred yards from us and Johnny ran towards them, screaming like a banshee for help. It was fucking comical seeing him shout to Motherwell, 'come on, help me here, this mob are shit'. Every ten yards or so he turned round and threw a dummy punch like he was holding off thirty of us himself. It was worthy of an Oscar. Here was this anorexic Rambo swinging at us as we followed in his footsteps. As the first SS lad arrived to 'save' him Johnny turned to him and 'crack', the poor cunt went down like a sack of spuds. Of our thirty about twenty doubled up laughing, leaving them a fair way behind as Motherwell got to the Rangers lads closest to them. As Motherwell piled in we had to get a grip and to realise the Benny Hill sketch was now over and done with. We had a job to do. The front lads began backing away as Motherwell, who were about forty-handed, piled in, They obviously hadn't found Johnny's little charade as funny as we did!

As the Motherwell punches flew in our front lads were struggling badly. This was now urgent and the rest of our firm eventually stopped laughing and joined in the fray. Motherwell had a bit of momentum but we stopped that in its tracks as we got our act together. The fight seemed to go on for ten minutes but in reality it was probably more like five. This was a genuine toe-to-toe. There was another comical moment when it seemed like an invisible bell had sounded, because all of a sudden both sides stopped for a rest. We re-engaged and, slowly but surely, pushed a very game Motherwell firm back. By this time quite a few of them were going down, relying on their mates to pick them up. Then, when the shout of 'ICCCCCF, ICCCCCF' went up they lost it completely. The momentum was ours and we weren't giving it back.

As they ran two things struck me. Firstly, only about five of our lot actually gave chase as everybody was totally fucked after the longest non-stop row I've ever experienced; secondly, I noticed that two coppers were sitting on a grass verge watching us go at it. Fuck knows how long they'd been there, but it was probably quite a while because they looked very comfortable.

We made our way back to the station and bumped into another firm of Rangers, about a dozen or so, who told us they'd also had a top-notch toe-to-toe with bigger numbers of Motherwell. Fair play to the Motherwell lads. They *certainly played their part in a very lively dash and, in addition, their team very nearly cost us the title.*

For the record Walter led us to the 1990/91 title, and many more besides, as Rangers continued to dominate Scottish football under his leadership.

The most recent encounter with the SS took place in 2006. They were making something of a comeback as a mob and had been involved in a number of skirmishes with the Rangers Youth. We knew they would be fronting up and we put together a tidy firm for the short trip to Lanarkshire. Some boys got tickets for the game, others didn't, so thirty ticketless ICF, including me, landed up in the Electric bar in Airbles Road, next to the train station.

After the game ended we got the call from the Saturday Service to say they were on their way. I got on the blower to the boys who had been at the game and asked if they had seen any Motherwell heading in our direction. 'No, we haven't seen them,' I was told. To be doubly sure I got a small group together – Swedgers, Bomb Scare, Willie the Bat and half a dozen others – and decided to go for a wee look. I told the rest of the boys to stay in the pub until we had seen the lie of the land.

As soon as we walked out the front door of the pub there they were, right in our faces. Twenty Motherwell, all of them well up for it. No one had time to think. No one had time to speak. No one had time to get apprehensive. It kicked off in a nano second.

Swedgers and I were confronted by two SS. As my opponent came at me I backed him off with a bottle of Miller while Swedgers was left to take on this cunt with the height and build of an all-in wrestler.

'I'm British Army,' Giant Haystacks proudly proclaimed.

'Oh, that's good,' Swedgers replied, before smacking him full in the face, a blow that put the big man right onto his arse. I doubt if any of the rest us could have knocked the soldier boy down but Swedgers is a roofer to trade and no shrinking violet.

The fun didn't last for long. Within minutes the sirens were blaring and we ran back into the pub, ready to play the innocent bystanders when the cops turned up. I took a call from Big Boris.

'The outside of the pub is black with Old Bill. Get your arse outside and I'll pick you up,' he said.

Swedgers and I sneaked out of the side door and jumped into Boris's car. It was just in the nick of time because as the police questioned the ICF boys in the pub it became clear they were out to get yours truly.

'Where is Sandy Chugg?' they asked. 'We have information that Sandy Chugg was drinking in this pub.' The boys of course blanked them and by this time I was long gone.

For me that day sums up Motherwell. We didn't have to go looking for them, they came to us. Despite the fact that we were now the number-one mob in Scotland they had the guts to front up without being shamed into it, which made a refreshing change from some other mobs I could mention.

More power to their elbow.

Kilmarnock

I wouldn't put Kilmarnock's mob in remotely the same league as the Motherwell Saturday Service but they had a couple of reasonably good years in the mid Nineties.[17] However, my first skirmish with them was 1986, when they were in the lower leagues. Six of us Rangers Soccer Babes, all from the east end, got the bus into the city centre and got off at George Square. The plan was to hook up with more RSB at our usual meeting place in St Enoch Square and look for someone, anyone, to fight. We didn't expect to meet a mob of Kilmarnock on the way – Rangers weren't playing them – but that's exactly what happened. On our way to St Enoch's we ran into thirty boys, obviously casuals, and although at that point we didn't have a clue which club they were attached to we weren't going to let that stand in our way.

There were more of them and they were older and bigger than us. But with the confidence of youth we threw caution to the wind and steamed in. It was a disaster. I got decked and on my way down I took a few more punches and kicks. In fact all six of us got a kicking before the Killie boys decided they had taught us enough of a lesson and went to catch their train. Bruised, battered and groggy we got up and inspected our injuries. I discovered that I had a burst nose, a chipped tooth and a black eye and that my five pals were in a similar state. What made me even angrier, however, was that one of the sleeves on my bright-red-and-blue Aquascutum shirt was caked in dirt. Those fucking Ayrshire bastards! That shirt was my pride and joy.

---

[17] Their mob had a fucking weird name, something like Painaro, after a song by the Pet Shop Boys. Well, each to his own I suppose.

As we cleaned up in Buchanan Street public toilets we agreed that Kilmarnock were not going to get away with turning us over in the middle of our city. Given their age and the numbers they had with them it was a suicide mission but we were fucking raging. We sprinted round to Queen Street and caught them at the low-level station, where they now had a police escort.

'We want a rematch,' we demanded.

They didn't take us entirely seriously.

'Fuck off wee men. Did you not have enough round the corner?' one of them sneered.

His mate was a bit more complimentary.

'Fair play to you, wee men. You're keen but youse have no chance.'

By this time the cops had seen what we were up to and we were told to get lost or we would be locked up. We got lost.

As I said Killie were at their peak in the mid Nineties and in a two-year period between April 1994 and May 1996 we had three outstanding offs with them. The first was on 10 April 1994, when we met them at Hampden in a Scottish Cup semi-final. The game was a rather drab goalless draw and to spice things up we went to look for their mob among the supporters' buses that were parked on red blaes pitches not far from the stadium. To our delight we came across a bus with about thirty of them in it. We picked up stones and did our best to smash every window on the bus. To their credit Kilmarnock didn't bottle it. They poured off the coach and, to our surprise, gave as good as they got before the cops arrived and broke it up.

We weren't done yet. Hiding up a side street we waited until the convoy of buses started to move off. Then when we saw their bus passing some of us launched a volley of bottles while the rest charged round to the front of the bus, stopping it in its tracks. Once again I was surprised when they trooped off the bus to face us and once again I was surprised at just how fucking game they were. In fact I would say that over the piece honours were even. A few ICF got nicked but I got lucky and managed to sneak away.[18]

Unfortunately, I missed the middle off in the trilogy, which took place in November 1995 when we played them in a league game at Rugby Park. I was told the whole story by someone who was there and what a story it

---

[18] Rangers won the replay and went on to face Dundee United in the final. If we had won it would have given us back-to-back trebles but, as I note in the chapter on the Utility, United sneaked it 1–0.

is. Twenty ICF went down to Kilmarnock, including some of our heaviest hitters, but they came unstuck against a forty-strong home mob. Even allowing for the numerical disparity between the two groups that surprised me, because I knew the calibre of the ICF who had gone down there. It was by all accounts a particularly nasty fight, in the course of which one of ours, Craig C, got his arm broken after taking a full-blooded blow from a baseball bat. I was beside myself with anger when I heard what had happened to Craig. Taking a baseball bat to someone who is not tooled up is a real liberty. And one, I vowed, that would be revenged.

As Kilmarnock didn't trap for the return fixture at Ibrox we had to wait until the end of the season to get our own back, but by Christ it was worth waiting for. It was now 4 May 1996 and we were due to face Killie on their patch in the last league game of the season. This time there would be no mistake, no underestimating them, no going with an under-strength mob. We also went well tooled up, with coshes, knives, CS gas and flare guns. They had chosen to follow that path and would now reap what they had sown.

We got on the train, stopping off at Barrhead to let the latecomers catch up and, by noon, when we got to Kilmarnock station, we had about forty with us. There was no way we were going to the game. We were there for one reason and one reason only: to kick fuck out of Kilmarnock. In the pub the forty became forty-five and then fifty and finally sixty as more and more boys arrived. I wasn't the only one who had been angered by what Kilmarnock had done to Craig.

We were in that pub for three hours, getting drunker and drunker and angrier and angrier. Then the call came. Kilmarnock were on their way. We piled out and sprinted round to the pedestrian precinct in the town centre. There they were, about sixty of them. There was no eyeing each other up, no gestures of defiance; no songs or chants. Fuelled by righteous indignation we charged. They had no chance. We smashed them and when they regrouped we smashed them again. I don't even remember throwing a punch, such was our dominance.

Only one of their boys put up any real resistance: a well-built cunt with a shock of red hair, who I believe goes by the name of Beastie. He was a really game lad, and even managed to mix it with Carrick, which, let me tell you, takes some doing. But I am afraid that after his heroics he blotted his copybook by pointing out a few of us to the Old Bill, who by this time had us corralled. It was no doubt an attempt to take the heat off his own mob but to me it is grassing. End of.

Not that we gave it much thought as we marched happily to the station, chanting raucously as we went. But we had to cut short the triumphalism. We knew that we were likely to be penned in again by the Old Bill as we waited for our train, which might lead to questioning and searches. Given that we were armed to the teeth that would be inviting trouble and, as a result, some of the boys decided to ditch their weapons in a clump of bushes. It resulted in a flare gun going off, causing a fire in the shrubbery, which cracked us up.

But none of that mattered. We had settled the score with Kilmarnock. The cunts would think twice before taking a baseball bat to Rangers.

Partick Thistle

Life is hard for Motherwell and Kilmarnock, both on and off the pitch. But for Partick Thistle, in the shadow of the Old Firm behemoth, it must be fucking soul-destroying. Glasgow's third force have always been up against it and they always will be. So respect to the club and to their mob, the North Glasgow Express, for even turning up. The NGE has always been competitive with the likes of Airdrie's Section B and Dunfermline's Carnegie Soccer Casuals but like their team they are also-rans where Rangers, Celtic, Hearts, Hibs and Aberdeen are concerned.

I like many of the Express. They are nice lads and I have particular respect for one of their main faces, who I will call 'Big H'. Two Asian brothers are also prominent in the NGE – Ben is one – and they too are stand-up guys. While they and their mates have never got the better of the ICF, in recent years they have taken on the Rangers Youth in a number of minor skirmishes.

That is not to say they weren't up for the challenge. They have been willing to front up to us, with the result that we have had to put them in their place on a few occasions. Back in 1993 they began to mouth off, saying how much they wanted to do us. At first we tended to ignore them, having bigger fish to fry, but they kept going on and on about it and we thought to ourselves, 'Fuck this. If they want it they are going to get it.' The good thing was they were in the same city and we didn't have to wait for a match day. So this night twenty-five of us went up to Maryhill, some in cars, the others by tube. Our plan was to attack their boozer, the Pewter Pot, which lies between Great Western Road and Maryhill Road and is close to Firhill stadium.

We mobbed up and made straight for the Pewter Pot and when we got within twenty yards of the place the front door swung open and fifteen NGE came out. They must have known we were coming because every one of their boys was carrying a baseball bat, a knife or a pool cue.

If they were trying to intimidate us it didn't work.

The cry went up.

'ICCCF, ICCCF'.

We steamed in, pushing them back, right up to the front of the Pewter Pot. They regrouped and charged but once again we pushed them back, forcing all but five of their mob back inside the pub. As the doors of the pub were barricaded we turned our attention to the five stragglers, relieving them of their weapons and giving them a slap for their trouble. There were still the other mouthy cunts cowering inside the Pewter to be dealt with. We laid siege to the pub, battering the front door and smashing the windows. But it was no use. There was no way through and encouraged by the sound of police cars in the distance we made ourselves scarce. A decade later, after a Scottish Cup semi-final, we did the same thing again, but this time we got into the Pewter Pot and waited for the NGE. When no one appeared we left for another pub and then went back to the Pewter Pot when they showed up. We mullered them, and it *was* them, despite their claims that none of their boys were actually in the pub.

There were always long gaps between our encounters with Thistle – we were invariably in different divisions – and if it was going to go off it was going to be a cup competition, which is how we came to face them in September 2008 after a League Cup tie.

Not for the first time the NGE had been taunting us, telling us they would have a mob out; daring us to front up. And once again we obliged. Before the game we assembled in Wintergill's, a cracking old-fashioned pub on Great Western Road, while Thistle were ensconced not far away in the Woodside Inn. Their location was a bit of a problem, as the Woodside was owned by relatives of one of the Rangers Youth.

We were on and off the phone to the NGE, who told us they were trying to put a mob together but were struggling for numbers. At this point Boris and I decided to recce the Woodside and while we were doing that we had a chat with one of Thistle's youth, 'R', who confirmed they were doing their best to pull a decent mob but were having problems. Boris and I told R that the trap would have to be in the street because the Woodside was a no-no in view of who owned it. We went back to Wintergill's and waited for their response.

When we heard nothing we left the pub and began to walk to Firhill, making sure that we went past the Woodside so that the NGE would see us. We swung right up a side street, where we bumped into a tall, balding, athletic lad, who asked:

'Are you Rangers?'

'Of course we are,' we replied.

'I am Thistle. We've got a mob for an off.'

'Go back to the Woodside and get your lads out of the pub. We'll have it on the street. Make sure youse are all out,' I told him.

We waited for a couple of minutes to give them time to mob up before going to the arranged rendezvous. But as we approached the side street that the Woodside was on we saw that fifteen NGE were standing around the door of the pub.

'Come on if you want some,' we shouted.

They didn't seem keen and although the Woodside was packed to the gunwales only ten Thistle came out onto the street. I noticed the bald dude from before; he was carrying a spring cosh while his mates had bottles and chairs from the pub. We ran towards them, chanting 'ICF, ICF,' and almost immediately they backed off. The strange thing was that some of the regulars from the pub came out to help them and I remember being confronted by a guy in his forties, who was wielding a chair. But when the reality of the situation hit him he just threw the chair at me and when it missed he quickly backed off.

Meanwhile the rest of the boys had pushed the NGE and assorted drinkers back, right up against the front door of the Woodside. The baldy lad, with the help of his cosh, was doing his best to rally them and they even managed a charge. I picked up a folding chair, which I threw at Mr Bald, narrowly missing his head. Some of the other ICF were more accurate and several Thistle and a few of the locals were knocked unconscious after being hit by chairs.

Our mood by now was to hell with who owns the pub let's attack it and give the cunts a right good leathering. But we could hear the cop cars screeching down Great Western Road, sirens blaring. It was time to make ourselves scarce.

The next day I got a call from the NGE, who told me the reason the pub was so busy was that a wake was being held in the bar. That would explain why the other customers joined in; they would have been raging that we had had the audacity to attack a pub packed full of people paying their respects to a deceased friend. One mourner however saw the funny side. My NGE contact said that while we were attacking the Woodside one of the guys in the funeral party filmed the whole thing on his mobile phone, complete with a humorous running commentary on the fight, which he later uploaded to YouTube. The mourner has a strong Glasgow accent and when we saw it we pissed ourselves laughing. 'Look at that. Look at that. Look at the fucking state of that. He's been pure knocked out man.'

It is typical Glasgow patter. Fucking pure dead brilliant.

St Johnstone

St Johnstone's Fair City Firm have a big rivalry with Aberdeen and they always pull a good mob for that fixture. However, they did turn out for us a couple of times, the most memorable occasion being the Scottish Cup semi-final in April 1989 (the day of the Hillsborough disaster) a game that was played at Celtic Park. We had forty boys out and we mobbed up at Queen Street station, hoping for a spot of FV but not expecting St Johnstone to be there in big numbers. But credit where it's due, they had a good firm out and there were skirmishes all the way from Queen Street to London Road. Their inspiration was a lad known to all and sundry as Mad Graham, who stood out in any crowd thanks to his long, flowing locks and his undoubted leadership qualities. He has now changed his allegiance and comes with the ICF but he was outstanding for the Fair City Firm that day, rallying them every time we steamed in. I think we fought each other to a standstill, which is commendable for a mob of their size.

Other Scottish mobs

Of the other mobs I have encountered the **Airdrie** Section B Boys stand out, not just for their fighting ability but also because so many of them are good Loyalists. **Falkirk** had a tasty mob – the Falkirk Fear – and they did well in the lower leagues but their day in the sun was a very short one and the same could be said about the Love Street Division, the mob attached to **St Mirren**; we have however had some memorable offs with both. Little **Stranraer** once gave us problems in Glasgow, as did **Ayr United** down at rickety old Somerset Park.

As I said I have a great deal of respect for the little teams who, despite invariably being heavily outnumbered, have often fronted up for the big boys. Only lack of space prevents me going into more detail.

Good luck to them all.

15

ENGLISH CLUB MOBS

The media have always made a big deal out of the ICF's links with the Chelsea Headhunters. Both mobs are right wing, both mobs are British and proud of it and both mobs hate Celtic and the IRA. All of that is true, especially the last bit about Celtic and the IRA. And it is also true that some of our lot would gather in the Toby Jug in Glasgow city centre and travel down to west London to give the Headhunters a hand. Some of our top boys, Davie Carrick included, were frequent visitors to Stamford Bridge.

Although I am a home bird and Rangers through and through, I have a lot of time for Chelsea. That said I consider my English team to be Manchester City, many of whose lads have real Loyalist leanings. Over the years I have also become aware that most English hooligans have a soft spot for Rangers. They love the way that we proudly fly the Union Jack and proclaim our Britishness. It is no coincidence that when a Scottish Defence League was set up – mirroring the much bigger English Defence League – Rangers fans dominated its membership. While English firms respect Rangers they loathe Celtic. In particular they hate the way that so many Celtic fans continue to venerate IRA murderers. And after the bombings in Warrington, Manchester, Birmingham and London can you blame them?

There is a myth propagated by many of the Celtic minded that they have a special bond with Man United. They base this theory on the fact that at one time United was owned by a Roman Catholic family, the Edwards, and that Matt Busby and Tommy Docherty and some of its other managers have been Catholics. Even Celtic's best-known hooligan, John O'Kane, has swallowed this claptrap. In a recent newspaper interview he said that the Celtic mob had never had any problems with the Red Army or the Men in Black. It is of course shite. In fact it is shite on stilts. I have spoken to many Red Army and they despise Celtic and the (very) large minority of their fans who belt out the Republican hate anthems.

All of this does not mean that the ICF, me included, did not enjoy taking on English firms. We did, and with as much relish as when we faced Aberdeen, Hibs or the Utility. We have always enjoyed going down south, rubbing every cunt's nose in it, from Spurs in 1962 to Manchester in 2008. There is no doubt about it, taking on the English, especially in England, is a big fucking thrill, both in a football sense and as a hooligan. In fact one of my biggest disappointments as a young teenager was when my mum refused to let me go down to White Hart Lane for a pre-season friendly in 1986. I was gutted when my brother came back from London and told me they had it all day with Spurs, not to mention the shoplifting expeditions in Oxford Street.

So I am sorry to disappoint the conspiracy theorists. Rangers have always taken on English mobs. And we always will.

Sunderland

In fact it was a game against the Wearsiders that put the ICF right in the centre of the media spotlight. It was July 1993 and Rangers were supplying the opposition for Gary Bennett's testimonial at the old Roker Park. The main body of ICF got a bus from the city centre, while I got a seat on a scarfers coach from Shettleston. I was excited to be going down there because I knew it would be tasty. My only problem was that I had had a heavy alcohol-and-ecstasy session the night before and was faced with the inevitable low. To combat it I had taken three Temazepam tabs and when they were mixed with the copious amounts of lager I managed to get through on the road to the north-east of England I was feeling even more aggressive than usual.

The ICF met up at twelve in a pub called Digby's, where we stayed until late afternoon, before moving to a pub next to a shoe shop. The bar was down a flight of stairs and as we walked in we saw a group of local lads, clearly annoyed that their pub was being taken over. Those same lads would later portray themselves as angels. They weren't.

The atmosphere grew more and more poisonous. Two locals in particular were giving it big licks, making all sorts of smart remarks about Scots. I could sense that something serious was about to go off and, when someone shouted 'Orange bastards', it did.

In a flash, two of the Sunderland boys got slashed across the cheeks. I didn't see the slashings but I did chase some of the other loudmouths up the stairs and along the street, where we pelted them with shoes we had lifted from the neighbouring shop. At the time it didn't seem that big a deal. Just one mob sticking it to another mob. Little did we know.

Realising that the cops would be on the way we left the area pretty quickly and mobbed up again, ready to walk to Roker Park. There were many more skirmishes on the way to the ground including a fight with Rangers scarfers, a fight that threatened to become very nasty indeed. It wasn't just us. It seemed to be going off all over Sunderland. *The Sun* later printed a helpful 'Timetable of Terror', which gave the time and place of dozens of incidents, including a man being glassed, a robbery at bookie's, a car being stolen, Rangers fans urinating in gardens and of course more fights than you could shake a stick at.

My only recollection of the game – I was behind the goals – is of a Sunderland fan running onto the playing surface and trying to get into our end. The funny cunt then whipped off his jacket to reveal a Celtic strip underneath. We were fucking raging and the cops had a real job on their hands to stop me, several other ICF and a large number of Rangers scarfers from getting onto the pitch and giving our uninvited visitor a right kicking.

The trip back up to Glasgow was uneventful but as we drove home a media storm of immense proportions was blowing up. The newspaper headlines said it all.

'Rangers Night of Shame'

'A Bloody Disgrace'

'Thugs United'

'Police Probe Gers Casuals'

'Slash Probe Cops At Ibrox'

As usual the whole affair was shrouded in a fog of confusion. Some people, most notably the police, blamed Rangers hooligans from Scotland for the trouble. However, representatives of Rangers supporters groups claimed that casuals attached to English clubs, but wearing Rangers strips, were responsible. Rangers Football Club took a different tack, with David Murray aiming his guns at the press coverage, 'It has been blown out of all proportion. I think the media caused this reaction . . . A few fans were arrested for being drunk and disorderly. That is not going mental.'

Even the police fell out about who should be blamed for the trouble. The top cop from the Criminal Intelligence Service, based in London, stated that 'a 50-strong mob of supporters [from Scotland] with links to the ultra-right-wing British National Party caused most of the violence'. It was rubbish of course. Some of our guys may have voted for the BNP, and others may have sympathised with some of their views, but there was no formal link between us and the BNP or any other political party. The English cop then showed just how clueless he was by claiming that 'police saw a vehicle with a flag sticking outside the window with ICF on it' and that 'ICF stood for Ibrox City Fan Club'. What a plonker. He obviously didn't know that our firm is, like West Ham's, called the Inter City Firm. Where he got 'Ibrox City Fan Club' from I will never know. Criminal Intelligence right enough!

The ludicrous claims by the English police that we are fascist sympathisers was given short shrift by the man responsible for policing at Ibrox, chief superintendent Lawrence McIntyre. He told the press that 'I have no intelligence saying there is a Rangers group linked to the BNP. It might have been nice for people who are going to make comments like that to come to the man who polices every game at Ibrox.'

The furore refused to die down, with the focus now switching to the two boys who had been slashed. They were featured in many newspaper reports, and on television, with their slash marks clear for all to see. Pedro, one of our boys, saw this as a good chance to enhance our media profile. He contacted the *Daily Record* and arranged to meet their reporters in a Glasgow pub. During the meeting Pedro boasted about the trouble the ICF had caused all over Scotland and went to say that it had been ICF boys who had slashed the two Sunderland fans. The reporters persuaded him to hand over photos taken both inside and outside Digby's, which they used in a front-page splash that also took up two pages inside the paper.

Yes, Pedro got publicity. But not the type you want. He and three other ICF, all brothers, were arrested and charged with the slashings. As far as the authorities were concerned it was all done with an eye to maximising the public-relations possibilities, with the police turning up at their homes complete with camera crews and batteries of press photographers to witness the arrests. That to me is trial by media and it makes a mockery of the justice system. The four guys then had to endure a few months of hassle in their private life and at work; in fact they all lost their jobs. The only consolation was that when the trial finally came around they were all acquitted.

Sunderland put the ICF on the map. It shifted the focus away from Hibs and Aberdeen, the traditional bogeymen. It also taught us how easy it is for the media to fuck up your life.

They say that elephants never forget. Believe me even a pachyderm with total recall has nothing on a football hooligan with a grudge against another firm. When Sunderland came north in July 1999 to provide the opposition for Ian Ferguson's testimonial they were still raging about what happened in 1993, six years before. We heard that they were looking for revenge and we were delighted.

It was a time when we were regrouping. The Scottish National Firm, to which many of us had been attached, had been disbanded and the boys from Rangers had returned to the ICF fold, hoping to build it up again as a fighting force. My involvement with the SNF helped. The publicity it created prompted boys to rejoin – being a casual was in vogue again – and we hoped that we would go from strength to strength.

Our main problem was getting a mob out early enough. It was a midweek game with an evening kickoff and as many of our boys lived outside of Glasgow it was difficult to get everyone there on time. So I was pleasantly surprised when I walked into our pub of choice – Dr Brown's in Queen Street – and found a fair number already ensconced. By seven the group had swollen to fifty, of whom twenty-five, me included, went to Ibrox. The plan was that the other half would join us after the game to take on Sunderland, who, we had again been assured, were well up for it.

I was in the Broomloan for the game – which Rangers won 3–1 – directly above Sunderland's scarfers and their mob. It looked promising; they had a tasty-looking crew out. We decided to leave at half time and go back to Doc Brown's to get things organised. We were given the honour of a police escort out of the ground and, bizarrely, the Old Bill walked us right past the Sunderland fans on the bottom tier. I looked at the other ICF in disbelief. We thought it was a set-up, as no doubt did Sunderland, who were gobsmacked by the police tactics. We all thought the cops wanted us to have a go at Sunderland, at which point we would be arrested. I was only a few feet from their mob but the only action was of the verbal variety.

'Glad to see you're here. Hope we'll see you later on,' I sneered.

'Yeah. See you soon,' they replied.

By the time the game had finished, at about half-past nine, we had regrouped in Doc Brown's. Some of the boys went out scouting but saw no sign of Sunderland. We didn't, perhaps surprisingly, have a phone number so we couldn't call them. I was still confident it would only be a matter of time before they turned up. However, by quarter past ten, with no sign of our friends from the north-east, some of the boys were getting restless. A few even drifted away. At half past, with nothing on the horizon, I advised those who lived furthest away to go and catch a train, which reduced our numbers to thirty. Fifteen minutes later, with the rest of us ready to call it a night, I took a call. It was one of our spotters, who told me that fifty Sunderland were in the Bristol bar, a well-known Loyalist pub in Duke Street.

'Game on,' I thought.

Most of the group piled into taxis, while I went in a white Mercedes owned by Colin Bell, an ICF member who sadly is no longer with us. We bombed the two miles to Duke Street, and got off at the Louden Tavern, another Rangers howff.[19] There were fifteen of us, with another fifteen en route.

Colin and I were waiting for no cunt. He went into the boot of the Merc, pulled out a baseball bat and with a shout of 'Let's have these fucking English bastards,' we steamed right in, ably backed up by the other boys. Sunderland had obviously been expecting us and had dozens of bottles to hand, which they threw at us in volleys. It didn't deter us in the slightest and the front five ICF, of which I was one, soon had them on their toes. I had a bottle in my hand, which I was swinging about for all I was worth, until I launched it at the head of one of their boys, missing him narrowly.

Sunderland must have realised how few of us there were because they regrouped and charged, surrounding me and another five ICF. Colin had been wildly swinging his bat, doing an excellent job of keeping them at bay, but some sneaky twat hit him on the shoulder with a bottle, causing him to drop the bat. 'Shit,' I thought. 'It was fucking silly not to wait for the rest of the mob.' By now there were bottles whizzing past my head and I could hear the unmistakeable sound of boys trying to trip me up. Colin meanwhile had already been tripped up and was taking a pasting from fists

---

[19]   The Louden is meant to be *the* Rangers pub but when I went into ask the regulars and staff for some bottles and glasses, they refused. I found that very disappointing.

and feet. Worst of all he took two sickening blows to the head from his own baseball bat. It wasn't looking good.

Then the cavalry arrived. After what seemed like an age but in reality was only about thirty seconds, the ICF taxis pulled up and our boys stormed out. A cry of 'ICF, ICF' went up and we re-engaged, helping Colin to his feet in the process. One of our boys found a set of aluminium ladders, which we proceeded to use as a battering ram on Sunderland. We managed to trip some of them up and now it was their turn to experience a bit of pain. But give the Mackems their due. They came right back at us, with the advantage swinging one way and then the other. The air was thick with flying bottles and a few of our lads got hit on the head and went down. For some reason the Old Bill took an age, in FV terms, to get there, which meant that we were able to battle it out for a good fifteen minutes. The violence was so bad that buses had to stop on Duke Street as the rival factions fought toe-to-toe in the middle of the road. There was even time for a moment of comedy as the ladders were used as a missile by us and seconds later by them.

It was one of the best fights I have ever been involved in and it only stopped when we heard the wail of the sirens. Finally, the cops had arrived and it was time to get to fuck. In any event, by that time both mobs were exhausted.

In the days after the battle with Sunderland I found out that five of my ICF pals had been hospitalised. Colin Bell had concussion, others had cuts, one or two suffered broken bones. Sunderland 'won' that particular contest: twelve of them had to go to hospital, two with broken noses. It was just so ferocious. I wish every fight could have been like that but we were helped by two factors: Duke Street is slightly off the beaten track; and the police took a long time to get there.

Fair play to Sunderland. They were as game as anyone I have ever encountered. The last place we expected to find them was in a Rangers pub in the east end. I would say that honours were even that night even if they did outnumber us fifty to thirty. The ones I felt sorry for were the street cleaners because Duke Street looked like the aftermath of a war zone the next day. It was strewn with bricks, broken glass, stones and even items of clothing. I would also like to pay tribute to Colin Bell, a true Loyalist who did time for gun-running for the UDA. You are sadly missed Colin.

Everton

I had never been to Liverpool in my life so when, in July 1997, the opportunity came along to go down to Goodison Park for the Dave Watson testimonial I jumped at it. Liverpool Football Club has never had much of a mob but Everton had a fearsome reputation in hooligan circles, and an even more fearsome one for being blade merchants. The city of Liverpool is also renowned for its nightlife so what could be better: drink, great drugs, a riotous night out and last but by no means least a spot of football violence.

Despite Merseyside's admirable tradition of hosting Orange walks – the biggest takes place in Southport – many Rangers fans believe that both the city's clubs are pro Celtic. There may be some truth in that but despite their apparent sympathies I have always had a soft spot for Everton, the club that provided both Trevor Steven and Gary Stevens to Rangers.

It was an evening kickoff so we left at the crack of dawn on the day of the game. Some ICF went by car, others on the train, but I travelled down on the bus being run by the Shettleston Rangers supporters club. By one o'clock Rangers fans had taken over every boozer in the city centre as well as those close to Goodison. I was in a city pub with ten other ICF and a group of boys from Shettleston. Although it was generally quiet in the afternoon there was one incident of note. We heard that some Everton boys were giving Rangers scarfers the 'big one', which of course is a no-no as far as we are concerned. Without hesitation we steamed out of the pub and a little skirmish with Everton ensued. With the cops quickly on the scene it was nothing to write home about, apart that is from what happened to Harky, one of the most fearsome hooligans of them all. This wee ginger-haired, spec-wearing cunt knocked him on his arse with a punch that Floyd Mayweather Jr. would have been proud of. As you can imagine Harky got a severe ribbing for it later on.

Talking of the Merseyside police they took no shit from any cunt. Even the happy drunk wasn't safe with them. I remember seeing three pissed-up Ranger fans being dragged up an alleyway and getting a few slaps and kicks for their trouble. It was a fly move by the cops, making sure they were out of range of closed-circuit-television cameras as they indulged in a spot of casual brutality. In fact most of them had a zero-tolerance policy towards anyone of a blue-and-white persuasion, and didn't hesitate to lash out at the slightest provocation. I remember being surprised that the locals didn't bat an eyelid at the police violence.

At six o'clock we made our way to the game, having split up into small groups to avoid detection. Word was coming back to us that there was a lot of trouble in the pubs around Goodison and that the Everton mob were trying it on with our scarfers, who, to their credit, were giving as good as they got. We also heard that Everton were tooled up, although coming from Glasgow that wasn't exactly a big deal for us. Some of us were too; a couple of boys had CS gas while more than a few of us were carrying knives.

As we got closer to the stadium it was going off all over the shop between the scarfers. Then we saw them. Everton's mob. Forty strong. There were only twenty of us but that didn't matter. We charged, backing them off with comparative ease. I went toe-to-toe with this fat lad who was shouting his Scouse mouth off. 'You Orange cunt,' he was yelling, which I have to say surprised me as I landed one of several punches on his ugly coupon.

That was the last violence we saw that day, although by all accounts it was a tasty day all around the ground and in the city. The game itself was disappointing. It was Marco Negri's debut but we lost 3–2. I was surprised by how old and really quite antiquated the stand was because I had always thought Everton were a big-six club in English terms.

Manchester United

Sunderland and Everton are one thing. Man United are quite another. When we drew the Red Devils in the Champions League of 2003/04 the excitement in ICF ranks went right off the charts. The simple fact is that the three groups attached to United – the Red Army, the Men in Black and the Cockney Reds – make up the biggest one-club mob in Britain, perhaps even in the world. There was also, as I have explained in a previous chapter, our history with them, which goes back to the early Seventies when we took the Stretford End and gave them a right going over. As Tony O'Neill points out in his second book about the United mob (*The Men in Black: Inside Manchester United's Football Hooligan Firm*) they hadn't forgotten what happened thirty years earlier and were looking for revenge.

Many of a Rangers persuasion, and not just the ICF, equate Man U with Celtic. There is a little evidence for that view. The club was once known as Newton Heath and before adopting the name Manchester United consideration was given to calling it Manchester Celtic (an idea that was surely dropped on the grounds of good taste!). The Edwards family, which owned the club for decades, was Roman Catholic, as were most of its prominent managers, who included fanatical Celtic supporter Sir Matt Busby and former Hoops favourite Tommy Docherty. But I don't buy into the theory that United and Celtic are joined at the hip. Why would Mancunians give the time of day to the scum who glorify the Provisional IRA, the group that bombed the heart out of Manchester, murdering many of their fellow citizens in the process?

Some people ask why United planned to bring such a big mob to Glasgow for that Champions League game in 2003. They argue that it must be down to the fact that United are Celtic-minded and just as anti-Rangers as their friends from the east end. Nothing could be further from the truth. United turned out in force that night to avenge the Battle of Old Trafford in 1974. The other reason, of course, is that by this time the ICF were, by some distance, Scotland's leading mob and they wanted to take us on. Forget the politics. Forget the so-called Irish heritage. Forget Edwards, Busby, Macari, Crerand and Docherty. This was simply a case of one top mob desperate to take on another top mob.

The ICF didn't have its troubles to seek at this time. Half of us were on bail following mobbing-and-rioting charges for the fights with Hibs in Dundee and/or Aberdeen in Glasgow. I was the only one on bail for both, having been picked out by Kenny Scott, the country's top anti-football-hooligan cop, who it seemed to me was intent on breaking the ICF. If I was caught in a further act of football violence I was looking at an immediate 110-day remand, plus a good few years in jail when the Hibs and Aberdeen incidents were factored in. Whatever way you looked at it I was taking a massive risk.

Another factor was general police pressure, which at the time was intense. It was not uncommon for leading ICF to have their doors chapped in the early hours of the morning every six weeks or so and then be hauled down to Helen Street cop shop for questioning. In addition we had a strong suspicion that there was a grass in the ranks of the ICF and also that the cops were sporadically bugging our phones.

Our other problem was that we would be vastly outnumbered by United, even if all the boys on bail had been available. Big Boris, one of our top guys, knew many of the Red Army and he had been told that they would be fielding their biggest mob yet in Glasgow.

I take most of the responsibility for not getting something more concrete organised for United's visit but the twin pressures of bail and police harassment were almost impossible to overcome. I also had to be careful on a personal level: I was on my second life ban from Ibrox and another incident would surely have put me completely beyond the pale as far as Rangers were concerned. It might sound like I am making excuses but that was the situation on the ground at the time. Strangely, on the night before the game, the ICF drank with Red Army and Men in Black members; the friends of Big Boris. Our first port of call had been a pub in Sauchiehall Street but as we were about to order a drink we noticed five guys in the corner. One was Rab Hynds, the top football-intelligence cop in Glasgow. He was there with four other cops, FI officers from Glasgow and Manchester. Hynds was the bane of my life. He was constantly on our case. We beat a hasty retreat before they spotted us. The presence of the Manchester FI guys brought home to us the scale of the resources the police would be throwing at the game. Not only would we have to take on the biggest mob in the land, there was also a major police operation to contend with.

There was no set plan for dealing with Man U, just a loose one to mob up before the game and see where it took us. Boris's information about the size of United's firm was spot on, because more than seven hundred of the cunts turned up in Glasgow. A couple of hours before the game started I was a hundred miles away, between Arbroath and Montrose. I was working as a van driver and with my shift complete I was burning the rubber to get to Ibrox for the pre-match skirmishes with the Red Army and the MIB. Such was my desperation to get there on time that I barrel-rolled the Transit van I was driving. Amazingly, I walked away from the accident without a scratch and somehow got to Govan half an hour after kickoff.

In my absence Man United were taking the piss big time: striding around as if they owned the place; monopolising our pubs; attacking any-one they didn't like the look of. The only opposition to them was a group of twenty ICF, including Harky, Bomber and Boris. They put up a good show but were swamped by the sheer size of the mob ranged against them. When I heard what had happened I was gutted. I was a main face and the main organiser and I had missed the action, an action that saw our boys take a right pounding. I was determined that we would take it to them before they left Glasgow.

After the game forty of us mobbed up in the (now closed) Clachan pub in Paisley Road West and from there we walked to Copland Road tube station. We were desperate even for a small dose of revenge and our frustration was such that when a few Rangers scarfers, mistaking us for Man U's mob, attacked us, we gave them a bit of a slap on the train into the city centre. We got off at St Enoch's but were met by wall-to-wall police, which forced us to split into smaller groups. We knew United were drinking close by, in All Bar One, and although it was a suicide mission we were determined to have a go. Such was my anger at United taking liberties that I can only describe my mood as deranged. I walked towards their pub with only one thought in my mind.

I got within fifty yards of All Bar One when I was spotted by Rab Hynds and his fellow FI officers. Two of his colleagues grabbed me, and unceremoniously dragged me into a shop doorway. 'Get yourself to fuck out of the city centre or you'll be arrested,' one of them growled. They knew that because of my bail situation I had no choice but to obey their instructions and my mission had to be aborted.

I was gutted but was already plotting my revenge.

For the away leg I was confident of taking a hundred boys to Manchester, despite the fact that, quite scandalously in my opinion, the city centre was in lockdown and tickets were as scarce as the proverbial hen's teeth. I travelled down with Big Boris and Swedgers and we found superior lodgings at the five-star Midland hotel. As with the home leg we went out drinking with Boris's Red Army pals the night before the game and who was in our party but the legend that is Fat McLeod, who was now living in Manchester where he had become a member of the United mob. It was a great night, with no animosity. The next morning we heard that Mickey Francis – legendary leader of the Manchester City Guvnors mob – had opened his pub for us, thus flouting the mass-closure policy adopted by the Manchester authorities. We jumped into a taxi and went to Mickey's but when we got to our destination I was dejected. There were only thirty ICF in the place, a really poor show after what happened at Ibrox. To make matters worse it wasn't long before legions of Greater Manchester Police officers arrived. The game was a bogey as far as FV was concerned and to make matters worse Rangers went down by three goals to nil.

The two Champions League games in 2003 with Manchester United marked a real low point in ICF history. We hardly laid a glove on them, either on or off the field. Worse than that they took the piss and they haven't stopped gloating ever since, as you will discover if you read O'Neill's books. We did however get a small dose of revenge when we met them again in the Champions League of 2010/11. The skirmishes outside the Broomloan and Govan stands definitely went our way and that at least was something.

16

MARCHING THROUGH EUROPE

The Souness Revolution, which started in 1986, put Rangers back on the map not only on the domestic scene but also in European competition. In Europe there was now no comparison with the dog days of the early 1980s: we qualified every year; our runs were longer; the clubs we faced were bigger; the tournaments more prestigious. That meant there were endless opportunities for football violence with top mobs across the Continent. And we didn't miss a trick. The ICF did more than any other firm in the country (including those in England) to show our friends in France, Italy, Holland, Spain and Germany just what British hooligans were all about.

Bayern Munich

My first experience of going abroad with Rangers was, however, a somewhat low-key affair. It was 1989. I was seventeen, an apprentice welder at Kvaerner Govan shipyard and for the first time in my life I had some disposable cash. We drew Bayern Munich in the first round of the old European Cup and although we were well beaten by three goals to one at Ibrox in the first leg I was determined to go to Germany for the return.

The ICF didn't go abroad in great numbers in those days and I suppose I went out there as a scarfer. I was with two older boys from the Barrowfield/Bridgeton area, Spud and Hadger, and we got on the Toryglen True Blues bus that left from the Lin O'Dee pub in Rutherglen's main street. I was well warned that if I fell asleep I would get my eyebrows cut off so I stayed awake for the whole thirty-six hour trip.

We got to Munich at five in the morning and after being told we couldn't have a kip on the bus we slept in the main railway station, surrounded by vagrants. We got lucky though. The annual Munich beer festival was on and the atmosphere on the streets was vibrant, so different from normal away games in Scotland. The German people were in general very welcoming, despite the war and the sea of Union Jacks all over their city. There wasn't any trouble in the hours leading up to the game although there was one highlight. Many of us were keen shoplifters and we cleaned out a jewellers-cum-bureau-de-change of half its stock. I nabbed a men's gold bracelet, which I sold for £100 to another Rangers fan. That little bonus paid for my entire trip, including my ticket for the game.

The game was played in the old Olympic stadium, part of a big complex that includes swimming, gymnasiums and many other sports. The football stadium was impressive and I particularly admired its spider's-web design. There were thousands of Rangers in attendance and while there were many verbals of the 'who won the war' variety it was all fairly light-hearted. The Bayern supporters had a massive flag with 'Let's Go Bayern' on it and I have to say it looked very impressive. Rangers had a good chance to get back in the tie when Terry Butcher found himself unmarked in the box but he couldn't take it and although we managed a creditable goalless draw we were out of Europe at the first time of asking.

The ferry trip home was a gas. Rangers fans cleaned out the duty-free shop, which was a regular occurrence when we went abroad. In fact things got so bad that the shop had to be closed to avoid further losses. There was nothing the owners could do. With up to twenty supporters buses per ferry the staff were swamped by hordes of bluenoses eager for booty. When we got home we sold the goods we had stolen and the proceeds helped pay for our travel and match costs. Sometimes the boys kept the perfume they lifted and took it home to their wives, just to keep them sweet.

Munich had been exhilarating. I was hooked on Europe and couldn't wait for the next trip.

Bruges

1992/93 was a great season for Rangers. A domestic treble was secured, in which we won both the League Cup and Scottish Cup at Celtic Park while Hampden was being redeveloped. How sweet it was to win two cups at the ground of our oldest rivals. It was also our greatest European season for decades. In the newly created Champions League we came through two preliminary rounds, including the Battle of Britain, in which we beat English champions Leeds United home and away. A place in the group stages of the competition beckoned, and we were bracketed with Marseille, Bruges and CSKA Moscow.

It was a great chance for the ICF to make a mark on Europe and our first stop was Bruges. In the run-up to the game, which was played in March 1993, there had been a lot of coverage in the *Daily Record* about Bruges's well-deserved reputation for FV, including their penchant for attacking other mobs with baseball bats. Their top man was of Chinese extraction and was reputedly a fearsome street fighter. With great originality he had been given the nickname, The Chink. Going over there would be a real test but we were well up for it.

I travelled on the Shettleston Loyal bus, which was getting a great reputation for thieving, partying and fighting. Harky was there too along with several more ICF members and a contingent from the east end, while some of the other boys got a seat on the many supporters buses heading for Belgium. The drug of choice at the time was ecstasy and the bus was awash with the stuff. Not only did it make us feel good it was also brilliant for keeping you awake and alert, which, in the days before charter flights, was a necessity.

We got to Bruges on the morning of the game and despite the freezing cold we made for the main square of this historic city (think Edinburgh) where we plotted up in the midst of a healthy contingent of Rangers scarfers. Everyone was in high spirits. Rangers had played two games in the group stages, winning one and drawing the other and there was a feeling that we had a real chance of winning the group and going into the Champions League final.[20] The ICF of course had other things to think about, namely the Bruges mob, of whom there was, as yet, no sign.

The drink flowed, the tabs were swallowed. Still no sign of The Chink and his firm. It was getting near to kickoff and we decided to walk the mile to the stadium. Along the way, perhaps out of frustration, one of our boys threw a bottle at the wall of a bar. Luckily for us, it was the very bar in which Bruges were ensconced. They poured out, steam coming out of their ears. We chanted 'ICF, ICF,' and within seconds the air was thick with flying glass and aluminium chairs. We definitely got the better of it, pushing them back into their pub as dozens of individual duels went off around the front door.

---

[20] There were only two groups of four at that time, and the winners of each group went straight into the final. There were no quarter, or semi, finals.

Within minutes the Belgian Old Bill had swamped the area. It was time to move on. We streamed away from the fight zone but a couple of us had to go back for one of our mates, Craig C, who was scrapping with two Belgians, oblivious to the very real risk of arrest. I noticed that one of the Bruges lads was about to attack Craig from behind so I kicked the sneaky fucker right up the arse and bundled our boy away before the cops could nab him. As for our first skirmish with Bruges we won that one on points and didn't we let them know it.

> *Where's your fucking Chinky now?*
> *Where's your Chinky*
> *Where's your Chinky*
> *Where's your fucking Chinky now?*

That was our triumphant refrain as we marched to the stadium, hoping and praying that round two was just around the corner. Nothing went off during the game. We were put in a shed behind the goals and watched with some satisfaction as Rangers emerged with a creditable 1–1 draw, thanks to an equaliser from Peter Huistra. The holy grail of the European game was now a distinct possibility; with a bit of luck we could emulate the Soap Dodgers by getting to the Champions League final and winning it.

After the game Bruges came looking for it, enraged that they had been done in their backyard. There was a clash on some football pitches close to the stadium, which was made all the more dangerous and confusing because we had to fight in complete darkness. I got isolated and as I blundered around in the dark, trying to get back into the fight, a cop on horseback grabbed me by the hood of my Berghaus jacket. The hood was buttoned on and as he exerted pressure it came away, allowing me to escape from his clutches.

The cops quickly restored order and we walked back to our buses feeling that we had acquitted ourselves well. There were no other offs with Bruges but on the way home we emptied a sports shop of most of its contents in Zeebrugge and then did the same to the duty-free concession on the ferry.

Happy days.

Marseille

Having beaten Bruges 2–1 in the home leg (thanks to a fluky goal from Scott Nisbet) we were now well placed to reach the final of the 1992/93

Champions League. Our away game in Marseille – by now our only serious group rivals – would be crucial. There was no way we were going to miss out on that one.

We didn't travel as a mob of ICF. The plan was to meet up in Marseille and get down to business from there. I again went with the Shettleston Loyal and for this trip we shared a bus with Rangers fans from Renfrew. The usual boys from the east end were on board, including Big Craw from Drumchapel, Robbo and Mark Hendry. Given that we had a great chance of progressing to the final the atmosphere on the road south to Dover was electric, fuelled as usual by alcohol and drugs. Of course we liberated the duty-free shop on the ship, with Big Craw stealing enormous amounts of perfume and designer sunglasses.

In France, with a journey of almost five hundred miles ahead of us, the bus convener decided that we would stop off in Paris for a couple of hours to break the monotony. We parked up in the Palais d'Opera, a wealthy and exclusive area, where we split into small groups, eager to take in the sights. Little did we know it would be our worst pit stop of all time.

I was in a group of twenty boys and as we were exploring we found ourselves in a back street, where we were confronted by the biggest collection of pimps, prostitutes and transvestites this side of Sodom and Gomorrah. It was an amazing contrast with the elegant boulevards just yards away and after a quick drink we decided that it was too dodgy even for us. We headed back in the general direction of the bus and with forty-five minutes to spare we went into one of the many pavement cafes for a drink. The Renfrew boys were already in there having a quiet beer and at that stage there was no sign of the mayhem that was to follow.

Having paid our bar tab we strolled out of the cafe and were heading for the bus when the owner came rushing out, holding a receipt and gesticulating wildly. He claimed that some boys hadn't paid their bill and although we insisted that everyone had squared him up he was having none of it. We couldn't calm him down. He was in a total frenzy, and, as the argument continued, the commotion attracted dozens of onlookers, ordinary Parisians going about their everyday business. It became clear that neither side was prepared to back down and in sheer frustration the cafe owner grabbed an ICF boy and tried to drag him back inside, while shouting 'police, police' at the top of his voice.

Cue bedlam.

One of our guys decked the owner, sending him spinning onto the pavement. That spurred the onlookers into action and before you could say cheese-eating-surrender-monkeys they attacked us, enraged by the assault on a fellow Parisian and perhaps also by the sight of so many Union Jacks on their streets. There were fist fights going off everywhere and, quite bizarrely, I was confronted by a portly businessman in a smart suit and overcoat. He swung his briefcase at me for all he was worth in what was one of the most surreal moments of my hooligan career.

Then a waiter decided to raise the stakes even higher. Charging out of the cafe he sprayed our faces with CS gas, which is certainly not the way to treat paying customers. Despite choking and spluttering from the gas I caught him on the side of the head with a neat punch, backing him off. It was at this point that our esteemed bus convener came on the scene. Before we got off the bus he had warned us to stay out of trouble and I thought we would get a right bollocking from him once the dust had settled. Not a bit of it. He picked up one of the round cafe tables and threw it through the cafe's big plate-glass window. There must have been something in the air that day.

When that window went in we realised it was time to make ourselves scarce before the French Old Bill arrived. We legged it to the bus and told the driver in no uncertain terms to drive. However, before he could make a move the coach was surrounded by locals, making it impossible for us to get away. The police weren't far behind and they frogmarched us off the bus and into an impromptu identity parade. I was the second-last person to get off and by the time I was on the pavement the arrest count was in double figures. With my eyes still streaming from the gas I knew I would be next and when the fat businessman I had been fighting turned up and identified me, my card was well and truly marked. I was slammed against the side of the bus, handcuffed and thrown into a police van.

Fourteen of us got lifted and with our coach as part of the convoy we were driven to the nearest police station and bundled into two holding cells. There was a great deal of confusion about what would happen next. Someone said that if we met the £1,000 cost of repairing the window we would be allowed to go on our way without being charged. Given there was a possible deal on the table Harky couldn't understand why we were still in the cells.

'What do you think we're getting held for?' he asked Robbo.

'I don't know Harky but I think they want us to play for their five-a-side team,' Robbo replied.

It was a light-hearted moment in the midst of a very serious situation.

After some toing and froing it was agreed that eight of the arrestees would be released but that the six main protagonists – Harky, four of the Renfrew contingent and yours truly – would face charges. It was particularly hard on two of the Renfrew lot as they had been fast asleep the whole time we had been in Paris and hadn't even got off the bus. The bus was allowed to go onto Marseille and before it left the boys had a whip round for us in case we were short of cash.

I was gutted. We had no chance of getting to the game. And in addition the cops told us they were about to launch a full investigation, which they said could lead to us facing very serious charges including assault with a deadly weapon, criminal damage and mobbing and rioting. Welcome to France! The police held us for twenty-four hours, interviewed us and then charged us with those three offences. We were told that we would be taken to court the next day, at which time the judge would decide whether or not to go ahead with the case. To be honest we feared the worst. Why would they hold us for two nights and then turn us loose?

During our second night in detention a cop told me that we were to be taken to a bail hostel. Like a mug I believed him but then, to my horror, we were driven at high speed in a police convoy, flashing blue lights and all, to our destination. It was way over the top, as was our accommodation for the night, a huge Barlinnie-like prison. We were hustled into a holding area with a massive cell, into which we were unceremoniously deposited. The cell was packed. I would say there were forty other guys in there, all of them either blacks or Muslims. By this point we had been given our money and jewellery back, which made us think it was a set-up. Our cellmates could rob us and the police would deny all knowledge.

The French criminals and the cops on guard did their best to intimidate us. None of us could understand a word they were saying but we knew it wasn't 'welcome to Paris'. We let them know in no uncertain terms that we wouldn't be fucked with and despite the language barrier from French to Glaswegian they got the message loud and clear.

After the game kicked off in Marseille the cops kept us up to date with the score and when Rangers equalised the whole cell erupted. And I mean the whole cell. The French criminals were PSG fans and they had no love for their southern compatriots. We quickly worked out the consequences of getting a draw in Marseille: going into the last round of games it meant that if we beat CSKA Moscow and Bruges beat Marseille in Belgium we would be through to the final. It brightened our mood considerably despite a lingering doubt about whether Rangers would ban us.

The police made us sweat for another twelve hours before letting us go. Of course they never had any intention of taking us to court. We had been held for forty-eight hours – the legal maximum – just to piss us off and to make sure we missed the game. We eventually got back to Glasgow on the Friday night, after an overnight stay in the London borough of Hackney, where we were given a bed for the night by relatives of one of the Renfrew boys. His niece and nephew saw the funny side of our incarceration and painted an old bed sheet with the words, 'The Paris six are innocent'. I kept it as a souvenir until quite recently.

It was a relief to get home after the European trip from hell. To make matters worse Rangers didn't get to the final, mainly because of some right dodgy dealings involving the Marseille chairman. So we didn't get to emulate Celtic, although I am still hopeful . . .

Juventus

Our trip to Turin in November 1995 proved beyond all doubt that trouble has a habit of finding me, even when I am not part of an ICF mob. The consequences of that little escapade could have been life-threatening and although I can look back and laugh at what happened, it was far from a joke at the time.

As far as the football was concerned we were knackered. The Champions League draw had bracketed us in a very tough group with Steaua Bucharest, Borussia Dortmund and of course the Old Lady of Turin. This was our return with Juve, who had already trounced us 4–1 at Ibrox, and we had also lost away to the Romanian champions and then scraped a draw with Borussia at home. Even with Gazza and Laudrup in the side there were no European heroics that year.

Perhaps our non-existent prospects on the field prompted many ICF to give the trip a miss but whatever the reason we didn't go out there as a mob. I did go, and as usual I travelled on the Shettleston Loyal bus, this time with a few of my other pals. The trip was long and wearisome, and the only highlight was being detained in the Alps by the *carabiniere*. When we were stopped and saw the police uniforms we immediately stashed our drugs in the luggage compartments, only for our hearts to sink when one of the cops came on with a sniffer dog. Luckily for us the stupid mutt didn't find a thing, apart that is from one boy who had stuffed hash in his underpants. The dog went straight for him and he ended up being the only cunt who was caught. The only consolation was that after being relieved of the drugs he was allowed to go on without being charged.

In Turin most of our day was spent drinking piss-poor Italian beer in the main square. There was no trouble, mainly because many Juventus fans lived outside the city and didn't tend to travel in for midweek games. During the game I was in the middle tier of a three-tier stand and for the purposes of segregation there were empty sections to our left and right. It was surprising but even with 42,000 in attendance – including thousands of Rangers fans – the stadium was still half empty.

Despite our dismal form in the competition the mood among the Rangers support was jolly. I wanted to get some photos of the other Shettleston boys as a souvenir and I asked one of the Rangers fans to move so that I could get a good shot. He was a mean-looking dude, with a personality to match, and he didn't budge an inch.

'Come on mate. Want to get out of the road. Stop taking the piss. I just want to take a photo of the boys.'

My request fell on deaf ears. He just stood there, without saying a word.

I didn't see the punch coming. It shocked me because I thought the Immoveable Object was there on his own but in fact he was one of a group of twelve. But nor did they realise there was a healthy contingent of Shettleston around me and in a split second one of my pals caught my assailant with a perfect haymaker, bursting his nose wide open. Within seconds a full-scale fist fight had broken out and although they were no mugs our superior numbers soon told and we chased them up the steep slopes of the stadium. During the fracas I noticed that they were certainly not run-of-the-mill Rangers scarfers; they were hard-looking guys, the type you wouldn't want to cross. In the back of my mind there was a nagging doubt, a sixth sense almost. There would, I was sure, be repercussions of some kind, either in Turin or back in Scotland.

My premonitions were spot on. It turned out that we had smashed a gang of serious criminals from Paisley, a gang prominent in the underworld. Worse than that, it was their leader whose nose had been splattered by my pal. It didn't take long for the rumours to start flying. We would be shot when we stepped off the bus in Shettleston; a top Glasgow gangster had been approached by the Paisley mob to gather information on me; a £100,000 bounty had been put on our heads.

To be honest I didn't give a fuck. I was young, unmarried and had few responsibilities. I took the view that what is for you won't go by you. I wasn't going to run and hide just because I had upset someone, major face or no major face. It turned out that the rumours were just that: rumours. Nothing came of them and life soon got back to normal. A few years later I even had a drink with the Paisley gang boss, him of the burst nose, and no mention was made of our little contretemps.

Ajax

Amsterdam away in October 1996 was always going to be a big draw for Rangers scarfers and of course for the ICF. It is a great city, easy to get to, with numerous attractions and a vibrant night life. It was also a great time to be a bluenose. With players like Gascoigne, Laudrup, Gough, McCall, Goram and McCoist prominent we were on a run of eight titles in a row and would soon equal the nine achieved by the Great Unwashed. Although we had lost our first two games in the Champions League group stages we felt capable of winning anywhere with the players we had. Ajax, we reasoned, would be the start of our revival.

We had a great mob out for that trip, with the majority getting to Amsterdam the day before the game. Most of us stayed in hotels in the canal district with its 'coffee' shops, red-light district, strip clubs and sex shops. The night before the game Davie Carrick and I, and many other ICF, based ourselves in a small pool hall. There were a few minor altercations with ethnic minorities, who were trying to sell us every drug under the sun. Although stories reached us that Rangers fans were involved in fights across the city we didn't see any trouble. The highlight of the evening, to my delight, was an impromptu Orange Walk around the canal district.

The next morning we plotted up in Hooters bar, which is close to the main railway station.[21] Everyone was in a great mood, helped by the beer, dope from the coffee shops and generous snorts of cocaine, our new drug of choice. Then a local sidled up to us and said he could get us cheap ecstasy tablets at a bar which was close to Hooters. To get there we walked through a warren of back streets, past shops full of leather goods and bric-a-brac, most of them owned by immigrants from Holland's former Asian colonies. We did the deal for the E and then walked back through those same narrow streets.

---

[21] This was the very bar in which Glasgow gangster Lewis 'Scooby' Rodden was shot a few years later.

One of our boys couldn't resist picking up a bargain. The problem was that he didn't bother paying for it. It was the proverbial red rag to the bull. The owner, supported by his staff and other Asian shopkeepers, raced out and a battle royal kicked off. They were well tooled up with coshes and clubs and in the course of a very violent struggle several of our boys took sickening blows to the head. Harky came off worst of all. He got trapped in a shop doorway and his skin was badly gashed by one of the Asians.

Although we made it back to Hooters we had discovered that Amsterdam was a very lively place. And we hadn't even met Ajax's mob yet.

The reputation of the Ajax mob went before them. They were fearsome, as were the mobs attached to Feyenoord, Den Haag and PSV. In fact, not long before that game an arranged meet between two Dutch mobs had resulted in someone being stabbed to death. So we all knew what we were going up against. The problem was that for some in our group the aura generated by Ajax was overpowering, as we would soon discover.

There was no contact with Ajax beforehand but we knew they used the train station that serviced the new Amsterdam Arena. Our plan was to board one of the fabulous double-decker trains and get off at the stop before the stadium, in the hope that Ajax's firm would be around. Sixty of us got on the train but only fifty were still there when we reached our destination. Clearly, some of our boys had lost their nerve and had stayed on the train. To our disappointment there were only Ajax scarfers in the vicinity and, like Celtic's, they are peace loving, so we got no hassle.

We could see the Amsterdam Arena in the distance and decided to walk there, hoping that we might run into the opposition along the way. As we got closer there was still no sight of them so Whitey, one of our lads, approached a young Dutch dresser.

'Where are your mob?' he asked.

'Follow me,' the helpful young man replied.

He guided us towards the station that serviced the ground and as we approached it he suddenly got on his toes. We soon discovered why. There they were, larger than life. It was Ajax's mob, two hundred and fifty of the cunts. No one said a word but you sensed a collective 'shit' and a sharp intake of breath from the forty of us who were left, another ten boys having shat it and fucked off. I was scared. I don't mind admitting it. It certainly wasn't for the faint hearted.

Ajax charged, running full pelt across a grassy recreational area. We tried to gee each other up: 'Come on Rangers, let's stand. Let's do these

Dutch cunts.' It was no use. We did our best, or at least half of us did. Faced with the reality of a mob that size, and with that rep, another twenty ICF panicked and ran. The boys who were left put up stern resistance but we got a right doing. Fair play to Ajax: when they put us down they didn't kick us to fuck, which they could easily have done. As for the boys who melted away – some of them even before the going got tough – they pissed me off. It made me less likely to take one for the cause; when others aren't as committed why should I risk my neck?

After being routed we regrouped outside the Rangers end. Despite being surrounded by a line of riot police the Ajax mob were undeterred. They steamed right into the police line in an attempt to get at us. This allowed the 'gallant twenty', and a few Rangers scarfers, to land a few punches and kicks on Ajax but it was no more than a token gesture.

I went into the game well and truly gutted. We hadn't shown our true colours and had been humiliated. With the exception of Slateford it was the worst day of my hooligan career. The annoying thing was that everyone had been well up for it in the pub the night before, or so they said. It just goes to show how powerful an emotion fear is. The easiest thing in the world is to panic and run away, as so many of our boys did, many of them before they clapped eyes on Ajax.

To make matters worse Rangers went two down and then Gazza was sent off, with Ajax winning 4–1. We just couldn't leave it there. A potent combination of anger and shame made our minds up: we would stay for another night and get our own back on the Dutch. So after taking Harky to the hospital the gallant twenty went back to Hooters, where fifty Rangers scarfers were also drinking. The police were taking no chances and positioned a hundred riot cops round the bar. It was a wise move because at the entrance to a lane to the right of Hooters sixty Dutch hooligans were trying to force their way through the police lines. We did our best to push through from the other side but the line of cops held firm.

The Old Bill were there all night and at one point I got into a conversation with one of the senior officers, who explained there was a mob of sixty Ajax desperate to attack us.

'Watch out,' he warned. 'They might be carrying guns.'

'Don't worry,' one of the boys replied, 'We carry blades,' which left the head cop rather bemused.

The night petered out after that, leaving us with bitter memories of defeats both on and off the field.

Shelbourne

In July 1998 we met Shelbourne in the UEFA Cup. Any game against a club from the Republic of Ireland was likely to generate huge interest from us. For obvious reasons our antagonism towards that country knows no bounds. We were also well aware of what happened when Rangers travelled to play Bohemians of Dublin in the UEFA Cup of 1984/85: fans from Scotland and Northern Ireland were subject to sustained attack both inside and outside the stadium and that could not go unanswered, even if it was a decade and a half ago. The other reason that the Shelbourne game was so attractive was that it was Dick Advocaat's first competitive game in charge, the dawn of what we hoped would be a glorious new era for the club.

In view of the potential for trouble the away leg of the tie was switched from Ireland to Merseyside and would be played at Prenton Park, home of Tranmere Rovers. That was a bummer. Nothing would have given us more pleasure than taking our brand of violence to the Republic and sticking it to them over there. It would have been awesome, Daniel in the lion's den. 'Fuck it,' we thought, 'we'll just have to take them on in Birkenhead.' But the authorities tried to close down that option as well: the Shelbourne fans were to be held in a seaside town in the north-west of England and bussed straight in to the ground. Despite all the obstacles being put in our way we were still very excited about the game. The trouble potential was high; it was too good to miss.

However, what should have been one of the most memorable days of my life turned out to be one of the most devastating. And for reasons that had nothing to do with football.

With there being no opposition fans in Liverpool city centre we spent the day getting drunk before jumping in a taxi that took us through the Mersey tunnel into Birkenhead and dropped us at a bar called the Clipper, which is close to Prenton Park. There were thirty ICF in the pub but we also noticed that a large number of ordinary Rangers fans were hanging about, hoping to bait the Shelbourne contingent before going to the stadium. Sensing the danger the police were on the case pretty quickly. They barged into the pub and told us to get out, sharpish. We gave them a quick reply – a hail of bottles and beer glasses. Within minutes they were back, this time with the riot squad. A vicious fight broke out between us and the Old Bill, in which endeavour we were ably assisted by Rangers scarfers. It got so bad that, and I kid you not, a mounted policeman, horse and all, tried to get inside the Clipper. Eventually, the Old Bill managed to restore order and we reluctantly headed for the ground.

The early part of the game was a nightmare. Rangers were 3–0 down to what is essentially a semi-professional team playing in a Mickey Mouse league. The ICF was behind one of the goals, at the opposite end of the park from the Shelbourne fans. Amid the anger there was talk of invading the pitch to get the game abandoned, while others expressed their frustration by throwing missiles onto the pitch, including a bottle of tomato ketchup stolen from the refreshment stall. At the same time arguments broke out between us and Rangers scarfers, which culminated in a huge fist fight at the pie stall at half time. Swedgers and I were in the thick of it, rolling about on the floor with two pricks who had accused us of not getting behind the team. Even members of the ICF didn't approve.

'This is a disgrace. Fighting with your own fans,' one of them shouted.

'Fuck off. Mind your own business,' we told them, in no uncertain terms.

Swedgers and I knew arrest was imminent so we left at half time, missing the great Rangers revival and a 5–3 win. We ran into Boris and some of the other boys, who had been involved in scuffles with Scousers and were now doing their best to avoid the many riot-squad officers on the streets. Given the distinct possibility of being arrested a decision was made to head into Liverpool city centre for a piss-up. After a few beers the other boys decided to head home to Glasgow. I had intended to go back up that day by car but Swedgers and I decided to stay on in Merseyside and go home the following day.

We had arranged to meet another mate in Birkenhead, where we were to spend the night. It was time to make a move so we got up and walked out of the pub. And what a shock we got. There right in front of us, a few feet away, were the Rangers fans we had been fighting with at Prenton Park. They were now part of a group of twenty. I turned to look at Swedgers, as if to say, 'Oh fuck. Just our luck when the other boys have gone home.' A fraught discussion followed, in which the earlier tussle was heatedly discussed. Then, just when Swedgers and I were ready to start throwing punches, one of the scarfers said:

'I know Chugg well. I'll get on the phone to him to get youse sorted out.'

We fell about laughing. We let the boy rabbit on before Swedgers put him out of his misery.

'That's Chugg. That's him right there.'

I showed him a tattoo with my name on it but still he was unconvinced. 'You must be Chugg's brother,' he insisted.

But he looked embarrassed, as did his pals, and to save their blushes they fucked off. What could have been a very moody situation turned out to be a right good laugh.

The next day, with hangovers Charlie Sheen could only dream about, we went to Lime Street for a train, where we met Pedro McL, a good mate, who very kindly offered us a lift back to Glasgow in his minibus. Before we set off I made a quick phone call to my mum, who gave me some shocking news.

My best pal had been shot dead.

His name was John McNair and we had been friends for years. I was shattered and what made it even worse was that I had an altercation with John over a trifling amount of money the week before. The row escalated and as I walked away my last words to him were, 'I'm gonnae shoot you.' How I regretted those words now.

John had been having a running feud with a young gang member from the Duke Street area, a guy who boasted to me that he had a handgun and was going to use it on my friend. I didn't take the threats seriously but I should have done. John was enticed to Bathgate Street in Dennistoun and then fatally shot in the abdomen. It was such a waste, one young guy dead at the age of twenty-five and another in jail for his murder, all because of male bravado.

I could write a book about John McNair. He was a larger-than-life character, one of the best fighters I have ever come across and totally fearless. His killer could never have taken him without the gun and he knew it. I have never got over my friend's death and not a day goes by that I don't think of him. How I wish I had never uttered those last words, spoken in the heat of the moment.

John, wherever you are, I hope you can forgive me.

PSV Eindhoven

With our previous experience of Dutch hooligans we knew that a trip to Eindhoven in September 1999 for a Champions League fixture would be tasty. The PSV mob may not have had the same fearsome reputation as their compatriots at Ajax, Feyenoord and Den Haag but they were still formidable. At that time, in the wake of the 1998 World Cup, the ICF regularly pulled a hardcore mob of sixty, home and away. The vast majority were pure Rangers but some were ex Hibs boys who had been with us in the Scottish National Firm.

As usual in that era it was trains, planes and automobiles for the trip to Holland. I flew out with the east-end contingent and some other boys, including Fat McLeod and Colin Bell. We plotted up in Amsterdam the night before the game and enjoyed the usual shit of beer, coke and cannabis. The next day forty of us met up in Hooters while another ten of the mob went ahead to Eindhoven to look for match tickets. With two-and-a-half hours until kickoff we walked to Amsterdam station to catch a train for the hour-long journey to Eindhoven.

On the way I took a phone call from one of our boys in Eindhoven. He had spotted a mob of two hundred PSV hooligans in a nearby pub.

'How far away are you?' my pal asked, knowing that he was likely to need help urgently.

'Five minutes,' I replied.

At that precise moment PSV attacked. Our mates were in deep shit and we couldn't wait to get off that train and help them. When the train stopped we almost ripped the doors off and tore out of the station. It was a race to see who would get to PSV first: the ICF or the Dutch Old Bill.

In the pub it was fucking mayhem. The ten ICF and a few Rangers scarfers were just about holding their assailants at bay, ably assisted by a big half-caste boy called Jan, who turned out to be one of Feyenoord's main faces. We got there about the same time as a huge contingent of cops and our presence allied to theirs soon had PSV on the back foot. Davie Carrick was as usual in the thick of the action and he got himself arrested for smashing a bottle off the head of a Dutch tail-ender (which would actually work in his favour later that day). After ten minutes PSV were well and truly defeated and they left the scene with a big police contingent in hot pursuit.

We were raging. Instead of scattering the back of PSV's mob we could have been having it with two hundred of them. If we had got there a few minutes earlier it would have been mob on mob and a full-scale battle would have been on the cards. Maybe we would get a second chance. Jan – along with a German guy known for running with foreign mobs – guided us through the back streets of Eindhoven, where Feyenoord had previously had it with PSV. Unfortunately, we drew a blank and instead of meeting a group of hooligans we ran straight into a police cordon, where match tickets were being checked.

It was clear the chance of a return with PSV had passed, at least for the time being, and so our thoughts turned to the football. I had a ticket but had also promised six of our boys that I would be able to get them a corporate ticket thanks to a deal I had made in the run-up to the game. However, they thought that with the heavy police presence and the potential for more trouble the tickets might not materialise. Just as they were debating whether to go to the pub to watch the game I told them to hang fire and that I would go through the cordon and get the tickets. 'I'll be back in ten minutes,' I assured them.

I was allowed through the cordon and went to look for the main entrance to the stadium, where the ticket office was located. I asked a steward for directions and he said, 'Follow me but keep quiet or you will be in great danger.' When I got to the office I asked the clerk for my six tickets, which were in the name of William Reid. The guy couldn't believe his eyes. Standing in front of him was a football casual, out of his face on cocaine, asking for six corporate tickets. He refused to hand them over even though I pointed out the envelope with 'William Reid' written on it to him.

Gutted, I phoned Big Boris, who was stuck behind police lines.

'No joy. I can't get the tickets,' I told him.

'Cool. The boys who can't get in are going back to the pub where PSV attacked us to watch the game. The rest of us will get you at the Rangers end. There is fuck all happening here.'

He couldn't have been more wrong.

I was escorted to the Rangers end by the same Dutch steward and after I thanked him for his help he wished me good luck. It was now twenty-five minutes to kickoff and I waited there with a couple of the other boys for Boris and his contingent. When no one showed I phoned Boris again, but this time got no reply. I was then approached by three of the PSV mob, two of whom were wearing Umbro, which to us was the dodgiest of dodgy gear. The other boy to his credit was in Stone Island and looked the part. They must have picked me out because of my clothes. I was wearing a Stone Island jacket, a Paul and Shark jumper and Hugo Boss jeans.

Pleasantries were exchanged.

'Do you want it Scottish cunts?'

'Fuck off you Dutch cunts. We will see you after the game. You're big and brave with two hundred police behind me. Fuck off before you get me arrested,' I snarled.

For some reason a chill ran down my spine. It was a premonition.

Young Rico McGill appeared. He was ashen faced. Something had gone off, that was obvious.

'What the fuck's happened? I can't get hold of Big Boris on the blower.' Rico gave me chapter and verse.

It all went off big time. You've just missed one hell of a fight. All the lads have been rounded up by the Old Bill. I managed to sneak away. Just after you phoned Boris to tell him you hadn't got tickets the boys started to go through the security cordon. The place was crawling with what looked like normal PSV fans. They had surrounded us and on a pre-arranged signal we were attacked from all sides. But credit where it's due: despite being outnumbered four-to-one, the boys kept steaming back into PSV. Our boys were in the thick of some fierce hand-to-hand fighting while some of them got hit by bottles and bricks, which cut them up badly.

The cops did fuck all. They allowed the fighting to go on for five minutes before stepping in, which surprised me. When they did get involved they quickly separated the two factions before rounding up our guys, helped by a Scottish football-intelligence officer who pointed out the ICF to them. It was then I sneaked away and got through the cordon by showing my match ticket.

I was gutted. I had missed one of our best-ever fights. I also felt guilty for leaving the boys to go on a wild-goose chase looking for match tickets. Later, while I was watching the game, I realised there was another problem: the one-mile walk back to the station could be very dangerous if PSV attacked again, given that so many of our boys had been taken out of the equation by the police. With all due respect to the Rangers scarfers I didn't think they were going to come to our rescue. My mood was lightened, albeit temporarily, when Jorg Albertz scored the only goal of the game, enabling us to emulate John Greig's triumph in Eindhoven in the late 1970s.

At the end of the game most Rangers fans were herded onto buses and given a police escort out of town. Those of us going by train were held in the stadium and then escorted back to the station by a large contingent of police, who successfully thwarted the efforts of the PSV mob to attack us. We walked past the cop shop where the rest of the ICF were being held and at that point the size of the escort diminished rapidly, which allowed some minor skirmishes to go off.

We got to the railway station and were herded onto a platform, from which the Amsterdam train was due to leave in about half an hour. There were four ICF there, plus a contingent of Rangers scarfers and a small knot of police. Further along the platform there were some guys from the PSV mob, who were also waiting for a train. One of them was a huge, burly body-builder type, who had a couple of girls in tow.[22] He and some of his mates started on the verbals with our scarfers, which of course was a right liberty in my eyes. So I said to Rico, 'I'm going to have these cunts.' A couple of our scarfers were from the Coventry Loyal and they were guys I was very friendly with. They had a carry-out at their feet and I said to them: 'Sorry lads, I might need these,' and with that I picked up two bottles of beer.

Rico and I strode over to the PSV boys, accompanied by a well-known face from the Glasgow underworld, a man who could handle himself. I confronted Eindhoven's answer to Arnold Schwarzenegger, making sure he could see the two bottles I was carrying.

'What the fuck is your problem? Do you want these?'

The Terminator said nothing, carefully sizing me and my two pals up.

'You are going on that fucking track,' I warned him.

I could see that he and his gang were debating whether to have a go. Then, after a few seconds, they made their decision.

'We don't want any trouble,' they rather meekly told us.

'Well fuck off before you get thrown in front of a train,' I replied.

And fuck off they did, which surprised me given their size and the reputation of the PSV mob. They just weren't up for it against three very keen Glaswegians.

Shortly thereafter the Amsterdam train pulled in and we got on. I was standing at the open doors looking down the station when to my surprise I saw Davie Carrick bounding down the platform. He jumped onto the train just as the doors were closing. It turned out that Davie had been released from police custody just as the rest of the ICF were being processed. However, as he was being released the FI cop from Scotland tried to have him rearrested because of his involvement in the mass brawl at the stadium. The Dutch police refused as Davie had been arrested for a separate incident, namely hitting the boy with a bottle outside the pub. To me it was a typically sneaky move by the Scottish police, who later did

---

[22]   The Dutch hooligan is generally a massive cunt.

their best to get custodial sentences for some of our lads, and that was after they had spent two weeks on remand in Dutch prisons.

After I got home I was depressed for a few days. I was still gutted about missing the fight outside the stadium and not being there to help the boys. I wondered if I should have noticed that was something was amiss before I went to get the tickets. After all I was an experienced hooligan and should have been able to read the runes. My mood wasn't lightened by an article in the following week's *Sunday Mail*, which splashed my face across the news pages. The gist of the piece was that the trouble in Eindhoven was my fault and that I was planning revenge at the return game in a fort-night's time.

Chance would have been a fine thing. The problem was that three-quarters of our mob were languishing in a Dutch jail. Revenge was out of the question.

17

MARCHING THROUGH EUROPE: TWENTY-FIRST-CENTURY BOYS

In terms of European competition, the twenty-first century brought significant challenges for Rangers and its fans. It was the dawn of a new politically correct era in which certain clubs – Rangers among them – were singled out by UEFA for special measures. This in turn encouraged the police, for whom Rangers fans became fair game. It was now wholly acceptable to use force on anyone of a Rangers persuasion, even when they had done nothing wrong. To me it was a process that reached its logical conclusion in Manchester 2008, when many Old Bill lost the plot and launched gratuitous attacks on my fellow bluenoses.

Paris St Germain

Our first real foray of the new century came in December 2001, towards the end of the Dick Advocaat era. We had drawn nil–nil in the first leg of our UEFA Cup tie with Paris St Germain and therefore needed a score draw or better in the return if we were to be in Europe after Christmas for the first time since 1992/93.

The boys made their own arrangements to get there. I was going with six other ICF on a flight from Prestwick to Paris and we planned to spend three nights in the French capital including the night of the game. But, at six o'clock on the Monday evening, just as we were boarding the plane, the French air-traffic controllers performed their usual party trick and called a strike, throwing our plans into chaos.

What happened next shows how dedicated ICF boys are to our mob and to our club.

Some guys booked flights from Dublin to Amsterdam and got a train from there to Paris. Me and my pals got on a train to Glasgow and then jumped into a taxi at Paisley Gilmour Street, which took us to Glasgow airport. From there it was a flight to Luton airport, followed by a train for London. When we got to the Smoke in the early hours of Tuesday morning we hopped onto the Eurostar, which took us to Paris. I am sure most people would have turned round and gone home the minute they heard about those lazy French bastards and their wildcat strike. But when you are part of a mob you don't want to let your mates down, especially when they are going up against a great mob like PSG.

In fact PSG has two great mobs, defined not by football but by politics. One is a left-wing tendency; the other is on the right of the spectrum. Politics or no politics these cunts can fight. Liverpool and Arsenal had both got a hiding in Paris in recent years, so we would have to be at our best.

After booking into our hotel we went straight out on the piss and the coke, keeping closely in touch with the other ICF who had yet to arrive – and waiting for news of the thirty Chelsea boys who were said to be joining us. After a surprisingly quiet night – I think we were exhausted after all the travelling – we got a good night's kip and were straight back onto the drink and drugs the next day. Our numbers grew steadily to forty and we were sitting in a cafe near to the old Parc des Princes stadium having a beer and awaiting the arrival of Warren and Carrick and forty more boys, some of whom were the Chelsea contingent. About an hour before kickoff the two halves of the ICF came together, giving us a fighting strength of eighty.

By this time we were hearing stories about PSG's mob attacking Rangers scarfers so we decided to hotfoot it to the ground. As we walked we were given the same spiel by the Rangers fans: 'You're a bit too late boys. They have been taking liberties for hours. We could have done with your help before.' That really fucking pissed us off because attacks on scarfers are bang out of order. The PSG mob would have to be taught a lesson.

Approaching a junction we turned right and suddenly we saw what was going on. We had reached the periphery of the stadium, which was heaving with police. That wasn't the only thing that caught our eye. There was a huge commotion because PSG's mob were again attacking our scarfers. Our reaction was instantaneous. We fucking charged the cunts. The French Old Bill fanned out, doing their utmost to stop us getting to PSG.

Then a weird thing happened. Someone lobbed a smoke bomb at us, sending thick plumes of white smoke billowing into the air. We thought it was the police who had thrown it but whether it was or not they suddenly stepped aside and let the two mobs go at it unhindered. As we came together I noticed that most of their boys were ethnic North Africans, with just a few whites in their ranks. Perhaps because we were disorientated by the smoke they got the upper hand and I suppose it was bit of a let off when the police re-engaged, pushing us back down the road and away from the ground.

We weren't finished yet. Not by a long chalk. Running down a side street in a flanking movement we came up behind their mob, who were out in huge numbers, about four hundred-strong I would have said. That meant fuck-all to us. We steamed in, screaming 'ICF' at the top of our voices and smashed them completely. I was about halfway back and I didn't need to throw a punch, such was the disarray in their ranks. I noticed that the Chelsea boys were well to the fore and that they gave a good account of themselves, so respect to them.

I don't think any of us could believe how easy it had been. Maybe it was down to the sheer ferocity of our charge. Or maybe PSG thought they had done their job after the first skirmish. We will never know. The Scottish football-intelligence officers assigned to the fixture then turned up and warned us not to go near the French mob, simply because there were so many of them. 'You'll get a fucking doing,' they confidently told us. Little did they know that we had already given the cunts a right chasing.

During the game I was with a group of thirty ICF, right in amongst the French fans. Surprisingly, and despite the poisonous atmosphere, it didn't go off with them but there was a little disagreement with the stewards. At half-time some of our boys got into a fight with the men in luminous yellow jackets, at which point they sprayed us with CS gas. Enraged by this over-the-top action we picked up a metal crash barrier and pushed the stewards right down the stand steps. After that they left us alone.

As we mobbed up after the game – in high spirits after winning a penalty shootout and progressing to the next round of the competition – we were sure PSG would be out for revenge. But the second front never came. I, however, ran into a spot of bother. After slipping through the police cordon I was marooned in a sea of PSG scarfers. One of them started mouthing off at me in French, gesticulating wildly as he hurled insults in my direction. The guy was obviously looking for a fight. He was a rugby-player type, six foot four and seventeen stones, and he was wearing a leather waistcoat and sporting a fine moustache. If you can imagine a combination of Desperate Dan and one of the Village People you will get the general idea.

Within seconds Dan and I were going at it. The big cunt wrestled me to the ground and we rolled around trading punches and kicks before we staggered to our feet ready for round two. I launched a karate kick at my opponent but it just bounced off his vast bulk. We grappled again and I thought to myself, 'I'm going to get a kicking off one of the Village People right in front of the rest of the mob. I'll never live it down.' The gendarmes were only feet away and I was sure I would get arrested but they seemed to be enjoying the spectacle. Maybe they took pity on me because a couple of minutes later they dragged the big Frog off me and marched me back to the massed ranks of the Rangers support.

Of course the rest of the ICF had seen exactly what had transpired and were pissing themselves at my antics. And no, I never did live it down.

But the fisticuffs with the man mountain couldn't put a dampener on my day. We had got a right result, on and off the park, and that night in a Paris cafe we celebrated like there was no tomorrow.

Feyenoord

The ICF had been getting some good results by the time Feyenoord came to Ibrox on UEFA Cup business in 2002. Our main problem, as ever, was the Glasgow Old Bill. We were getting some serious heat from them. Boys would get a knock on the door at six in the morning and then be dragged off to Govan police station for questioning on this incident and that fight. It was part investigation, part intimidation. So although we knew Feyenoord would bring a mob we would have to be cute to avoid early detection by the cops.

In common with most of the other main faces I was banned from Ibrox so any thoughts we had of attacking them before kickoff were quickly discarded. I went to a pub in Sauchiehall Street to watch the game on television along with the rest of the banned contingent, while the 'unbanned' boys went to the game. Imagine our surprise when a news report came on, stating that Feyenoord had broken through the police lines inside the stadium and were taking on Rangers fans and, presumably, the ICF. It was the first time for years that anything had gone off inside Ibrox and it ended with thirty-four people being arrested, eight Dutch and twenty-six Rangers fans.

The news gave us a boost of moon-rocket proportions. Although we had no phone contact with them the Dutch were clearly up for it and there was the potential for Glasgow city centre to be a war zone later that night. Feyenoord are a formidable mob but we fancied our chances, having been buoyed by our recent exploits against PSV and PSG. And the bonus was that, thus far, we had managed to avoid the police.

When the game finished we decided to sit in the pub and bide our time. That would not only give Feyenoord the opportunity to get back into the city but would also ensure that we avoided detection by the boys in blue. After an hour we were ready to make a move. We were thirty-strong but to make ourselves less conspicuous we split up into groups of four or five and headed for Central station. It was as good a place as any to start our hunt.

We got lucky. When we got within a hundred yards of the station we saw them. Seventy Feyenoord, standing around the entrance to the Central hotel. Even though it was dark we could see they were all big, hard-looking lads, including two giants who were clearly of a South Pacific or Polynesian background. We quickly mobbed up and walked at a fast pace towards our Dutch visitors.

At first they didn't spot us. It was only when we got to within fifty yards that the penny dropped. This was it. We had to take the initiative. 'ICF, ICF' we chanted as we charged. I expected, and hoped for, a severe test. It never materialised. Feyenoord turned tail and ran. Not one of us got to throw a punch. I was disappointed, given our previous experiences with Dutch hooligans. I can only put it down to the element of surprise. That and the fact that we were close to the top of our game in those years.

As the police sirens whined we made ourselves scarce, dividing once again into small groups. I was with Davie H and Neilly S and we kept in close contact with Carrick and Boris and the rest of the boys. I was sure Feyenoord would be pissed off at having been run and would be looking for revenge. I was right. While I was striding along Sauchiehall Street, talking away to Carrick on my mobile, my two pals and I walked right into sixty of Feyenoord's finest. They ran across the street, surrounding us. We looked at them, they looked at us and then they made their decision. Instead of giving us a hiding they took the piss. I was given a couple of clips behind the ear. 'Go away little Scotty boy,' one of them said. There was nothing I could do. I had to stand there and take my medicine.

Fair play to them. They could have taken a right liberty and demolished us. It had been a lucky escape. I should have been relieved but my blood was boiling. I had sleepwalked into the middle of a foreign mob in my home city. I was dying to fight them but there would have been no point. My night was over.

I didn't go to the return leg in Rotterdam. Nor did the rest of the ICF. After what had happened in Eindhoven we were threatened with instant arrest if we set foot in the city. It turns out there was a lot of fighting between Rangers scarfers and Feyenoord's mob, before and after the game. When I heard that I regretted my decision not to travel, as did the rest of the boys. Even though we would have been well outnumbered we would have given a good account of ourselves. We might even have avoided the clutches of the Dutch police.

Osasuna

The fans in Spain don't have a tradition of organised football violence – they leave that to the police! In the spring of 2007 Rangers became the latest British club to suffer at the hands of Spanish cops. Not only did we get a battering from the riot police, but also when we got home the Scottish media were ready to give us another kicking. For once, however, we were innocents abroad.

The scenario was that Rangers had reached the last sixteen of the 2006/07 UEFA Cup and had drawn 1–1 with Osasuna in the first leg at Ibrox. About thirty ICF decided to make the trip to Spain, not really looking for FV, but first and foremost as fans. Like all bluenoses we were desperate for Rangers to reach the quarter finals of a European competition.

Osasuna play in Pamplona (the ancient and very beautiful capital of Navarre, which is in the north of Spain) and we flew out there, landing at an airport about sixty miles from the city. When we got to Pamplona we spent the day drinking and having a right good laugh. Some of the boys had fake 50-euro notes and were able successfully to pass them off in the local bars and shops, making the whole trip a hell of a lot cheaper. We ended up in a bar-cum-bowling-alley where one of the boys had a novel idea: he stripped naked and threw himself down one of the lanes. Of course the police were called but we were away by the time they got there. While the bulk of the Rangers support was transported to the ground in buses we walked, which gave us ample scope for more high jinks. In a cafe someone let off a fire extinguisher, covering everyone in thick white soot. Once again we left before the cops arrived.

During the game the ICF boys were in different parts of the ground, the reason being that Osasuna, in defiance of UEFA regulations, had sold tickets to anyone and everyone. Most of them were in a corner of the ground in the upper tier of a stand and across the stadium from the main body of Rangers fans. I was in a corner among the home support with a few more of the ICF. At first the Osasuna fans were amused by the vociferous support we were giving our team but when a couple of the boys hung up a huge Union Jack, with the letters ICF on it, the mood immediately darkened. Neither the home support nor the Spanish police liked that flag and both groups became openly hostile.

It was however the cops and not the Spanish supporters who got violent. The police waded into the ICF group at the other end of the stadium, lashing out indiscriminately with their batons as they went. Our boys were on the receiving end of sustained brutality and clearly in need of help and so at half-time our smaller group vacated its seats and went into the section where the trouble had kicked off. I was surprised that we were able to do that without being hindered by the stewards or the cops but the Spanish have their own way of doing things.

We joined up with the other group of ICF, who by this time were positioned in front of the main body of the Rangers support. They had been battling manfully with the cops, who with the usual heavy-handedness of the Spanish police were taking no prisoners. There were now two empty rows of seats at the front of the upper tier, simply because the fans had been pushed back by the riot squad. The atmosphere was very tense. I was having verbals with a cop in full body armour when I felt a dull thud. It turned out that one of his colleagues had hit me on the head with a steel baton. He wasn't satisfied with that because he caught me with two more sickening blows, knocking me to the floor. Luckily for me one of our boys helped me to my feet or the cop might have come back for more.

'I am going to throw you into the bottom tier of the stand,' I raged at my assailant, but I don't think he understood English as she is spoken in Glasgow.

There was then a ten-minute standoff after which the police charged us again. We held firm and even tried to snatch the batons out of their hands and after a few more scuffles an uneasy peace was restored.

Rangers lost 1–0, eliminating us from Europe, and at the end of the game the stadium announcer put on 'Simply the Best' by Tina Turner. His choice of music surprised me. It is of course a favourite of Rangers fans everywhere not only because it sums up how we feel about the club but also because it gives us the opportunity to add some cheeky lines of our own. It later became clear to me why he had played our unofficial anthem. When the song reached the part where Rangers fans add the line 'Fuck the Pope and the IRA' it seemed to me that the volume from the PA system was turned down, making it easier to hear the little improvisation. That led to Rangers being fined £8,000 by UEFA for so-called discriminatory singing.

After the game the police again used their batons in a quite indiscriminate way, on both scarfers and ICF. We learnt they had done the same before the game. The buses carrying our fans had been penned into a car park and when they tried to get off the police had set about them for no reason at all, hitting even women and children with their batons. Eventually, after taking yet more whacks from the thugs in uniform, we reached our designated coach, which was to take us to the airport for a flight home that night. The airport terminal was bristling with cops – there were literally hundreds of them – and I felt sure round two was on the cards. But it turned out they just wanted us out of the country as quickly as possible.

The aftermath was fraught to say the least, hardly surprising given the scale of the disturbances. For once the Scottish media recognised that Rangers fans were the victims of brutality. Although they did of course take the ICF to task (of which more later) most papers were highly critical of the tactics use by the Spanish cops. The *Evening Times* described the police as 'outrageous'; Jim Traynor in the *Daily Record* insisted that 'the behaviour of those cops was savage and extremely dangerous'; while in *The Sun* Rangers captain Barry Ferguson (who was suspended for the game and watched from the stands) told the paper that 'he feared for Rangers fans as he watched them being battered senseless by Spanish riot cops'.

Despite the overwhelming evidence about the conduct of the Spanish police the Scottish media just couldn't help themselves. They picked up on the ICF banner at the game and made us out to be as bad as the cops. One reporter noted there were 'banned thugs in Gers crowd', another churned out phrases like 'lunatic fringe' while a third talked about 'a calculated bid to cause mayhem'. All shite of course. We were reacting to extreme provocation. I believe that if the ICF had not been in the thick of it defending normal Rangers fans things would have been much worse. There might even have been some people coming home to Scotland in body bags.

If you think I am exaggerating just consider a document released by the Foreign and Commonwealth Office in the wake of the game. As several newspapers reported, the Foreign Office feared there would be mayhem at the game and had put in place emergency measures to deal with the injured and even the dead. The document states that 'Injured British survivors to receive prompt, adequate medical attention. British fatalities to be identified formally and rapidly.' The British government knew of course how shambolic the Spanish authorities were likely to be in terms of issues like ticketing and segregation and also that the police would adopt a zero-tolerance approach to Rangers fans.

That cut no ice with the Scottish papers, which sadly is par for the course where we are concerned. The resulting media stushie resulted in three ICF, including me, getting letters from Rangers, informing us that we were banned from Ibrox for life.

Astonishingly, it was my third lifetime ban.

Manchester

The headlines said it all.

> 'Night of Carnage' *Evening Times*
> 'Shameful' *Daily Mail*
> 'It's Like a Bloody Civil War' *The Sun*
> 'Light Blues Black Night' *Daily Star*
> 'Mob Like a Pack of Wolves' *Daily Record*

That was the reaction to what happened in Manchester after the UEFA Cup final between Rangers and Zenit St Petersburg on 14 May 2008. Rangers fans fought back in the face of brutal attacks by some police officers and a riot ensued in the city centre. It was without doubt the most sustained and vicious battle with the constabulary on British soil since the great Hampden riot of 1909.

The irony was that the ICF missed the party. We were too busy watching the football.

Given what happened after we lost to Zenit it is surprising that in our run to the final there was very little organised violence either at Ibrox or at our away games with the likes of Werder Bremen, Sporting Lisbon and Fiorentina. As soon as it was confirmed that we were going to the final we got straight on the blower to Man U to see if they were up for a dash. By this time however it was becoming clear that the city was going to be swamped by Rangers fans from all over the world and so the Red Army and the Men in Black politely declined our kind invitation. We weren't that bothered. After all it would be our first final for nearly forty years and another bonus was that we had emulated Celtic's run to Seville in 2003. We were just happy to be at the centre of the football world.

With up to two hundred thousand Rangers supporters about to descend on Manchester the biggest problem was getting hold of a ticket. They were like the proverbial gold dust. Luckily, a mate of ours, Myles Sarward, runs a travel company in London and he got his hands on forty precious briefs. At £400 a pop they weren't cheap but it was well worth it to see our team in a prestigious European final. Because of the historic nature of the occasion I decided to give tickets to family members and close friends who I knew were regular attendees at Rangers games, then to pass on any that were left to other ICF members. The other ICF leaders did the same, which shows that, despite what people may think, we are genuine football fans. I can assure you that trouble was the last thing on our mind.

We had booked into the Blackpool Hilton and by the time we arrived at the seaside town's railway station it had become clear that Manchester was about to be swamped by the biggest away support in history, much bigger than the contingent of eighty thousand that Celtic took to Seville. There were many thousands of Rangers fans in Blackpool so what the fuck was Manchester going to be like?

As getting on a train would have been impossible we got a coach to Manchester, arriving there about 12.30 p.m. I would have said there were already a hundred thousand Rangers fans in the city centre, with more pouring in by the minute. It was obvious the infrastructure that had been put in place to deal with a gathering of that size was totally inadequate.

We found a pub in Deansgate and spent the day there drinking, where we met up with lads from mobs throughout the country, the main group being the Chelsea youth firm. There was only the occasional interruption by Glasgow and Manchester football-intelligence officers. They were keeping an eye on me and the other forty ICF in the city but they were probably reassured when they clocked the family members we had with us. They would also have been glad to learn we had match tickets and that football seemed to be our priority. Maybe they would have a quiet day after all.

There wasn't any trouble during our drinking session, although we did hear that thirty Zenit skinheads had kicked it off in a nearby bar. We weren't tempted. It was all about the game and adding to our haul of tro-phies. We left the pub about two hours before kickoff and made our way to the City of Manchester stadium (as it then was). When we got there we discovered there was a problem. Our tickets were for the Zenit end and some of our party had already been knocked back by the stewards.

We improvised. We bought scarves from the Zenit supporters and pretended we were Russian. In the end, everyone got in but not before I had a run-in with a jobsworth steward. As I passed him he decided to question me.

'Where are you from mate?'

I mumbled something that sounded vaguely Russian.

'Look mate. I'm from Coatbridge,' he replied.

'And no doubt you're a Celtic supporter as well,' I thought, as he con-tinued giving me the third degree.

'It's obvious you're from Glasgow. I can't let you in,' Jobsworth con-cluded.

'Well look mate. You'll know the score. I'm from Shettleston in Glasgow and I paid £400 for my ticket. And if you're not letting me in I'll plant the nut on you and bite your ear off. Then I'd be getting the jail for something worthwhile.'

I have never seen someone's demeanour change so quickly. He turned as white as a ghost and waved me through.

In the stadium, as more and more Zenit fans arrived, it became clear there might be a problem. Looks were exchanged, lines in the sand drawn. We quickly realised we would have to move if a full-scale riot was to be avoided. Normally, we would have been right in there but we didn't want our dads and our other friends and relations involved in something like that. To my surprise, given that the game was a sell-out, we managed to squeeze into seats near to the halfway line and settled down to watch the most important game of our lives. It was a truly wonderful atmosphere, created almost entirely by the Rangers contingent, which made up around 80 per cent of the crowd. The hairs on the back of my neck stood to atten-tion as the traditional songs and chants rang round the stadium. It could have been our finest hour since 1972.

Sadly, it wasn't to be as the Rangers players, exhausted by their sev-enth game in twenty-one days, went down by two goals to nil. I still find it hard to talk about that game. Unlike Celtic fans, who, with their usual twisted logic have turned Seville into some kind of moral victory, I associate Manchester 2008 with failure. It was the most disappointed I have ever felt after a Rangers defeat.

I left the ground utterly dejected and almost immediately I took a call from an ICF boy to say they had just chased Manchester riot cops all over the city centre. In the depths of despair I thought, 'Thank fuck I am not involved. They will no doubt pin the blame on us [the ICF].'

We walked back into Manchester, heading for the same pub we had been drinking in before the game, but ended up instead in the Deansgate Hilton. The city centre resembled a war zone. The streets were littered with broken glass and empty cans and there were riot vans full of police speeding this way and that. Having used our keys from the Blackpool Hilton to get in to the Deansgate equivalent we drowned our sorrows in the bar. All the while I was taking calls from ICF boys telling me what happened that afternoon with the giant screens, the toilets and the over-crowding. Another message that came across loud and clear was how heavy handed the Manchester police had been in their dealings with Rangers fans, even those who had not been involved in the disturbances. To be honest my pals and I were so crushed at losing to Zenit that we couldn't even think about getting involved. Apart from anything else the cops had things under control by that stage. After a couple of hours we got a taxi back to Blackpool.

My verdict on the debacle that was Manchester is quite simple. The city got what it deserved. Right from the word go the authorities made it clear that Rangers fans weren't welcome. It was only when they realised that we would travel in unprecedented numbers that they got their act together and started to prepare. By then, however, it was a case of too little too late. I have been told that the giant screens were deliberately turned off and I believe it. Some people wanted to give the Rangers fans a good hiding and when they quite understandably expressed their disap-pointment about the loss of the pictures that gave the police the perfect justification for wading in. What the cops didn't expect was that we would fight back, and fight back hard. I don't condone everything our fans did in Manchester but if you go around whacking people with a metal baton what do you expect?

Although we played very little part in the fighting we still got most of the blame. I know for a fact that the first mugshots the police asked for were those of the ICF. Instead of looking at the piss-poor organisa-tion and their own brutality to explain what went wrong they wanted a convenient scapegoat. I am afraid I have nothing but contempt for the city of Manchester. It was bombed by the IRA but still welcomes Celtic fans. Yet it continues to treat us with contempt and has stopped Rangers from playing a couple of friendlies down there in recent years. I would of course not include Man City fans in this; to me they are sound, pro Loyalist and pro Rangers. It just goes to show that no place is all bad.

18

THE SCOTTISH NATIONAL FIRM (1): DOMESTIC DISTURBANCES

During the early-to-mid Nineties organised football violence went into decline, ravaged by football intelligence, the rave scene, acid house and old Father Time. Boys became men, got married and took on mortgages. The ICF wasn't immune. By the middle of the decade our numbers had fallen sharply. Sometimes we were lucky if ten boys turned up, even for big games. Other mobs too were feeling the pinch, most notably the all-conquering Capital City Service, which hadn't been helped by the long jail sentence handed down to its most prominent member, Andy Blance, in 1991.

Radical solutions were required if we were to keep the good ship football violence afloat. It meant thinking the unthinkable. And that's what happened after Davie Carrick and one of the best-known faces from Hibs, James 'Fat' McLeod, got together on a night out. Between them they concocted the idea of a Scotland-wide mob, to be called, you've guessed it, the Scottish National Firm. Although it would mean joining up with our most implacable opponents, guys we had been fighting with for years, there was some logic to it. The ICF had lost many good boys, including stalwarts like Barry Johnstone and Harky, while Hibs too had seen a decline and had not been helped by a vicious power struggle between factions led by Blance, now released from jail, and Fat McLeod. It was also proposed that some boys from the Hearts Capital Service Firm would be invited to join.

I almost choked on my cornflakes when Davie told me about the proposed 'super' firm. I am Rangers through and through and the thought of boys from other mobs coming along with the ICF made me distinctly uneasy. Here we were, effectively disbanding the ICF and setting up a new mob with our sworn enemies. Gradually however, I came round to the idea. It wasn't as if we had that many alternatives and in addition working with other mobs also had a certain novelty value. So, after a lot of deliberation, I threw my lot in with the fledgling SNF. Some ICF objected strongly to the new organisation but only guys who weren't that active and so we just ignored them. With the benefit of hindsight it turned out to be a master stroke from Davie and McLeod, because it kept the flame of hooliganism burning and eventually led to the renaissance of a new and more powerful ICF.

It was also through the auspices of the SNF that I got to know some of the most hardened thugs that Scotland has ever produced. Step forward the aforesaid 'Fat' McLeod. The big man was the most dedicated football hooligan I have ever met. He was a larger-than-life character, and I am not just talking about his twenty-stone bulk, a natural leader who completely dominated his faction of the Hibs mob. Starting off in Blackley's Baby Crew, James graduated to the CCS, in which he became a leading light thanks in no small measure to his great organisational skills. It was clear from the first day I met him that football violence was the main driving force in his life. He was excitable and he came alive when he talked about hooliganism. In fact I would say he almost got a sexual thrill when he was discussing it: he would put his hands over his eyes, rub them and squeal like a pig as he discussed steaming in. I know that some of his former Hibs pals say he was never a true front liner but that is shite: I have seen him in action many times and he was game, of that there is no doubt.

Among many other fine thugs I was particularly impressed by Bobby T, a Hearts boy, who, ironically, hailed from the Hibs heartland of Leith. Bobby was reputedly one of the hardest men in Leith and people talked of his fighting abilities in reverential tones. Like Fat McLeod, Bobby had a big personality to match his prowess as a street fighter and for those reasons people willingly followed him. His brother too was a prominent member of the Hearts crew and he was another good recruit for the SNF. Another guy I should mention here is 'English' Steve, who despite a cockney accent and a boyhood supporting West Ham was another former Hibs boy. English Steve was another handy guy to have around; he is massive and I always thought he put the brick into brick shithouse. I am pleased to say that he now comes with the ICF.

*

The SNF's first outing was to Aberdeen during season 1996/97, for which two minibuses were hired, one for the ICF members and the other for the CCS contingent. I was living in Cumbernauld at the time and so I was the last to be picked up. It was actually quite depressing. There were only nine of a bluenose persuasion on the bus and given that it was a Rangers fixture that was very disappointing. It showed how sharp our decline had been and that was pointed up even further when I saw there were more from Hibs than from the ICF. That saddened me because a club like Rangers should never be the junior partner in anything. I was also concerned because in total only twenty SNF were making the journey to Pittodrie, despite the undoubted calibre of those in the buses.

When we reached Dundee we decided to mix things up, with former CCS piling into our bus and some of our lads going into theirs. If we were stopped by a normal cop – football intelligence would have been a different matter – it might confuse them to hear Glasgow and Edinburgh accents in the same bus. There was another advantage. It helped us to get to know our new colleagues. Over a few beers and a couple of lines we got on like the proverbial house on fire, swapping stories of battles past and looking ahead to the violence to come. The Hearts and Hibs boys were like-minded individuals, and the only difference from us was their Edinburgh accent. The fact that I remembered fighting a few of them didn't seem to be a problem and as the alcohol and the drugs worked their magic it seemed that the 'unholy alliance' might work after all.

But it all came to a shuddering halt. We got pulled over on the A90 between Arbroath and Stonehaven by traffic cops from Grampian police. It was a routine check on football fans, which was a fairly regular occurrence. Minutes later they were joined by a ginger-haired cunt, who I recognised as an officer in Grampian's football-intelligence unit. He started to reel off our names, 'Chugg, Carrick, McLeod, Trotter . . .' before the penny dropped. Rangers and Hibs hooligans travelling together! He just couldn't believe it. His face was a fucking picture.

'What the fuck is this all about?' he asked Fat McLeod.

Someone at the back of the bus shouted out, 'What do you think we're doing? We're going to the match.'

'I'm glad you think so,' the cop replied.

We were marched off the bus one by one to be searched and checked for outstanding warrants on the police national computer. The Old Bill noted down our details, which were then recorded in FI files.

Perhaps naively we thought we would still be able to go to the game. I had a ticket, which I showed to the FI cop but it did no good. We were escorted out of the Grampian area with a police escort and even when we got out of their jurisdiction every exit on the motorway was blocked by a cop car. After the disappointment we needed a drink and we stopped off in Falkirk, where we visited a few pubs and clubs. I was still there drinking and snorting at one in the morning with the four boys who had not made their way back to either Glasgow or Edinburgh. Although our first expedition hadn't been a success in FV terms it served one very useful purpose: it broke the ice between the different contingents. Next time we would be better.

Two of Scotland's leading mobs took nothing to do with the SNF: Aberdeen and the Dundee Utility, and as far as we were concerned they were fair game. So when Aberdeen and Dundee United were drawn together in the League Cup semi final of 1997/98 we saw an opportunity to kill two birds with one stone. The game was at Tynecastle and I travelled through to the capital with a group of fifteen ICF. We met the Edinburgh contingent on Broughton Road in an industrial estate, Fat McLeod, the brothers T and Warren B among them.

The Utility were our first target and we fully expected them to trap. They were normally reliable and they had given us a clear indication they were up for it. We left the pub in small numbers to avoid detection and went in search of the men from Dundee. It just didn't happen. They were nowhere to be seen. Perhaps they had heard that the SNF was the crème de la crème and they just didn't fancy it.

Plan B was quickly hatched. We made for the Wheatsheaf, well known as a Hearts pub. The plan was to plot up in there until after the game and to attack Aberdeen, who we knew had come down in a coach.[23] At time up we left the Wheatsheaf and mingled with the thousands of Aberdeen fans who were streaming away from Tynecastle. We were planning to sneak up to the ASC bus and to take the cunts by surprise. With any luck they wouldn't know what had hit them. It would have been our first major coup.

On the way however some of our boys just couldn't help themselves. They laid into the Sheep scarfers, no doubt still angry with the many dirty tricks they had pulled over the years. Still, it was out of order. You don't

---

[23]   We didn't give a fuck about the game, as our own teams weren't involved in the semi-final.

attack the non-combatants; it is a liberty. But that was as nothing compared to what happened next, which must go down as the most shameful event in the short history of the Scottish National Firm.

There is no other way to describe what was done.

One of the SNF slashed a female Aberdeen fan across the back. I was disgusted, as were the other main faces. To attack a woman, never mind stabbing her, is beyond the pale. It was disgraceful and I am still ashamed of it to this day. It is little wonder the incident made headlines the next day.

Meanwhile Carrick and Fat McLeod had spotted the ASC bus, which was in the middle of a long line of Aberdeen scarfers buses. I saw them jump onto the bus, which was only about a quarter full. I expected the ASC who were on board to attack Davie and James but they bottled it. All that our two guys could do was to tell them to 'get your fucking mob down here sharpish'.

By the time the main body of the ASC arrived the cops had worked out something was amiss and had flooded the area around the coach park. But in the dark, with thousands of fans milling around, it was chaos. The filth couldn't get a handle on what was going on, especially as we were in small groups, making detection even more difficult. We seized our opportunity and attacked Aberdeen. Fights went off everywhere. I remember steaming into a group of the cunts and while some of them stood and fought others shat it and ran like fuck. It was so dark that some of our boys, perhaps still unfamiliar with their new mates, fought each other.

As the skirmishing continued some of us mobbed up again and ran towards their bus. But when we got closer we could see that the Old Bill were in control and had lined up the Aberdeen boys against a wall. Those Sheep were a sorry sight. Some had black eyes, others looked dazed; many were bleeding. We didn't get away scot free because two of the 'Hibs' SNF had been arrested and were being held in a police van. But one of the boys made a break for freedom and I will never forget the sight of him being pursued by a burly cop while handcuffed. It was hilarious, like something out of a Keystone Cops movie.

With the Old Bill now well on top, Carrick and I and a contingent of the Hibs boys hid out in Factor's Park until the heat died down. While we were hiding one of the top FI officers was shouting: 'McLeod, McLeod, we know it's you. I will get you for this.' We were pissing ourselves and I was surprised that the cops didn't hear us laughing. But they didn't and after hiding out for an hour we managed to make good our escape.

*

We were innovators in the Scottish National Firm. There is no doubt about that. We would try anything and everything, going boldly where no Scottish mob had gone before. One of our most audacious forays came in January 1998 (it could have been 1997), when we took fifty-five boys down to fight Middlesbrough, who were playing Manchester City at Maine Road in the FA Cup. It would be the first time that a mob from outside England had targeted an English club game. We tied it in with a day out in Blackpool. The boys were always keen on a good piss-up at the seaside and that made the whole trip a much bigger draw.

The coach left from Pitz five-a-side soccer centre in the Townhead area of Glasgow, where twenty-five ICF were joined by the cream of Edinburgh's hooligans, including Fat McLeod and Bobby T. We now felt comfortable with the whole concept of the SNF. After the trips to Pittodrie and Tynecastle a real camaraderie had developed; there was trust and mutual respect. When I looked around the bus at some of the faces on board I knew we would be a match for anyone. These guys would back down for no cunt.

Gallons of beer were drunk on the road south, and those who had it were sniffing coke as if it was going out of fashion. But you can never have too much of a good thing and when we got to Manchester – where we parked outside the famous, but now closed, Hacienda nightclub – it was straight to the nearest pub for another session. After half an hour Boro's spotter – a big, baldy, formidable-looking guy – walked in to do a headcount. Bizarrely, he was accompanied by two attractive women. The moment he left plans were made to have it with the Frontline after the game. We were genuinely excited. Boro were one of the most respected firms in England, with a reputation for always fronting up. If their spotter was anything to go by we would need every single boy to be at the top of his game.

We stayed in the pub for another hour, by which time there were five minutes to go in the cup tie. We decided to go looking for the Frontline, rather than have them come to us. It would give us the element of surprise and ensure that the Old Bill didn't rumble us. We split up into small groups and made our way up Oxford Road in the direction of Maine Road. After ten minutes we mobbed up and to avoid detection we walked at a fair rate of knots. We were passing groups of City scarfers coming back from the game and when we got to the edge of the Moss Side district there were thousands of them milling around a road junction adjacent to a park. But where were Boro?

Bang! There they were, in the middle of a police crocodile. We thought, 'It's show time,' while for some strange reason someone started to chant 'Scotland, Scotland'. That lit the touch paper and the two mobs charged. I saw one of their main boys trying to slow them down, and then Bobby T decking him with a punch that would have done George Foreman proud. But, as we later discovered, he wasn't a lad; he was an undercover cop!

By this time the two firms had collided with a ferocity and momentum that put me in mind of one of those battle scenes from *Braveheart*. There were individual skirmishes all over the street and from the looks on the Frontline's faces I could tell that they were shocked by our ferocity. As the fight went on I tried to drop kick my immediate opponent, who immediately backed off. It was the same story with the other SNF; they were getting the better of the exchanges and pushing the Frontline back.

Time froze. It always does when it goes off. It seemed like five minutes before the cops arrived but in reality it was probably less than a minute. They penned in the Frontline, who rather meekly accepted it, which surprised me after all I had heard about them. Then the cops turned their attention to us. They drew their batons and charged, trying to push us back up the street and away from Boro. Fuck that. We were taking that treatment from no cunt so we regrouped and charged the baton-wielding bullies. I fronted up to one of them, a massive plod, doing my best to goad him into lashing out. 'Come on then, let's have it.' But he didn't respond. Nor did I hit him because I knew that would mean certain jail time.

The police weren't interested in making arrests. Their plan was to split us up into smaller and smaller groups and disperse us. Having said that, however, one SNF boy did get picked up for hitting a cop with a lump of wood while another got lifted for affray. Several baton charges later they had managed to push half-a-mile up the road, at which point the cop I had been having verbals with started trying to clip my heels. 'Fuck you, you big English bastard,' I sneered. That was the proverbial red rag to a bull and he lunged at me, baton flailing. He had lost the plot and his dispersal tactic was a distant memory. He wanted Scottish meat, which to his way of thinking meant arresting me with a couple of baton blows thrown in for good measure.

Fuelled by coke, lager and sheer adrenalin I legged it, pursued by an indignant, six-foot-plus boy in blue. I could feel his breath on the back of my neck and I could also hear him trying to swipe my feet away with his size eleven standard-issue police boots. I had another problem; in my pocket there was a quarter (seven grams) of Colombia's finest. 'Shit,' I thought, 'I don't want to get caught with this on me.' So as I was sprinting I threw the gear into a bus shelter.

He didn't see me dumping the coke but he was still fucking raging and determined to put me in handcuffs. 'You're for it if I catch you, you little Scotch cunt,' he assured me. I was zigzagging like fuck trying to prevent him from tripping me up but I was now exhausted.[24] As we passed a side street I saw my chance and made a sharp left, into ground owned by Manchester University. My heart sank. It was probably a dead end, which would mean arrest and a few digs from my pursuer's baton.

Thud! What the fuck was that. I turned round and saw that the big bastard had run straight into a bollard and taken a tumble. He was writhing around in agony, clutching his knee. I didn't miss him and hit the wall. 'Aye, ya stupid big English prick. That'll teach you,' I gloated. By this time a few of the boys had arrived to help me evade arrest. But they weren't needed now and we all had a right good laugh at the plod with the gammy knee.

Back at the bus we were buzzing. Everyone had a tale to tell about Boro, which was one of the best episodes of FV we had ever been involved in. But my elation was short-lived. I was minus three-hundred-quid's-worth of Charlie. 'Fuck it. I am going to get a taxi and find it,' I told the others. I hailed a cab and it took me back to the bus stop. And there it was, shining like a diamond. My gear. When I got back to the pub I was ecstatic. Getting the better of the Frontline, seeing the cop injure himself, recovering the coke. What a day.

But it wasn't over yet. We still had Blackpool to look forward to, where half of us went to one nightclub and the other half to another one. The group I was with didn't have any hassle but when we came out a couple of hours later it was mayhem. There was a pitched battle going on between the other half of the SNF and a group of bouncers. It started when a bouncer got wide with one of our boys in the toilets. The bouncer saw him snorting coke and tried to eject him. Little did he know who he was fucking with and it all kicked off outside. We immediately steamed in and

---

[24] Who says cocaine is a performance-enhancing drug?

the reunited SNF chased the bouncers back inside the club, just as the Blackpool Old Bill came flooding onto the scene.

The cops escorted our bus out of Blackpool and from there we were passed from force to force for the four-hour journey back up the road to Glasgow. It made a nice story for the local television news the next day and we also made the front page of the local papers, 'Marauding Scots hooligans,' etc. We had made our mark.

There is a postscript. The two boys who were arrested faced up to two years inside for assault and affray. At their trial the jury couldn't make up its mind and a mistrial was recorded. At their retrial they were found not guilty after only forty-five minutes of jury deliberation.

19

THE SCOTTISH NATIONAL FIRM (2): TAKING ON THE TARTAN ARMY BAMPOTS

Given its name the Scottish National Firm was never going to be satisfied with matters domestic. We needed to branch out, to perform on a bigger stage, and there is no bigger stage than international football. In May 1997 Scotland travelled to Gothenburg to play Sweden in a friendly. We were determined to make sure it was anything but a friendly and we hoped to track down either Stockholm's notorious Black Army, or Gothenburg's own thugs, and take our first scalps on foreign soil.

I had better explain my attitude to the Scottish national team and to the bank clerks, accountants and other ne'er-do-wells who follow them, known to one and all as the Tartan Army. I have never had more than a passing interest in the national side, perhaps because it has never been that good in my time as a football fan. The SFA doesn't help either: to me the blazers, egged on no doubt by high-profile Celtic supporters within the Scottish establishment, have always treated Rangers and Rangers players like shit. I would support Scotland in a game against England but in major finals I would want all four home nations to do well. (I exclude the Republic of Ireland, a foreign country, from that list.)

Then there is the Tartan Army, a cultural phenomenon about as welcome as acid rain. With their kilts, glengarries and 'See You Jimmy' wigs, and the repertoire of songs from the *Sound of Music*, they are a permanent embarrassment to Scotland. Nor are they the friendly, cosmopolitan bunch of media myth. I have seen them getting pished and exposing themselves to women and children. There was an infamous episode in the Algarve in the early 1990s (heavily reported in the Scottish media) in which hordes of them ran naked through the streets of Albufeira shouting abuse at locals and urinating in public, while other Tartan Army 'foot-soldiers' played football naked in a park. Strangely enough, the Portuguese no longer see them as friendly ambassadors for Scotland.

The Tartan Army's 'anyone but England' philosophy is also objectionable. Why do they get away with abusing our English cousins? The media would come down on Rangers fans like a ton of bricks if we spouted similar anthems of hate about the Republic of Ireland. But for some reason anti-English racism is acceptable in modern Scotland.

When twenty-five of us got to Glasgow airport for our flight to Gothenburg the tension in the terminal building was palpable. The Tartan Army could tell by the way we were dressed and by our aggressive demeanour that we weren't foot-soldiers. They knew right away who we were and what we were. We felt like gatecrashers at a wedding and they did their best to ignore us in the airport and on the plane. We didn't give a fuck about getting the cold shoulder, especially after a few beers and some of Colombia's finest.

In Gothenburg we stayed at a floating hotel on the river, called The Ship, and once we had unpacked we went out on the town. The women were lovely, right at the top of the gene pool, and it may sound corny but they really did remind me of the blonde one from ABBA. The only problem was that they were obsessed by the Tartan Army and what they had on underneath their kilts. We were in a nightclub full of TA and the women swarmed around them like flies on shite. We didn't get a look in, although we still had a good night fuelled by coke, ecstasy and beer.

Despite the presence of the Tartan Army babe magnets one of our boys, Kinky Keek, did manage to pull. He got off with a highly attractive local woman, or at least she seemed to be a highly attractive woman. Some of the boys noticed that Keek's bird had a very pronounced Adam's apple and a rather square jaw. He got the third degree when he came back to the hotel the next morning with a big smile on his face.

'How did you get on last night,' we asked.

'Aye fine. I done her up the arse,' Keek replied.

'Are you sure it wasn't a 'him'?'

But he wouldn't admit it, telling us only, 'That she made me a cracking breakfast.'

Keek had pulled a transsexual but it didn't seem to worry him and I have heard that he keeps in touch with him/her by e-mail. It was the beginning of a beautiful friendship.

Later that morning a few of us went out for a walk and found the ideal place in which to set up base camp. It was a combination of sex shop, bar, lap-dancing club and porno cinema, a very handy establishment if you ask me! When we went in we found Gags, a Hearts boy, trying to fend off a beautiful woman. But once again appearances proved to be deceptive because 'she' was also a transsexual; it must be a popular pastime in Sweden. My pal Swedgers and I had a look in the cinema, where three of Gothenburg's dirty old men were wanking furiously as they watched a hardcore movie. The smell of stale spunk was nauseating.

It really was a weird place. Swedgers heard loud, animal-like noises coming from behind a locked door. It turned out to be chickens clucking, with a man moaning in ecstasy. Could he really have been fucking hens? He shouted over the rest of us and we did our best to open the door to see what was really going on. But there was no handle, only a Yale lock, and we couldn't get inside. It gave us a right good laugh though.

About two hours before the game we mobbed up in a bar in Gothenburg's main square. Some SNF had already been arrested for fighting but had been released and had now rejoined the main group in the bar. We needed them because a few minutes later a group of Swedish hooligans appeared, obviously spoiling for a fight. We didn't hesitate. We weaved through the passing trams and the thousands of Scotland and Sweden fans to get at them. I have no idea to this day if our opponents were Black Army or locals but we scattered them, despite a volley of bottles being thrown at us.

The cops were quickly on the scene and although I hid out in one of the many watering holes on the main square I was arrested along with one of the Hibs lads. We were taken to a nearby police station, which quickly filled up with more of our SNF colleagues. The cops informed us we were going to be strip-searched. 'Shit,' I thought, 'they will find my drugs' but I quickly calmed down when I realised I had none on me. I did, however, have something that was even worse: a nine-inch, black-mamba vibrator! I had forgotten all about buying it in the sex shop earlier that day. To add to my potential embarrassment, because of all the drinking and snorting, my dick had shrivelled to the size of an inverted belly button. When the Swedish cops who were doing the searches found the two very different appendages they had a right good laugh at my expense. I nearly died of shame; I would rather have faced fifty Black Army on my own than have gone through that embarrassment.

I was held in a cell and peering out of the window I could see the old football ground and also the new Ulleval stadium, where Scotland and Sweden were playing the inaugural match. It was the only time during the trip that I gave any thought to the football; I had come to Gothenburg ticketless looking for drugs, drink, fighting and banter. My flight home was very soon after the final whistle and I was desperate for them to release me so that I could get to the airport on time. With five minutes left at the Ulleval I was ushered out of my cell and told to get a taxi to the airport. As we walked through the electric doors at the terminal building I was aware of a commotion at check-in.

The Tartan Army were loudly singing, 'If you hate the fucking English, clap your hands.' Our pal, English Steve, understandably, didn't take too kindly to their little ditty and told them, 'I'm fucking English you know,' and was met with foul-mouthed racist abuse for his troubles.

Within seconds there were scuffles between the SNF and the Tartan Army, with a huge crate of beer on the terminal floor acting as a sort of no-man's land between the two groups. It might not have escalated beyond a bit of pushing and shoving had not Rob Roy McGregor lit the touch paper. This huge red-haired cunt, wearing the full regalia of kilt, sporran and Glengarry, entered the fray. He challenged any of the SNF who fancied it to a square go. It was an invitation that one of our boys couldn't resist.

Whack! English Steve caught Rob Roy on the chin with a peach of a punch, sending him spinning to the floor. The touch-paper lit, fights broke out all over the place and although we were vastly outnumbered we smashed them to fuck, using the cans from the crate of beer as weapons. To me they just weren't up for it, despite all their tough talk.

Luckily for them the police arrived and split the two groups up, corralling us into a corner of the building, as far away as possible from the Tartan Army. There was peace for ten minutes and during the lull hundreds more of the kilt-wearing numpties arrived. Then out of nowhere they started chanting, 'Baldy casual bastards,' and at the same time moved menacingly towards us. They obviously reasoned that as we were now outnumbered by at least twenty-to-one they would have a chance. We were well up for it but by now the airport was flooded with cops and they managed to keep us apart.

Of course, we got the blame for everything that happened. The pilot wouldn't let us on the plane, claiming there was potential for violence in mid-air. The only one who flew out of Gothenburg that night was Carrick, who, by the simple expedient of turning his Harrington inside out to reveal the tartan lining, was able to sneak onto the plane. The rest of us had to go back on the overnight ferry, which took thirty hours, and had no bunks. It was nightmare journey, made worse because I had to fend off a very ugly Swedish schoolgirl with a moustache problem.

We disembarked at Harwich, where we were separated from the other passengers and were then escorted to the railway station. Along the way the cops tried to goad us into a fight but we ignored them and when we reached London we got on a train for Glasgow.

20

THE SCOTTISH NATIONAL FIRM (3): THE ROAD TO SALOU AND THIRTEEN YEARS OF GRIEF

Despite my initial misgivings the SNF had been a great experience. Apart from anything else it was a privilege to fight alongside real front-liners, to be in a firm that had no passengers. We had also been innovative, trail-blazers, taking it to two leading English mobs, in England, and giving a good account of ourselves. But we had no intention of resting on our laurels so one night we put our heads together and came up with the idea of taking a mob to the 1998 World Cup in France, in which Scotland had been drawn to play Brazil, Norway and Morocco in the group stages. We knew Aberdeen were going, as were the Utility who would no doubt have Stoke's Naughty Forty to back them up. There was no way we could miss the biggest party of them all.

Little did we know that it would turn out to be the most hysterical media circus in the history of Scottish football violence. On a personal level it also made me the country's most talked-about hooligan, a status I have been living with from that day on.

Our first priority was to pull the numbers. Our cunning plan was to tie in the football violence with a holiday in Spain. Who could resist a week in the sun, with drink, drugs, women and a fight thrown in? The next item on the agenda was to decide which match, or matches, to target. Scotland's first game was against Brazil, in Paris, which we concluded was too far away from Spain, as was the game in St Etienne with Morocco. That left the Norway tie, which was being played in Bordeaux, about nineteen hours from Salou by road. Halfway through the week we would take a coach to the stadium, do the business and then drive back to finish our holiday.

We thought we had managed to keep our plans under wraps (although there had been an article in the *Edinburgh Evening News* about our expedition a few months earlier) but when we got to Glasgow airport for our flight to Reus we were immediately targeted by special branch. While we were having a quiet drink they took our names and addresses and asked where we were going. I just couldn't work out how they had got onto us so quickly. It was only later that we found out there was a grass in the camp. However, despite the questioning we weren't fazed. We thought we would be able to sneak over the border, do the business and get out undetected.

There was real excitement on the plane. It was not only a lad's holiday in the sun but also we had been in touch with both the ASC and the Utility, both of whom said they would trap in France. I was confident of a result. There were sixty of Scotland's finest boys on that plane; a true elite.

The first few days in Salou were great. We were boisterous and we certainly enjoyed ourselves but we kept a low profile. We watched in the pub as England played Tunisia and then enjoyed the running battles between the English mob and Arab immigrants after the game. But some boys were worried about what happened in the aftermath of that violence. The England boys who were arrested were named and shamed by the media and the worry was that if the same thing happened in Bordeaux some of us would lose our jobs. I didn't think there would be much of a problem. The England violence involved thousands of lads while there were only sixty SNF. The media profile surely wouldn't be as high. In addition we weren't targeting either Norway fans or the locals; if it did go off it was likely to be our fellow Scottish thugs on the receiving end, which would be of less interest to the papers.

We set out for Bordeaux early in the morning, planning to get there around six the following morning. A lot of the boys had been out all night partying and hadn't slept a wink but they were so full of adrenalin (and coke) that it didn't show. Every man jack of us was pumped up and raring to go; I had rarely felt such excitement on a FV expedition. All we had to do now was to keep out the way of the French police, which we all thought would be a piece of piss.

The first sign that things might not go according to plan came at the border between Spain and France, where we were met by a hundred gendarmes, French soldiers and plain-clothes officers. An official from the French immigration service came onto the bus and demanded to see our passports. I took it upon myself to collect the passports, but deliberately held back eight of the fifty-eight I had just collected. There was great hilarity at some of the older passport photographs. One guy had an Eighties mullet and a moustache and looked like one of the Scousers from the *Harry Enfield Show*. He got some fucking stick. Within minutes Inspector Clouseau had come back onto the bus to demand the other eight passports. That was worrying. They seemed to know all about us: what time we had left Spain, our route, the bus we had hired, the number of boys.

After the passports had been examined they sent us on our way and we got on the motorway for Bordeaux. As we got drunker and drunker, and higher and higher, our worries about the security operation began to fade. We reminisced about the old days and looked forward to writing a new chapter of infamy when we got to our destination.

The sun came up. We were now within fifty miles of Bordeaux. We knew the Utility and Aberdeen were both in the city and that they were almost certain to front up. There was even the outside possibility of having it with those Tartan Army creeps if they stuck their noses in where they didn't belong. Spirits and confidence were both high. The general consensus was that even if we did get stopped the police would simply take a few photographs and jot down our names before sending us on our way. This would be a day to remember.

The expected pull did come. The coach was surrounded by a phalanx of police motorbikes and the driver was ordered to pull over. Although we had been expecting it there was still a feeling of dejection because we hadn't managed to get to the centre of Bordeaux, where we could have split up and blended in with the hordes of Tartan Army and Norway scarfers. 'Never mind,' I thought, 'once they have checked us out we'll be on our way again.'

We were on our way, but not to the centre of Bordeaux. To a fucking cop shop, where we were stuck in a holding pen complete with crash barriers. After that they took us inside to get processed and then marched us up a flight of stairs into a room with five cops. Strangely, one of the officers was wearing a cap and a scarf over his face, as if he was some kind of undercover operative. After answering the usual set of questions some of us had a category put next to our names: A for the least serious hooligan and C for the most serious. I was given a C, along with six other boys, including Fat McLeod, Carrick and Warren. Then we were put into another holding pen.

It all clicked at that point: being stopped at the border by a task force encompassing three different agencies of government; the inspection of the passports, which showed they knew how many of us there were; taking us straight to the holding pens. They had known all about us, right from the start, and we were now ensnared in the biggest anti-hooligan operation of all time. We later found out that, in the wake of the England game, an emergency law had been passed the day before by the French parliament, authorising the police to stop and detain suspected hooligans.

What we didn't know at the time was that our detention had become a media sensation in Scotland. As we languished in the pen Martin Geissler of STV was outside with a camera crew reporting live for *Scotland Today*. The Scottish public – who had been labouring under the misapprehension that football violence was an English phenomenon – were being whipped into a frenzy. It wasn't just us: several Aberdeen lads had been arrested and jailed in Paris, and they too had been named and shamed. The politicians responded, with Tony Blair proposing that a law should be introduced making it easier for hooligans to be sacked from their jobs.

Meanwhile, in our holding pen, we still thought we would be set free and allowed to complete our journey to Bordeaux. After an hour, with no indication that we were going to be freed, tempers got frayed. Some of us rattled the crash barriers, others goaded the cops, then everyone started singing 'We want food.' Seconds later a squad of riot police appeared. With their body armour, helmets and long-handled batons, they looked like Robocop. There was a tense stand-off, and it seemed like we were on the verge of an ugly confrontation, but then a senior officer came on the scene and managed to defuse the situation.

'You can't hold us. We know our rights,' we insisted.

But he told us it was all legal and above board, thanks to the new law. He also said that we would be taken to a primary-school gym on the outskirts of Bordeaux, where we would be fed and then allowed to watch the game. After that a decision would be taken on what was to happen to us.

Our ball was now well and truly burst. Six months of planning and anticipation had been swept down the drain. Nor did we believe their assurances about watching the game or about a decision being taken on what to do with us after it. That was just to placate us and make us more manageable. We knew that in France you could be held without charge for days and we thought that's what was going to happen.

The riot police, the CRS – real naughty cunts with their batons, helmets and armour – herded us onto a bus. We were then given an escort that would have done Al Qaeda proud: six motorcyclists plus a vanload of riot police. The convoy swept through the centre of Bordeaux, taking us alongside the stadium where we passed the Tartan Army, some of whom booed while others clapped us. A few of the lads dropped their trousers and bared their arses as an insult, showing them that we hadn't forgotten what happened in Gothenburg.

We reached the outskirts of the city and drew up outside the primary school, just as we had been told. The place was teeming with riot cops and as we got off the bus we got that sinking feeling. We weren't going to get food and we weren't going to be watching the game either. Based on what had happened to the ICF in Marseille earlier in the 1990s they would probably single out a few boys and give them a hiding, probably on the pretext that we had started the trouble. Inside the school we were ushered past dozens more riot goons, which made us even more convinced we were going to be attacked.

In the gym we all moved to the centre of the floor, psyching ourselves up for the onslaught we felt sure would follow. I was in a foul mood, having had a blazing row with one of our boys, Gary the Gimp, over a fag. As the minutes passed we got tenser and tenser, expecting the doors of the gym to open and a squad of Robocops to burst in. Then we heard footsteps and as they got closer we prepared to defend ourselves. When the door did swing open the cops made an entrance, but they were carrying trays wrapped in foil. It was chicken (or more likely rabbit) dinners! We were all fucking starving and the food cheered us up no end, as did the sight of a massive television being wheeled in for us to watch the game. The cops had been telling the truth after all. Scotland drew 1–1 with Norway, which meant there was still a chance we could qualify for the second stage if we managed to beat Morocco in the third and final group game. Some of us even thought of staying on for that game, which would have given us a great opportunity to fight Moroccan immigrants.

But first we had to find out what plans the riot police had for us. An hour after the game had ended we were still stuck in the gym and our patience was running thin. We asked what the script was and were told that we could be held for twenty-four hours. The cops had a problem. Because of some legal technicality they could only deport us back to our country of origin, which of course was Spain. And that's what they did. We were put back on the bus, which would take us back to Salou. That at least was some consolation. We could now enjoy what was left of our holiday and soak up the Spanish sunshine.

As I took my seat on the bus I got the first indication of the media storm that was to follow. Through a crack in the window I could see a photographer taking shots with a long lens. 'I hope to fuck that's just the French papers,' I said to the boy next to me.

For the journey back to Salou we had an escort worthy of a visiting head of state. There were several police cars, riot vans, motorcyclists and even a helicopter. Talk about overkill. The Scottish media had also parked their tanks on our lawns. Our little expedition was the top story on the BBC and STV news and it was plastered on the front page of almost every Scottish newspaper. We thought that the English lads would attract the attention of the media, given the huge numbers involved, but not us. Our mob was minuscule by comparison. But by now the writing was well and truly on the wall.

Back in Salou at our hotel we got a phone call from a *Daily Record* reporter, which I took. I told him that I had no comment to make and I refused to confirm who else was there. He then reeled off the names of people he believed were in our group, including mine. That was a shock to me as I thought the reporter didn't know I was there. 'I don't know what you are talking about,' I curtly replied, and put down the receiver.

The next day I phoned Mum to tell her that I might be named in the *Daily Record*. But the paper had beaten me to it. 'I've already had them at the door and they tricked me into giving them a photograph of you. But I didn't tell them anything that could hurt you,' she told me. I did my best to reassure Mum, trying to convince her that everything would be all right. I didn't do that great a job; in fact I didn't even convince myself. I knew the papers would have a field day at my expense.

The irony was that I had been making a real effort to turn my life around. I had met Kerry, the woman who was to become my wife, and I was doing an HND in sports coaching at college, where I had been at the top of my class. I realised however that I was kidding myself. Football violence was still the driving force in my life, to the detriment of everything else.

Sure enough, when I got a hold of a copy of the *Record* I was cast as the villain of the piece. 'Chugg is the leader of the 58-strong group who were detained in Salou,' it told its readers. And it wasn't just the *Daily Record*. I was named as the SNF leader or ringleader by every Scottish media organisation from the BBC to *The Sun*. I also now discovered that our detention in Bordeaux had been given blanket coverage, something we had been blissfully unaware of at the time.

Reporters had even approached the college, and my employers, Clyde Football Club, to get their reaction, and while both had said I was highly thought of it must have been embarrassing for them. I knew there was a possibility that I might be kicked out of college and sacked from my job.

More importantly, Mum and Kerry were upset. I felt sorry for them but I wasn't ashamed of what I had done. After all I had only gone to France to fight like-minded individuals, not scarfers or ordinary French people. In fact as the calls poured in from journalists in a strange way I almost felt proud. FV was what we were all about; it was what we lived for and to be recognised for that was very satisfying, if you follow my logic.

It was at this point we discovered the extent of the police operation. We got the night porter at our hotel drunk and he told us that two under-cover cops had posed as hotel workers to keep an eye on us. It was little wonder they had been so clued up about the coach trip to Bordeaux. But the authorities had known all about us from day one at Glasgow airport, despite our best efforts to keep things quiet. We were convinced that someone had grassed us up. Our main suspect was Andy Blance, leader of those Hibs boys who had decided to stay with the CCS after Fat McLeod had broken ranks and formed the national firm. To tease the media we put a £5,000 'contract' on Blance's head. It was shite of course but it kept the pot boiling and it gave us a few laughs when we saw how seriously the papers took it.

We didn't go the Morocco game and instead flew home from Reus on the Saturday. Our expectation was of a huge media stushie at Glasgow airport and a scramble to get photos of us for the Sunday papers and news bulletins. We were right on the money. The place was awash with journal-ists, most of them looking out for 'SNF ringleader' Sandy Chugg. Customs and Excise, however, did me a big favour. 'Right, Mr Chugg, come with me,' I was instructed. They had targeted me because I had a conviction for selling drugs and they hauled me into an office and conducted a full body search. They probably did it to annoy me but in fact they saved me from the abuse the rest of the boys were getting from pressmen and the general public in the main concourse. The place was thronged with tour-ists waiting to fly out on their annual holiday and when they spotted the SNF with their 'three-lions' England T-shirts they didn't hold back. Our lads were roundly abused and called 'scum' and 'a disgrace to Scotland'. Inevitably, fights broke out between the SNF and the holidaymakers, which the police did their best to contain.

By the time I was released by Customs several more flights had dis-embarked and when I was walking out I was part of a huge crowd and therefore hard for the few remaining pressmen to spot. My stepdad had come to meet me and he told me to put on my hat and sunglasses and that also helped. I am convinced that many of the reporters were expecting me to be six-foot two and built like an all-in wrestler. They wouldn't have been looking for a guy at five-nine with a slight build. The result was that they didn't get a photo of the SNF bogeyman, because I was bundled into a car and driven off.

Avoiding the press at the airport was a minor victory because I knew from that day on I would be a marked man: not only for the media but also for the police. Despite me having given up active involvement in football violence, I am still a target. Thanks to Salou I have endured thirteen years of grief.

21

TALES FROM THE MOB

Some of the boys were kind enough to provide me with their memories of life with the ICF. Towards the end of the chapter I have also included a couple of stories from the youth wing of the mob; after all, they are the future.

Here is a selection.

How the ICF Was Formed (by Pedro)

It might upset some of our boys but the famous Rangers ICF was inspired not by a Rangers fan but by an Aberdeen fan, or casual.

It was 1983. I was fifteen and I remember that a boy at our school supported the Dons. As part of a group of what would later become known as casuals he followed them home and away. Every Monday morning he would come into the playground wearing big thick trainers, split jeans and a Peter Storm cagoule and regale us with tales of taking a mob to Edinburgh and Dundee, and how it would go off big time with the locals.

Fashion and fighting. A fifteen-year-old's dream.

We wanted some of that. In Glasgow we were in a bit of a void in fashion terms. Most of us were just getting out of Sta Press and two-tone.

A small group of us from school had been going to Ibrox for a few years and sitting in the Broomloan stand, where the away fans were housed. In those pre-Souness days Rangers didn't have such a big following and so you got to know the guys around you pretty quickly. At that stage there was no organised football violence as such.

Anyway, this day my school pal 'Aberdeen P' told us the Aberdeen casuals were going to be in town (on their way to Paisley for a game with St Mirren) and a dozen of us went in for a look. We clocked them at Queen Street station. They were thirty-strong, all of them aged from about fifteen to twenty-two. They were wearing brightly coloured clothes and they all had serious haircuts, with a few even sporting moustaches. Looking back there was a huge difference between us. Most of them were adults and we were just kids. Aberdeen P introduced us to them and after a closer look at their clobber, some chat and a bit of Glasgow lip a few blows were thrown. We lost but we didn't run; we stood our ground and had another go . . . and lost again.

At this stage a few of the older Aberdeen mob got bored and went to the pub. We licked our wounds and headed for Enterprise, an amusement arcade, where we met up with some other young Rangers fans from the north side of Glasgow. Looking for reinforcements to take on Aberdeen we told them about the incident and when they heard about what had happened they were right up for it. So it was a bigger, altogether more confident group that marched the three hundred yards back to Queen Street, where we had it with the younger Aberdeen lads. We did well initially, belting quite a few of them, but they bolted to the Pig and Whistle pub where they called out their big guns.

Although we got another going over when their older lads re-engaged we were hooked. That night four or five of us decided that we wanted to become casuals, although some of the boys who had been in Queen Street decided against it, simply because they didn't fancy a bent nose every weekend. Those who were up for it spent the next few months saving our spare dosh from the milk round and investing it in footwear like Adidas New Yorkers, Puma G Vilas and Adidas Wimbledon. We also dressed ourselves in Lacoste T-shirts, flared jumbo cords and some decidedly dodgy Paisley-pattern granddad shirts. It was hard to find the right gear, Glasgow not exactly being awash with this type of attire at the time.

Before we knew it we had twenty guys from our area who knew each other well and who would back each other up, whether they were in the right or the wrong. On our first few forays to Rangers games as casuals we were met with open hostility from some of our own scarfers. But we brassed it out and didn't shy away from the inevitable confrontations. Most of the older Rangers fans realised that we were bluenoses too, just like them, and eventually the aggro calmed down.

The boys who sat alongside us in the Broomloan also started to dress casually and the whole thing just spread from there. We regularly got thrown out of the ground for misbehaviour and sometimes we struggled to get into the away end at Ibrox, even though few teams brought much of a support. It went on like that for the rest of the season and for most of the following season too. Being arrested was also becoming much more prevalent.

In terms of our name we called ourselves the Inter City Firm from day one. The reasoning was that we would get more credibility by copying the name of a real mob. Simple as. Then, in 1985, some of the guys suggested that we move into seats in Section Red of the Govan stand. It made sense. Section Red was the nearest area in the stadium to the away support and it gave us a good visible mob for both the visitors and the television cameras. We adopted the name Section Red for the mob and it really caught on, but, later that season we moved again to the terraced enclosure and the Section Red moniker faded into history. A few of the boys suggested an alternative name of Her Majesty's Service but it never took off. ICF just seemed to stick but although we were ICF in name we rarely used British Rail's expensive commodity, the Inter City train, and stuck to the old football specials due to the financial constraints of the Eighties.

The mob got bigger and bigger. For most of the boys it was back to nodding-acquaintance time. There was no organisation or hierarchy. Guys just went to the football, met up, had a wee ruck and went home to their estates on a Saturday night to do the same thing.

There is a postscript to the Aberdeen story. Later in season 1983/84 they were guests of Rangers and for weeks beforehand all the ICF boys were asking every nutter they met to come along. We were desperate to have another go at them. Before the game, Aberdeen, being an organised bunch of lads, came off the train, stuck together and took their usual liberties. However, after the match, Rangers got their act together. I can honestly say I have never seen a mob like it in Scotland. Maybe the quality wasn't there in some cases but in terms of quantity it was phenomenal. And it wasn't just casuals either. There were all sorts of nut jobs, from skins and punks to scooter boys and scarfers. We trailed Aberdeen all the way from Ibrox to the city centre, skirmishing with them as we went. Then, as they approached Queen Street, we knew it would be our last chance. The whole unruly Rangers mob went nuts and launched a mass charge. Aberdeen to their credit tried to face us up but they had no chance, due to our vastly superior numbers. The Dandy Dons took a right pasting.

The Rangers ICF had come of age.

A Busy Afternoon (by Andy McC)

My first outing with the ICF came when I was thirteen. It wasn't a great start because we got a right chasing from the Capital Service Firm who are, of course, attached to Hearts. Because I was always playing football on a Saturday I didn't go with the mob again until I was seventeen. For my 'comeback', which turned out to be a Rangers versus Motherwell game at Fir Park, I went with six other lads from my scheme.

I was wearing a pair of dungarees, a pair of green Kickers (Unlimited ones) and a short bubble jacket. I thought I was the dog's bollocks but looking back I must have looked a real prick. That said I wasn't as bad as some of the other boys, a couple of whom were sharing two pairs of Adidas Gazelles, one pair red and the other blue. They each had a red trainer on one foot and a blue trainer on the other foot, which (thank you guys) took the heat right off me.

We headed down into Queen Street to get the train and when we got there a couple of the guys who were with me noticed a few ICF at a table in the station bar. In fact the place was full of ICF, laughing and drinking. The ICF boys at the table invited us over and asked if we wanted to go to Motherwell with them.

'Why not,' we replied.

So, about two o'clock, with everyone having gulped down the last dregs of their pints, we went onto the lower deck of Queen Street to catch a train. There were around sixty ICF there, a pretty good mob. We stayed with the younger element and let the older ICF get on the train first. During the journey everyone was talking about what was going to go off when we got to our destination and what they were going to do to the Saturday Service, Motherwell's firm.

Everyone piled off at Motherwell station and marched up the hill towards Fir Park. To our left there were a few Saturday Service following us and they were giving us dog's abuse, letting us know in no uncertain terms what was going to happen to us when we got a wee bit further up the road. A couple of the younger firm tried to go across the road to have it with them but they got shouted back. 'Keep it tight,' they were told.

A few yards further on someone shouted 'It will happen here,' and with that we heard a loud roar from across the street. Fifty Motherwell were running at us. We started jumping about and clapping our hands, excited that it was about to go off.

'ICF, ICF, ICF,' we shouted, a chant that made the hairs on my neck stand up, and one that has the same effect even today.

We ran towards our opponents, who by this time had picked up traffic cones and were throwing them at our front line, but we were too strong and we pushed them right back. Fist fights broke out all over the shop and a couple of them got decked and then stamped on. It wasn't long before the Old Bill turned up in their vans and they held us there, before giving us an escort to the match. I went into the stadium but some of the older boys went to the pub. After the game we met up with the boys who had gone drinking and although we ran into some SS as we headed back to the train station they got chased and nothing major went off.

On the train back to Glasgow a lot of people were talking about how we might run into the CCS because Hibs were playing the Beggars at Celtic Park that afternoon. When we got to Queen Street we all came out together down the steps, then passed a pub called Berlin and on to George Square. We saw a few lads outside a pub called Chambers; they were CSC, Celtic Soccer Crew. More and more of them piled out of the pub and fronted up to us at the edge of the square. Before we could steam in there was a huge roar from the other side of George Square. It was the Hibs mob. Celtic charged them and we charged Hibs and Celtic. With three mobs going at it there was chaos. There were scuffles all over the place, with no one giving an inch. Out of the corner of my eye I saw a CCS lad get thrown through a plate-glass window by a couple of Celtic.

Next thing I knew the sirens were blaring and the polis were piling out of their vans to break it up. I have never seen so many cop vans in one place, when the reality is that it only takes a couple of Glasgow's boys in blue to break up even the biggest brawl. Everyone started running their own way (it was like something out of the movie 'Warriors') and as I made my way home with a couple of my pals I felt a warm glow of satisfaction about the day's events.

South of the Border (by Porky)

1989 was a big year for ICF going to Chelsea matches. One of the lads used to run buses from the city centre and they were always packed out. There was one particularly memorable day out in March 1989 when both Chelsea and Man City were in the old English second division and were battling it out for top spot. We left the Toby Jug early in the morning with a bus full of lads, but with a few scarfers on board as well, and headed for Maine Road. Most of us were going in the Chelsea end but a couple of lads had City as their second team and so there was plenty of banter on the road down.

The plan was to go to the game and then head to Blackpool for a night out and for that reason the bus wasn't hoaching with drink although as usual there were a few guys getting tore into a carryout. We hadn't arranged with Chelsea to have a go at City; it was a take-it-as-it-comes scenario, where, if it kicked off, then fair enough. As soon as we arrived at the ground we were shepherded inside straightaway and I will always remember the strange sight of giant inflatable bananas in the home end (there was a craze for inflatable objects at the time). Not to be undone Chelsea had inflatable celery sticks, which I presume was to do with a witty Chelsea tune that still gets chanted to this day:

> *'Celery, celery, if she don't come*
> *I'll tickle her bum*
> *With a lump of celery.'*

As it happened Chelsea won a five-goal thriller to go top of the league and we could go on our merry way to Blackpool.

Everyone was game for a good piss-up and after we parked up we hit the first pub we came across and started to get the lager down our throats. There was a £20 football card doing the rounds and Walesey (R.I.P.) stood up on a stool and pretended he was scraping the card to find the winner. 'Celtic' Walesey shouted and with that some bloke jumped out of his seat and cheered, thinking that a score was coming his way. The poor guy got the pish ripped out of him and he quietly slunk out of the pub, tail between his legs.

Just as we were getting ready to move to a pub down the road another mob walked in. Maybe we could have a little fun before we left. As they were getting the beer in one of our lads asked who they were.

'Derby. Why, who are you?'

'Rangers,' our mate replied.

'We hate Rangers.'

Bang. It kicked off big style and we gave those Derby boys a right kicking, with one of our boys using the confusion to go behind the bar and try to nick the till.

Job done we headed out into the night in search of a new pub. The jungle drums must have been beating because we struggled to get in elsewhere and a few bouncers got a sore face in the process for knocking us back. The only thing for it was to split up and I ended up going to a bar with a with a few east-end lads, where we had a great night.

Our bus was due to leave at midnight but although we were on time there were only about twenty lads there, which was a bit of a headache for SC who was the convener. Then out of the blue, ten lads appeared and were hanging about, looking menacing. Without hesitation we steamed in and as they ran we kicked them to fuck and back. We were later told they were Leeds but that was never confirmed.

It was 12.30 by the time the bus left, with about twenty of our party missing. This of course was in the days before mobile phones, so it was only over the course of the next couple of weeks that we heard how the rest of the lads got home, with eight of them hitching and getting a lift in the back of a lorry!

A great day out was had by one and all and on the way back SC was already planning the next trip. I know he got a lot of stick from Rangers security for organising these trips so fair play to him for doing so.

Sunderland and Celtic (by AL-K)

Sunderland away in 1993 was one of the most-publicised ICF events ever and depending on your perspective it either made us or destroyed us. We were flying and the mob was at a stage when the babes were no longer babes and the guys who had joined in the early 1980s were now the main faces.

We took a bus down, which was a mixture of new and old faces from all four parts of the city, although if I remember rightly Shettleston went down on their own bus. We got there early and had a walk round the city centre before heading for a pub called the Londonderry. The problem was it was packed out with Rangers fans so we found another decent pub and hung our ICF banner up on a window. There was no sign of any trouble and I can remember being more worried that our ginger-headed friend, who owed one of the top east-end boys money for a drug deal, might end up bumping into him and the Shettleston mob.

We moved onto another pub and went to the bar downstairs. It was the time when our little ditty 'Father's Advice' was being sung at games and we were giving it laldy when some Sunderland came in and started on a few of our younger boys. Then one of them shouted 'Celtic and the IRA' and that's when it kicked off. They got chased out and everyone left the pub thinking we had done their mob, but it wasn't them.

Sunderland had not yet shown their faces but as we walked to their end there they were, team handed. We backed them off towards their end of the stadium and I remember Carrick taking a punch from a bloke who may not have realised he was one of our top boys. Our attitude was that if a main face got punched it was up to the lesser faces to lash back, not back away, and that's exactly what we did. It went on good style for a couple of minutes before the Old Bill broke it up and escorted us into the stadium. During the game there were coins flying about everywhere with 'We're the Famous ICF' being the main song of choice.

We went back home to Glasgow thinking we had got a right result, not realising the maelstrom that was about to be unleashed by the Joke, sorry the Jock, press. It turned out three Sunderland lads had been slashed and to me the media, and especially the Daily Record, went right over the top. One group of people were however very happy with our trip to Sunderland: yes, you've guessed it, the Newcastle fans. We played them at Ibrox shortly thereafter and they loved us for it. The whole Toon Army sang 'Thank you very much for slashing Sunderland' to the tune of the Roses chocolate advert.

A few days later I remember standing in work and this boy who used to run with Celtic in the Eighties was holding up a paper. He was pointing to it and laughing. Lo and behold, on the front page there was a picture of the pub in

Sunderland along with a seven-page spread on the ICF. At first we thought it was cool and we kept all the papers. But as the weeks went on the dawn raids started and the three brothers who were suspected of doing the slashings were plastered all over the papers as they got lifted. Most of us ditched anything that could tie us to the ICF. I had an ICF tattoo and it suddenly dawned on my mum and dad that it was not an innocent football tattoo after all. After pressure from Mum I agreed to get my tattoo covered over and she paid for a new one, which now proudly guards my secret tattoo. I also got hassle at work. I got pulled into the office and was asked if they were to expect me turning up in the papers. I told them 'no', as I had given all that up years ago.

My assertion that Sunderland could have been the event that destroyed our mob is perhaps a bit harsh. Some of the boys packed it in around that time, no doubt because of the heat we got from the police but also because someone sold the story of the slashings to the newspapers, which caused a great deal of distrust among us. At the same time however some people had their resolve strengthened and it did put Rangers back on the map as a travelling mob.

The Youth (by Frankie W)

The ICF Youth, as we became known, came about one day in late October 2005, when we weren't even playing. It all happened when one of the younger lads in the firm tried to get a few of the newer members of the main ICF together and have a dash with Celtic, who were at home to Hearts that day.

We met up early and made contact with the CSC then moved around from pub to pub in the city centre trying to get them to front up. It soon became clear that the Celtic boy was a timewaster and that they had no intention of taking us on. They were having a drink in a pub at Glasgow Cross, he told us. So our little mob, numbering about twenty-five, headed down there and a few of us went into the pub to look for Celtic. Of course they weren't there, which is par for the course for the CSC.

Bridgeton was our next stop and someone had the bright idea that because Thistle were at home to Morton we could take on the North Glasgow Express instead. So we headed up to Maryhill and plotted up in their pub, the Pewter Pot, which the old-school ICF had attacked a couple of times in the past. Maybe it would be third-time lucky. Although we managed to contact both Thistle and Morton neither of them were interested in a dash.

In some ways it had been a wasted day but it started something that hadn't been seen in a long time: a smaller, younger, highly enthusiastic Rangers mob on *the prowl. That's how the Youth came about and over the next few years we would have it with a number of firms, including Aberdeen, Airdrie and of course the CSC, with whom we had several run-ins.*

The Celtic encounters were always the most enjoyable. In November 2005 we lost 3–0 at Celtic Park but a few hours later around forty ICF, a mixture of old guard and Youth, smashed a sorry CSC outside a city-centre boozer. This came after eighty of us had gone onto their patch with the aim of running amok, only to be frustrated when the Old Bill turned up, which meant that we had to split, with a lot of lads calling it a day and going home.

Another good dash with Celtic came when a lot of our main faces were away at a stag do near the end of season 2005/06 and we had drawn at Celtic Park. When we headed back into town the Celtic mob quickly realised that we had been weakened by the main faces being absent, which made them keener than usual to meet up. After a few hours it was game on and a decent-sized firm with a mixture of old school and Youth took them apart, pushing them back into the Gallowgate. Job done!

*

On 19 August 2006 Rangers were playing Hearts at Ibrox while Aberdeen were in Paisley to take on St Mirren. So we arranged to meet a busload of ASC in a field beside the Abbots Inch pub in Renfrew. We pulled a good mob that morning and plotted up in another boozer in Renfrew. But as time passed the Sheep were on the phone to say that not enough of them had travelled. Because it was getting close to kickoff the older lads among us either headed for Ibrox or for the city centre. They obviously thought that the prospects of FV were now remote if not non-existent.

That left eighteen of the ICF Youth plus two young boys from Hearts. We decided to phone our Aberdeen contact back and say that we would come to them. So here we have twenty young lads nowhere near Ibrox on the day of a game, jailbaiting ourselves up. But we just had to have a go. Our main problem was that getting to where Aberdeen were without getting caught by the Old Bill was a difficult task. Luckily, a few of the lads knew the area so we jumped on a service bus that took us to an industrial estate, where we got off. After walking through a residential area we were just two minutes from the ASC boozer.

The ASC boy was phoned again and told we would be there in a few minutes. 'Get your mob outside,' he was instructed.

I don't think they believed we would come because as we turned a corner there was an Aberdeen lad standing in the middle of the road. The look of surprise on his face was priceless. He ran round the corner, back to their pub. When we got there we fully expected the ASC to be waiting for us on the street but there were only a few of them there. Fair play, they had a go but they were no match for the twenty of us. The rest of their mob meantime were happy to lob bottles and glasses at us from the doorway of the pub, while others pelted us from the beer garden.

Some quick thinking was needed and so one of our boys shouted 'The Old Bill are coming.' We ran up the road and the boy who had shouted the warning told us he was only joking; it was his way of enticing the ASC out of the pub. It worked. After hearing the police were on the scene more of them piled out. That was our opportunity. We steamed into the newcomers and smashed them.

As it happened no Old Bill turned up and we headed into the city centre for a well-earned drink. We came away from that fight with a feeling that we had got a result. You can only fight what is in front of you. I don't understand why the Sheep didn't empty the pub and take us on mob-to-mob because it would have made it a better dash. Maybe they thought we wouldn't come to Paisley when Rangers were playing at home. Who knows? Whatever their reasons were they made a cunt of it that day. We did well and any row against Aberdeen is a result.

22

LOVE AND MARRIAGE

My first encounter with Kerry, my wife-to-be, was bizarre. We met in that well-known footballers haunt, Victoria's nightclub, in Glasgow's Sauchiehall Street, in July 1997. I was lucky to be there. I had been drinking in McKinlay's snooker club in Shettleston that night when one of my pals said he could get me into Victoria's because he knew the bouncer. That was the starting pistol for a mad rush to my house to put on clean shirts and good shoes. Actually, despite our best efforts, the four of us still looked like an accident in a charity shop due to the un-ironed shirts and ill-fitting footwear.

'Victoria's?' I asked myself. 'We've got no fucking chance.'

True to his word, however, my mate had a word with the bouncer and in we went. I wasn't at my most confident. My shirt was like a concertina and I was more than a little embarrassed by my appearance. It was while I was admiring myself in front of one of Victoria's many mirrors that I bumped into Kerry.

'You don't need to look in the mirror. You're looking good,' was my instant chat-up line.

'It's a pity you didn't look in the mirror before you came out. Your shirt is a state,' she retorted, quick as a flash.

One of my pals heard our exchange and he put his tuppence-worth in.

'You can't speak to him like that. He's Sandy Chugg, the top man in the ICF.'

'I don't care who he is. I'll say what I think.'

I remember being impressed by her frankness. Although as far as first encounters go it was hardly the stuff of a Mills and Boon novel.

I went home alone and didn't think much about what had happened. Then, the following week, someone arranged a blind date for Kerry and me. The look on our faces when we realised who we would be dating was priceless. Despite our inauspicious start we got on well that night. We both like to speak our minds and we also discovered there was a definite attraction. We started courting and before long it developed into a serious relationship.

Our next problem was one faced by many people in the divided West of Scotland: religion. Kerry is a Catholic and I am a Protestant and a committed Loyalist. I also profoundly disagree with everything the Roman Catholic Church stands for. That does not mean I hate individual Roman Catholics. My nieces and nephews are Catholics and avid Celtic fans and I often help them to get match tickets. In addition, some of my pals are Irish Republicans and while I hate their politics I don't hate them. In fact, they are very nice people and have turned out to be staunch friends, as I have noted elsewhere in this book.

When it came time for us to get married the ceremony was in St John's in Barrhead, which is a Roman Catholic church. Given my principles I thought that I might be struck by lightning when I walked into the place! Despite my misgivings I did it because of the love I have for my wife and also out of gratitude for the support her family gave me after the SNF debacle in Salou. The compromise was that my children would be brought up as Protestants. I wasn't about to repeat the mistake my brother Christopher made. His kids were brought up Catholic and they support Celtic (although I love them both dearly). The only cloud over our big day was that some of my Loyalist friends refused to go into St John's, preferring to stand outside until the ceremony was finished. That said most of my ICF and Loyalist friends did go into the church.

Marriage didn't change my lifestyle when it came to football, something that Kerry could never understand. She could never work out what drew me to violence and the casual culture although, in the early days at least, she found the scene intriguing. Over the years her attitude changed, simply because my love for Rangers and football violence meant that I put those things ahead of her and my family. I am not proud to admit it. I should have been a better husband and father and football and the violence that goes with it should have taken much more of a back seat.

Even today Kerry is still of the view that I put the ICF first, especially when, as she calls it, I go into 'robot' mode. She thinks I still have something to prove. But being such a prominent member of the mob makes it very hard for me to walk away. I will always be known as 'Sandy from the ICF' and, let's face it, I was a casual before we met, so she knew what she was getting into. That said I believe things have been getting better in the last few years although Kerry insists that I could do more around the house. I am still trying to find the right balance, and I admit that at times it can be a real struggle, but we are both making a real effort to make it work and that surely is the main thing.

She is a devoted mother and our three wonderful children are a great credit to her dedication and hard work. She hates the fact that police come to our door, as any mother would, and she doesn't want her children to get the idea that what I do is normal. Given some of the things we have been through I daresay some other couples would have been divorced by now. But there is a deep-rooted love there that has kept us together and long may it last.

23

DRUGS

Drugs have got me into more trouble than football violence ever did. I have spent fortunes on pills and powders of every description and using them has cost me several jobs; good jobs at that, jobs that could have set me up for life. My worst experience with drugs came when I was eighteen and trying desperately to fund an ecstasy habit: I was caught dealing LSD, ecstasy and Temazepam. I copped a three-year sentence and was sent to Glasgow's notorious Barlinnie prison.

The conviction is not something I am proud of and of course it had serious consequences: I lost a great job as a welder in the shipyards and it also put paid to my long-term aim of becoming a Royal Marine. Further down the road I was denied the chance to join my sister in Canada. Another problem is that the conviction is never spent. It was for more than two-and-a-half years and sentences of that length are never wiped from your record. That youthful indiscretion will follow me to my grave. Worst of all however is that drugs cut me off from my family, both physically and psychologically. My nearest and dearest paid the price for my drug use and that is unforgiveable.

I wasn't the only football hooligan who was heavily into drugs. Most boys in most mobs were. In what I would call the second generation of casuals – the mid-to-late 1990s – alcohol and cocaine were the drugs of choice. That was true in both Scotland and England; Chelsea, for example, were always partial to a bit of whistle, as they call Colombia's finest.

It was inevitable that as a working-class boy from the east end I would get into drugs of one kind or another. Given the poverty and deprivation in that part of the city – which goes back for generations – the people who live there have always been inclined to find solace in mind-altering substances. It is hard to get away from drugs in the east end: they are as easy to get a hold of as drink or cigarettes; in fact probably easier given that there are no age restrictions on street corners. I was actually a latecomer to the scene. I smoked my first cannabis joint at sixteen, whereas by that age most of my contemporaries were already well into stronger drugs, like heroin and LSD.

Cocaine was virtually unknown at that time in my part of Glasgow; it was a rich man's drug, costing £50 a gram, a small fortune to most east-enders. But then, in the early 1990s, after the ecstasy craze died down, the supply of cocaine increased and the price plummeted. I didn't need to be asked twice. I got right into it. Despite what the authorities will have you believe it had some beneficial effects. For one thing it helped me to stay sober. I have never been much of a drinker; I just can't hold it that well, which is a major disadvantage when you are a member of a pub-loving mob like the ICF. Cocaine helped me drink more and it stopped me get-ting paralytic. It also gives you much more confidence in social situations, helping you to interact with people, again helpful in a gang scenario in which large groups of people coming together is the norm.

At least that's how it was in the early days. With long-term use I started to become paranoid and I got into the habit of shutting myself away to snort on my own. In splendid isolation, and with a brain befuddled by coke, I would twitch constantly at the blinds; the slightest noise made me think that people were coming to get me. I often felt suicidal, especially when the cocaine was mixed with alcohol. I frequently cut myself off from my family and I have lost count of the number of family events I fucked up by being on a binge or coming down from one. And if by chance I did manage to attend an event I would be depressed and make everyone's life a total fucking misery.

When I started snorting coke was a social thing. I would have a few lines at the weekend and maybe one day through the week as well. Soon, that wasn't enough. Before long I was at it every day. In fact I was snorting so much of the white powder that I could have got a job as a test pilot for Hoover. At the peak of my habit I was going through a quarter (seven grams) a day. That is the equivalent of twenty big lines. Surprisingly, I was still able to work, but I lost a succession of jobs because of the coke. It was also expensive. Some weeks I would spend £600 on my habit. The money came from a variety of sources: some from my wages; some from introducing buyers to dealers; while some was payment-in-kind through debt collection for shady characters.

In my fifteen or so years as a user I tried everything to get off the coke, including various forms of counselling. I had to do something, partly because of the heavy price I was paying in terms of my mental and physical health but mainly because of the effect it had on my wife and family. Nothing I tried, however, had the desired effect and from time to time I still fell off the wagon. It is only in the last few years, as I neared forty, that I got a grip on it. I am older and wiser and of course I have three young children and a host of other responsibilities, including helping to run a boys' football team. At the time of writing I am delighted to say that I have been clean for six months.

Drugs may fill a void in your life, but the effect will only be temporary. Ultimately, they lead to pain and misery, especially for your nearest and dearest. So do as I say and not as I do. Stay off them. Having said that, I still think drugs should be as legal as alcohol is. That way the purity and safety could be guaranteed. The government would also derive huge amounts of tax and it would save enormous amounts of money on policing and on the criminal-justice system. There are also cultural considerations. Why not control drug use, rather than making it cool and anti-establishment? It couldn't make things any worse than they are today.

24

MY LIFE NOW

I don't see myself as anything special or extraordinary. I am still the same wee Sandy from the Gallowgate and it is only other people who put me on a pedestal. Looking back I am not embarrassed about anything I have done with regard to football violence, although as I have said already I am sorry that it took me away from my wife and family when they needed me most. My only regret is the drug conviction, which caused real pain and suffering to my nearest and dearest.

I would have loved to have made it as a professional footballer. I played at under-fifteen and under-sixteen level for Rangers Boys Club, where Eddie Annand, later of Dundee and Ayr United, was a contemporary, while Charlie Miller, who did make it with Rangers, was a couple of years below me. Some people thought I could have made it at some level in football but the reality is I was an average midfielder, the type who broke up attacks and played the simple ball to more skilful teammates. Not unlike a certain Mr Neil Lennon! When Rangers failed to offer me a professional contract I was of course disappointed but as my burgeoning career as a football hooligan was beginning to take off I didn't have time to dwell on it. Maybe it was for the best. I am a great hooligan but an indifferent footballer.

My love of football has endured to this day. I got an HND in sports coaching with development, and I put theory into practice by working as a community coach. I am now heavily involved with my son's team, which is called Drumsagard Football Club. It has allowed me to coach boys at under-ten level, and it is something that I love doing. Instead of taking from football I am imparting knowledge, putting something back in, redeeming some of the bad things I did. That gives me a lot of satisfaction.

The parents at Drumsagard know all about my background. I have been up front with them from the start. I have to thank all of them for not judging me, but especially Graeme Ireland and John Love, respectively the chairman and vice-chairman, and committee members Jill Donohoe, the Craigs, Houston and Queen, and Brian Miller. They stuck their neck out for me, letting me coach despite my background. I am proud that they now see me as a positive role model. Those parents who don't know about my background may be shocked by some of the things in this book but I can assure them that my involvement in football violence is all in the past. If, however, they had any objection to me being there I would walk away, sad as that would make me.

I have only let myself down once. Drumsagard were losing 4–0 and the opposition players were also putting in some hefty challenges on our kids. The other team's coaches and parents were rubbing it in big time and I think some of our lot expected me to say something. At first I restrained myself but when one of their boys put in a hefty challenge on my son, Elliot, it led to heated verbals with their coach. In the old days I would have laid him out but I restrained myself, although I did tell him to fuck off, something I am not proud of.

Despite a few lapses I now see myself as the dedicated family man. I have got much to be proud of, including a nice home, a wonderful wife and three beautiful children. I don't think of myself as a bad person and I would always try to help anyone who was in trouble. I proved that to myself at the Bellgrove train crash in 1989, when I pulled survivors from the wreckage. That led to an appearance on *Kilroy*, a popular television programme of the time.

There has been another great source of joy during the last two years. I have been reunited with my two sisters, May and Gina. In the process I have discovered that I have a number of 'new' nieces and nephews, as well as great-nieces and great-nephews. It has been a very nice surprise.

I hope you have enjoyed reading my book. Some of you will be angry at the things we did but all I have done is to tell the truth about what happened in those years. I hope that at least you respect me for being honest.

ICF HALL OF FAME

Aldo, Andy McC, Al Kair, Alan Bell, ADS, Action, Albertz, Adam, Ally G, Andy K, Billy Maitland, Browny, Bomber M, Big F, Big Gary, Brucie, Big Lawrie, Cagey, Colin Martin, Carmichael, Cooper, Con, Collins Bros, Craw, Clarky, Christie, Big Craig C, Deek K, Deryk S, Davie T, Danny W, Davy Imrie, Dougie Watson, Douglas Don, Donald, Daz, Del A, Ecky, Eddie C, Edon and Bro, Fearon brothers, France, Flemie, Forrey, Frankie Bear, Fraggle, Gadget, Grog, Geo McD, Grahamer, Graham Anderson, Gytobear, Garry F, Geemac, Graham O, General Jamie, Garry Miul, Graeme, Hoppy, Jeff, Johnny R, James C, Jim H, Jinx, John Lav, Jambo McG, Jay Munro, John McC, Jackie Mac, Joe, Jaimo, Jock, Jamie Andrew, Johnny Milne, Joe Daps, Kev (Greenock), Kev (Perth), Kenzie, Kegz, Kenny B, Lochy, Mark McL, Mitchell, Milligan, Mackay, MacRae, Murdo McL, Moose, Mark H, Millsy, Maxy, Mark McE, Nordo, Ozzy S, Pedros K and McL, Porky, Paul L, Praty, Percy, Paul Wilson, Rico McGill, Rab Anderson, Robbo, Ron D, Ross McP, Rab T, Riot, Ricky C, Rab McG, Swedgers, Scott N, Scott McL, Slim, Smoothy, John and Sam Bruce, Stirling, Wee Stoddy, Stu and Scotto, Stuart McL, Shug, Skelly, Sick Mick, Steph W, Strachan, Scotch Tosh, Steely, Shorty, Scott Clydebank, Terry, The Bat, The Chuckle Brothers, Tighe, The Gimp, Tommy and Big John (from Greenock), Whitey, Willox, WBA Scott, Wilson, Wullie C, Wee Ronnie

Apologies to anyone I have missed

To our friends from clubs all over Britain and beyond. Follow, Follow.